Censorship and Interpretation

Historians desiring to write the actions of men ought . . . to choose such an opportunity for writing, as it may be lawful to think what they will and write what they think, which is a rare happiness of the time.

—"Sir Walter Raleigh," *The Cabinet-Council,*
published by John Milton, 1658

Thank God that there are no free schools nor printing in this land, for learning has brought disobedience, and heresy, and sects into this world, and printing hath divulged them.

—William Berkeley, governor of Virginia, in 1677

I think it is disgusting, shameful and damaging to all things American; but if I were twenty-two, with a great body, it would be artistic, tasteful, patriotic, and a progressive religious experience.

—Shelley Winters on stage nudity

Annabel Patterson

Censorship and Interpretation

The Conditions of Writing and Reading in Early Modern England

With a New Introduction

The University of Wisconsin Press

The University of Wisconsin Press
114 North Murray Street
Madison, Wisconsin 53715

3 Henrietta Street
London WC2E, 8LU, England

Library of Congress Cataloging in Publication Data
Patterson, Annabel M.
  Censorship and interpretation.
  Includes index.
    1. Censorship—England—History.
2. Books and reading—England—History. 3. English
literature—Early modern, 1500–1700—History and
criticism. 4. Great Britain—Intellectual life—
16th century. 5. Great Britain—Intellectual life—
17th century. I. Title.
Z658.G7P37   1984   098'.12'0942   84-40156
ISBN 0-299-09950-4
ISBN 0-299-09954-7 (pbk.)

For Lee

Whose support means more than I can say

Contents

vii

Acknowledgments

This project was begun, all too long ago, with the assistance of a Canada Council Research Grant in 1977 and a special leave from York University; furthered by a Summer Research Grant from the University of Maryland in 1980; and brought as near to completion as it will ever be during a Senior Fellowship at the Society for the Humanities, Cornell University. Among those who have read parts or versions of the manuscript, I am grateful to Stanley Fish and Jerome McGann for their enthusiasm, to Ernest Honigman for a warning about Jonson and a suggestion about Rousseau, and especially to Earl Miner, in response to whose generous and detailed commentary the book became, among other amendments, more forthright. Paul Grendler helped with the history of censorship. Joseph Wittreich and Samuel Schoenbaum shared their knowledge of *King Lear.* Molly Emler, going beyond the call of duty, typed much more of the manuscript than anyone else. Ann Coiro, my invaluable research assistant, alone knows how many inaccuracies she has saved me from recording.

A shorter version of the first chapter has already appeared in *Studies in the Literary Imagination* 15 (1982); and some of the material on Jonson, on Donne's letters, and on Milton's relationship to romance has appeared, or may even appear concurrently, in the following contexts: *Rome and the Renaissance,* ed. Paul Ramsey (Binghamton, N.Y.: Mediaeval and Renaissance Texts and Studies, 1982); *Milton Studies* 17 (1983); *John Donne Journal* 1 (1983); *Lyric Poetry: Beyond the New Criticism,* ed. Patricia Parker et al. (Ithaca, 1984); and *Poems in Their Places,* ed. Neil Fraistat (Chapel Hill, N.C., 1984). In all instances I am grateful to the university presses involved for the right to engage in this partial overlap.

Censorship and Interpretation

Introduction

When this book was first published in 1984, it opened with the following statement:

> We live in a world in which much is taken for granted about freedom of expression, a concept that remains in fact theoretically and practically unstable. While the presence or absence of state censorship is widely assumed to distinguish absolutely the two major geopolitical structures of our time, it is by no means clear that the "Free World" has resolved such problem areas as freedom of information in relation to national security, intellectual liberty in the educational system, the rights of public servants to express their views on the institutions they serve, or the tense relationship between what the West regards as political freedom and the socio-economic upheavals in "developing" countries. At such a juncture, a book about the cultural impact of censorship in the past may seem both timely and peculiarly academic.

Six years later, part of this statement is mocked by the extraordinary changes that have occurred in Eastern Europe, rendering the "Free World" obsolete as a term of political differentiation. The most visible symbol of this change is the presence of Václav Havel, previously censored and imprisoned Czechoslovakian playwright, at the head of his own government. The premise of the West's superiority with respect to intellectual freedom has been shamed by several notorious developments in the United States and the United Kingdom, including the campaign led by U.S. Senator Jesse Helms against the exhibition of photographs by Robert Mapplethorpe, leading to constraints on the funding of artists by the National Endowment for the Arts, and the 1989 banning in Britain of the film "Visions of Ecstasy," produced for television by an independent film company, and refused a certificate by the British Board of Film Classification on the grounds that it depicts the erotic imaginings of Saint Theresa of Avila. School libraries and children's books have been increasingly subject to parental and citizen interference. On September 3, 1989, the *New York Times* reported that People for the American Way, a group that opposes censorship, had documented 172 incidents in forty-two states of attempted or successful censorship in schools, with *Catcher in the Rye* a perennial No. 1 on the hit list. But with respect to the third world, my earlier caveat can now be seen as uncannily predictive. Possibly the greatest case of literary censorship since that of Joyce's *Ulysses,* the 1988 banning of Salman Rushdie's *The Satanic Verses* in eleven countries, including India and South Africa, and especially the sentence of death pronounced upon Rushdie by the Ayatollah Khomeini, has forced the West to reassess its own principles of freedom of expression, and made the topic of censorship once again a matter of wide public interest and investigation.

The decision to republish *Censorship and Interpretation,* though it anticipated the events of late 1989 in Europe, was taken in the light of the Rushdie case; not for purely (or impurely) opportunistic reasons, but because the nature of *The Satanic Verses,* the stated and unstated reasons for its banning, the extreme punishment proposed for its author, and Rushdie's statements in his own defense, all transport us, in effect, back to the conditions of authorship and censorship in the sixteenth and seventeenth centuries, which historians call the early modern period. Rushdie's article "A Pen against the Sword: In Good Faith" supports my central thesis, that it is to censorship in part that we owe our very concept of "literature," as a kind of discourse with rules of its own, a concept that has for centuries been thought to be capable of protecting writers who have tried to abide by those rules. On February 12, 1990, in *Newsweek,* Rushdie protested that "people on all sides of the argument have lost sight of this simple fact," that "at the centre of the storm stands a novel, a work of fiction, one that aspires to the condition of literature." Instead, the book has been treated

> as a work of bad history, as an anti-religious pamphlet, as the product of an international capitalist-Jewish conspiracy. . . . It felt

impossible, amid such a hubbub, to insist on the fictionality of fiction. (p. 52)

Although one may certainly inquire whether *The Satanic Verses* was as resolutely fictional as Rushdie claimed, the more pertinent questions are why the conventions he invoked—modernism, fantasy, the dream, "pitting levity against gravity," the close affiliations with *Ulysses* (the paradigmatic censored text) and Joyce's "silence, exile, cunning"—were insufficient to protect him when, as he also argued, the real issue was not the supposed affront to orthodox Muslims but rather the internal political struggles in India, Pakistan, and especially Iran; whether such protective conventions are reliable when the political stakes are high; and whether they are ever transcultural. The failure of protective conventions was demonstrated in England in 1633 in a censorship case of comparable notoriety, when William Prynne's indirect attack on the Caroline court and its theatricals resulted in his trial for seditious libel. At least Prynne suffered only a scarifying fine, academic demotion, and the loss of both his ears. Whether such conventions can be transcultural is a question that has interested me greatly since *Censorship and Interpretation* first appeared; and much of this new introduction will be concerned with demonstrating precedents for, continuities between, or reinventions of what I found in early modern England in other times and places.

Even more than in 1984, then, one of the main objectives of this study is to break down the barriers between academic discourse and "real" issues, by recovering for inspection and theoretical understanding that stage in European culture when all the major European powers were themselves emergent nations, engaged in a struggle for self-definition as well as for physical territory, and when, in consequence, freedom of expression not only was not taken for granted, but was a major subject of political and intellectual concern. Because others have described them systematically, I focus only occasionally on the history of censorship as such, on law and the formal institutions and mechanisms whereby the press, or the pulpit, or the theatrical companies were supposed to be made subject to state control.[1] My topic is the *effect* of censorship in the broadest sense, as a cultural experience of limitation and threat, on the writerly psyche and its products.

Although I have chosen to focus this book on England from the middle of the sixteenth century to the end of the seventeenth, the story begins earlier (as, given our arbitrary sense of "period", it always does) and in Europe (as, for England, is usually the case). By 1518 the event that was to set all Europe at loggerheads and to render problematical all aspects of national and international discourse was already under way, as the works of Martin Luther began to circulate. The extent to which the Reformation—combined, of course, with an already well-developed printing industry—constituted a sufficient motive, indeed, the governing condition, for a new international interest in censorship can be well illustrated by its impact on France. In 1521, Francis I issued a law forbidding printers to produce or distribute any publications not previously examined by the Faculty of Theology of the University of Paris. In 1534, Lutheranist pamphlets of an extreme sort were distributed, nonetheless, on the streets of Paris and other cities, including Amboise, where the king resided—a flagrant provocation that could scarcely be ignored, even by a king who was not at all clear where he stood, especially in his political relationship to the pope. In January 1535 he issued a decree that was as clearly excessive as the provocation: all printing of any kind was to cease, upon penalty of hanging; all bookshops were to be closed; and a list was published of suspected Lutheranists who were immediately condemned to banishment, without trial, from French territory. Among these was the poet Clément Marot.[2]

Marot, who had been since 1519 a protégé of the king's sister, Margaret of Angoulême, already well known for her reformist sympathies, escaped first to her court at Navarre and then to Ferrara. But officers were sent to his home at Blois and his books and papers seized. It is clear that this event had a profound effect, conceptually as well as psychologically, upon Marot. In an exile's edition of his *Adolescence Clementine,* his enormously successful collection of poems first published in 1532, he inserted a new poem addressed to Francis I, "Epistre au Roy, du temps de son exil a Ferrare," which is both an appeal for clemency, an ideal to which his name symbiotically connected him, and a statement of his poetics. And central to these poetics, forged out of his recent experience, are two conjoined ideas: the *right* of the individual to privacy and the *responsibility* of poets to wade in dangerous waters; hence their special or privileged status in society, an immunity from censorship or laws designed for others:

> . . . O juge sacrilège
> Qui t'a donné ne loy, ne privileige
> D'aller toucher & faire des massacres
> Au cabinet des sainctes Muses sacres?

Bien est il vray que livres de deffense
On y trouva; mais cela n'est offence
A ung poëte, à qui on doibt lascher
La bride longue, & rien ne luy cacher
Soit d'art magicq, necromance ou caballe:
Et n'est doctrine escripte, ne verballe,
Qu'un vray Poëte au chef ne deust avoir,
Pour faire bien d'escripre son debvoir. (ll. 131–42)[3]

[O sacrilegious judge, who gave you the legal right or privilege
to go tampering and wrecking in the cabinet of the sacred
Muses? It is true that they found forbidden books there; but
that is no offence in a poet, who should be allowed a long rein,
and have nothing hidden from him, whether it be magic,
necromancy, or cabbalism; there is no doctrine, written or
spoken, that a true poet should not understand in order to do
his duty as a writer.]

In this passage, Marot not only complained to the king about the seizure
of his books and papers at Blois, but transformed that event into a symbolic paradigm of a profoundly mistaken relationship between culture
and authority. Marot's cabinet, literally his study, became simultaneously
his private space (the self); his workshop, where the tools of his erudi-
tion, his nascent classical humanism, were kept; and the cultural arena
where new imaginative work should have been allowed to proceed, connecting the documents of the classical past to the emergence of France
as a nation and the vernacular as its medium of expression. It is important to see, also, that the freedom of the writer in this passage is expressed in terms of the freedom of the reader (a crucial aspect of Reformation idealism) to read books which society prohibits as dangerous to
the *status quo*.

This humanist principle, that the writer has a right to be in advance
of or athwart his times, a principle which censorship itself has the self-
contradictory effect of suggesting to those who have not grasped it and
strengthening in those who have, is itself always in uneasy relation to
the problem of writerly influence and efficacy. In an earlier though unpublished poem, *L'Enfer*, which was also the product of state interference
with his liberties (a short imprisonment apparently for having eaten meat
in Lent),[4] Marot had reminded his monarch both of his own mysterious
connections with Vergil (Maro), and of the king's responsibilities for

playing the role of Augustus, literature's patron and protector: "O Roy heureux, soubs lequel sont entrez / (Presque periz) les lettres et Let-trés" ["O happy king, under whom are rescued from near obliteration both letters and lettered men," ll. 375–76].[5]

There is no reason to suppose that Marot was unaware of the theoretical problem so posed: that the ideals of which he speaks could be restored only through the patronage system. When Marot recovered the royal favor, as he did a year later, he wrote, among many other poems ad-dressed to the king, an *Eglogue au Roy soubz les noms de Pan & Robin,* in which the symbol of the cabinet appeared in a new form, the "verd cabinet" of the shrine of Pan, or the privy chamber of Francis I, the space, as in the phrase "cabinet counsels," where affairs of state are actually negotiated.[6] To such cabinets, writers, in certain circumstances and in certain media, quite properly have desired access. Marot's case, then, exhibits the equivocal and fragile relationship between writers in the early modern period and the holders of power, a relationship whose maintenance was crucial to all writers who aspired to have some influ-ence, either on the shape of the national culture or more directly on the course of events. At any moment that delicate balance between inde-pendence and involvement could be broken by imprudence or intransi-gence on either side, for what we are here considering was essentially a joint project, a cultural bargain between writers and political leaders.

There are, of course, a hundred similar stories that have been or could be told about writers of our own time, in the Soviet bloc and elsewhere; not least that of Václav Havel, who during the early 1970s endured a dreary kind of partial immunity. Though his plays could not be per-formed, and he refused the advantage of the lavish state support offered to those who censored themselves, he was at least still free, and free to write. In 1975, however, he addressed an open letter to Czechoslova-kia's president, Gustav Husák, protesting the country's "profound spiritual, moral and social crisis," and urging him to "realize just how much he himself was responsible for this general misery." This letter was written, Havel himself tells us, out of "the idea that it was time to stop being merely a passive object of those 'victories written by history' . . . and try to become their subject for a moment."[7] Its logic led to his four years' imprisonment,[8] and the astonishing *Letters to Olga*[9] writ-ten in prison (and through the rigorous prison censorship) which explore, among other philosophical problems, the nature of freedom, responsibil-ity, and the role of the theater in challenging the status quo. Havel's equivalent of the "bride longue" that Marot demanded for poets is found in his poetics of the theater, his definition of "that controversial 'probe' " that true theater makes beneath the surface of life. The test of a play's validity is "how inventively and daringly it addresses society." As a member of a profession which courts publicity, Havel would always have had to face more precisely than Marot the dilemma of audience and reception, the self-denying ordinance of the *avant-garde*. "The daring is far more important than how many people were originally addressed. From a certain point of view, a single performance for a few dozen people can be incomparably more important than a television serial viewed and talked about by the entire country."[10] But this sentence also defies, by claiming that scarcity enhances value, the *unwilled* banning of all his plays in his own country, a topic at which the *Letters to Olga* can only glance.

Nevertheless, there was one occasion on which, as the *Letters* confess, Havel partly, or almost, or apparently, submitted his independence. When he was first arrested in 1977 for his role in Charter 77, he wrote a request to the public prosecutor for his release:

> Prisoners in detention are always writing such requests, and I too treated it as something routine and unimportant, more in the nature of mental hygiene: I knew, of course, that my eventual release or nonrelease would be decided by factors having nothing to do with whether I wrote the appropriate request or not. Still, the interrogations weren't going anywhere and it seemed proper to use the opportunity and let myself be heard. I wrote my request in a way that at the time seemed extremely tactical and cunning: while saying nothing I did not believe or that wasn't true, I simply "overlooked" the fact that truth lies not only in what is said, but also in who says it, and to whom, why, how and under what circumstances it is expressed. Thanks to this minor "oversight" (more precisely, this minor self-deception) what I said came dangerously close—by chance, as it were—to what the authorities wanted to hear. What was particularly absurd was the fact that my motive—at least, my conscious and admitted motive—was not the hope that it would produce results, but merely a kind of professionally intellectualistic and somewhat perverse delight in my own—or so I thought—honorable cleverness. (p. 347)

This strategy backfired. The same cleverness that later enabled Havel to outwit the prison censorship here proved his temporary undoing. He was informed that he would indeed be released and that political use would be made of his release. The ambiguity of his request would "with appropriate 'recasting,' 'additions' and widespread publicity," be used to create the impression that he had given in to pressure, renounced his opinions, betrayed his cause.

The painful lesson that Havel learned in 1977, and that he chose to confess in a letter dated July 25, 1982, was that no utterance is autonomous, still less, once it is uttered, under the author's interpretive control. "Truth" or meaning "lies not only in what is said, but also in who says it, and to whom, why, how and under what circumstances." These insights also dominate that section of the annals of censorship that I investigate in this book, where historical circumstances, timing, the nature of the audience, not only inevitably affect the interpretation of a work but demand of the writer (a demand not always met sufficiently) a special kind of cleverness. What Havel saw as an event of "key significance" in his subsequent life can also, in his retelling of it, serve as a key to *Censorship and Interpretation*.

In particular, the rules about prison correspondence that Havel had to circumvent forced him to innovate. These rules, designed by the sadistic prison governor, were, while apparently arbitrary, evidently designed to prevent the conveyance of secret messages. The single, four-page letter home permitted "had to be legible, with nothing corrected or crossed out, and there were strict rules about margins and graphic and stylistic devices":

> (we were forbidden, for example, to use quotation marks, to underline words, use foreign expressions, etc.) . . . We could write only about "family matters." Humor was banned as well: punishment is a serious business, after all, and jokes would have undermined the gravity, which is one reason why my letters are so deadly serious. (p. 7)

By trial and error, Havel learned that a certain immunity was attached to the highly abstract, philosophical meditation on life, reflecting the influence of Heidegger, of existentialism and phenomenology, which, it is to be assumed, the censors either failed to understand or recognized as sufficiently detached from contemporary events to be harmless. Yet in fact this mode (from which Havel's readers are now privileged to learn his theory of artistic responsibility) was a code. "In time I learned," he wrote, to think ahead and arrange my thoughts in thematic cycles. . . . The letters, in fact, are endless spirals in which I've tried to enclose something. Very early on, I realized that comprehensible letters wouldn't get through, which is why the letters are full of long compound sentences and complicated ways of saying things. Instead of writing "regime," for instance, I would obviously have had to write "the socially apparent focus on the non-I," or some such nonsense. (p. 8)

In other words, Havel invented, perforce, a new genre and a new hermeneutics of censorship; as Janet Malcolm put it, prison conditions "compelled him to function as an artist where, under less extreme conditions of censorship, he would probably have merely functioned as a good letter writer; they elicited from him a strange, unclassifiable, inadvertent masterpiece, a work that . . . will outlive his plays and essays."[11]

It cannot be entirely a coincidence (though the importance of Havel's *Letters* to my argument only dawned on me while constructing a new undergraduate course on literature and censorship) that a new poetics of the familiar letter developed in the seventeenth century as a direct result of the interception of mail. The most extreme example of this breach of privacy in the service of political reorganization was the seizure of the correspondence of Charles I at the battle of Naseby and its subsequent publication by the revolutionary leaders, an event which occasioned a royalist poem entitled *The Kings Cabinet Opened,* an interesting reentry of Marot's "cabinet" as a symbol for intellectual freedom. And in my last chapter I describe how James Howell, one of the pioneers of the art of writing private letters for public consumption, complained of the breach of his own privacy in terms not at all dissimilar to those in Marot's complaint. One day in 1643 five agents of the revolutionary government arrived at his house, "rush'd presently into [his] Closet and seiz'd on all [his] Papers and Letters, and anything that was Manuscript; and many printed Books they took also, and hurl'd all into a great hair Trunk, which they carry'd away with them."[12] The result, less disastrous than in the case of Algernon Sidney, was an extended stay in the Fleet prison, and the evolution, in Howell's mind, of a concept of privacy as a key to the intellectual life. Howell's synonym for the cabinet is the "Closet," but the symbolic force of the two terms is equal; and as he sees the breach of the private space as one of the most obvious symptoms of the general political malaise, the "plundering of the very brain," so his solution is to create a new genre, an epistolary history of his time, in which the paradoxes of the intellectual, torn between privacy and publicity, will be most peculiarly manifest.

I argue throughout this book that the unstable but unavoidable relationship between writers and the holders of power was creative of a set of conventions that both sides partially understood and could partly articulate: conventions as to how far a writer could go in explicit address to the contentious issues of his day, and how, if he did *not* choose the confrontational approach, he could encode his opinions so that nobody would be *required* to make an example of him. It has frequently been claimed that censorship was not a significant force in early modern society. Such critics point out that legislated control of the press by such mechanisms as prepublication licensing tends to be virtually impossible to enforce, given the various stratagems to which writers and printers could resort to evade the laws—clandestine presses, books smuggled in from abroad—not to mention the costs and difficulties of administering such a system, and its constant undermining by commercial interests. The invention of printing alone created an instrument impossible to control precisely because of the power of the market. Added to that was an inchoate understanding of the relationship between church and state interests (where did campaigns against heresy intersect with anxiety about sedition?), and between spoken, sung, written, and acted offenses. The sheer multiplication of the objects of censorship—sermons delivered in the pulpit, ballads sung in the street, academic theses, political caricatures, plays, the oral circulation of news and rumors, use of "reformed" translations of the Psalms, almanacs and prognostications—made the task both capricious and quantitatively impossible. Alfred Soman, whose subtle account of the situation in sixteenth-century France and its neighbors gives examples of all such cases, also documents the chaos in the French censorship prior to Richelieu, and the consequent "reliance upon individual complaints . . . and upon exemplary punishment as the principal deterrent."[13] Exemplary punishment, of course, means only very occasional and hence arbitrary punishment. John Milton was one of the first to argue, in *Areopagitica,* that censorship could not work, pointing to the incompetence of censors as mere bureaucrats required to assess complex arguments, and the inadequacy of their numbers to the scale of the task if taken to its logical conclusions. But this did not prevent him from taking on himself the role of licenser for the Commonwealth a few years later.

There is no question but that early modern censorship was inefficient and incoherent, though its efficiency varied under different regimes and according to fluctuations in the political climate. Soman's entire argument anticipated (though not, of course, with pleasure) the arrival of systematic censorship under Richelieu. Philip Finkelpearl has argued, for instance, that the Jacobean stage was permitted considerably more license generally than Glynn Wickham and others have supposed;[14] this was perhaps a reaction against the last years of Elizabeth's reign, when, in response to a series of popular protests, published controversy over church government (the Martin Marprelate pamphlets), and ultimately the threat posed by the earl of Essex, security was greatly tightened.[15] A comparable period of repression recurred in the Restoration, focused on the control of Nonconformists, and spearheaded by Sir Roger L'Estrange, who lobbied successfully for the position of Licenser of the Press in 1663 and prosecuted his task with ideological zeal. But there is a whole range of publishing in England that can be better accounted for by assuming some degree of cooperation and understanding on the part of the authorities themselves, something that goes beyond the recognition that unenforceable laws were better than none, that the occasional imprisonment, however arbitrary, had exemplary or ritual force.

This, surely, is the significance of those famous puzzling incidents of *noncensorship:* Elizabeth I recognized the topical meaning of a production of *Richard II* on the eve of Essex's rebellion and two years after she had imprisoned Sir John Hayward for presuming to publish a prose history of Richard that appeared to encourage Essex; yet the players, after questioning, went free. James I "allowed" Middleton's *Game at Chess,* a notorious satire on his pro-Spanish policy, to play for almost two weeks to packed audiences, before acceding to the protests of the Spanish ambassador and closing the production down. One of Philip Massinger's plays, clearly critical of Caroline appeasement of Spain, was licensed for production after the most trivial gesture of appeasement, the replacement of Spain with Carthage.[16] Charles I himself read the manuscript of Massinger's *The King and the Subject,* and wrote in the margin of one passage that referred to forced taxation, "This is too insolent, and to be changed."

The history of theater censorship makes it clear that such allowances are continuous throughout the theater's history. When Philip Stanhope, earl of Chesterfield, fought the Stage Licensing Act in 1737, he cited an anecdote from republican Rome:

> The great Pompey . . . had certainly a good Title to the Esteem
> of the People of Rome; yet that great Man, by some Error in his
> Conduct, became an Object of general Dislike; and therefore, in
> the Representation of an Old Play, when Diphilus the Actor, came
> to repeat these Words, *Nostra Miseris tu es Magnus,* the Audience
> immediately applied them to Pompey: who, instead of resenting it
> as an Injury, was so wise as to take it for a just Reproof: He exam-
> ined his Conduct, he altered his Measures, he regained by degrees
> the Esteem of the People, and then he neither feared the Wit, nor
> felt the Satyr of the Stage.[17]

If this anecdote matches Elizabeth's self-identification with Richard II,
Charles I's personal scrutiny of Massinger's play was repeated by
George IV in 1820, when James Sheridan Knowles's *Virginius: or, The
Liberation of Rome* was submitted for licensing by Covent Garden, summoned "for inspection in a high quarter," and returned with erasures.[18]
In Russia in the mid-nineteenth century Nicholas I himself personally
censored some of the most important writers, especially Pushkin; but
in 1836, Nikitenko, himself a censor of extremely liberal tendencies,
recorded a performance of Gogol's comedy *The Inspector General* in
terms that support Chesterfield's anecdote:

> It is performed constantly—almost every other day. The emperor
> attended the first performance, applauded and laughed a great deal.
> . . . The emperor even ordered his ministers to see *The Inspector
> General.* . . . Many people feel that the government should not ap-
> prove a play in which it is so harshly censured.[19]

In 1936, the New Theater in Sydney, Australia, put on Clifford Odets's
Till the Day I Die, a famous expression of anti-Nazi sentiment. In a striking reenactment of the case of *A Game at Chess,* it was not until Dr.
Asmis, the German consul, complained to Chief Secretary Baddeley that
the play was "unjust to a friendly power" that the government banned
it; and when they did, the audience threw the police out of the theater,
and the play proceeded.[20]

It is true that all the above episodes concern the theater, and while
it is often argued that governments fear the theater more than other forms
of literature because of its capacity to stir up public opinion, they may
sometimes fear that closing down a play will stir up that opinion still
more dangerously. Yet there is plenty of evidence that tacit agreements

existed, in different countries at different times, whereby nondramatic writing that criticized the government in a recognizably *literary* way would or should be treated with a certain latitude. This principle was also understood in ancient Rome. As Frederick Ahl points out in his study of Lucan, formal rhetoric recognized a system of oblique political commentary. Quintilian introduced the system in his *Institutes* with this advice:

> You can speak as openly as you like against . . . tyrants, as long as you can be understood differently, because you are not trying to avoid giving offense, only its dangerous repercussions. If danger can be avoided by some ambiguity of expression, everyone will admit its cunning.[21]

In England, at the opening of the period I am investigating, this principle was reemphasized, significantly in a work that had itself been "hyndred" in the reign of Mary Tudor, but licensed at the very beginning of Elizabeth's initially more liberal regime. This composite work, the *Myrroure for Magistrates,* was, as its title implies, intended to promote reflection in the current political leaders, and its major theme is the tyranny of Richard III and the moral failures of those who surrounded him.[22] One of the figures who come back from the dead to give advice is, in fact, a rhetorical failure, who though aware of Quintilian's advice chose to ignore it: the poet Collingbourne, executed, we are told, "for making a foolishe rime." A reader today may be forgiven for feeling that Collingbourne's style deserves some major penalty; yet behind this execrable verse lie a number of significant statements. Three times Collingbourne invokes a concept reminiscent of Marot's complaint to Francis I, that poetry has from classical antiquity been granted certain privileges, certain freedoms of expression. He associates the "freedome of the auncient tymes" (l. 96) and the "Poetes auncient liberties" (l. 197) primarily with the Roman satirical poets, Horace, Juvenal, and Martial, and indeed quotes from Horace's *Satires,* "Ridentum dicere verum / Quod vetat" ["What law is violated if someone laughs while speaking truth?" I.i.24], a remark that helps to explain, for instance, the immunity of Gogol's *The Inspector General.* The ancient tradition of literature's freedom, Collingbourne complains, has been abrogated by the tyrannical government of Richard III, who allows neither the direct nor the indirect critique, neither rough Juvenalian nor deft Horatian satire: "Be rough in ryme, and then they say you rayle . . . / Touche covertly in termes, and then you taunt" (ll. 8, 15). Collingbourne protests that the culture that destroyed him was one defined by interpretive excess, by a constant ungenerous search for disloyal meanings: "To the wurst they all thinges construe styl . . . / They racke the wurdes tyl tyme theyr synowes burst, / In doubtfull sences, strayning styll the wurst" (ll. 60, 62–63). And like a many a writer in difficulties who used this disclaimer (the disclaimer was not, as I shall argue, to be trusted), he invoked the criterion of authorial intention as a guide to judicious political reading:

> This auncient freedome ought not be debarred
> From any wyght that speaketh ought, nor wryteth.
> The authors meanyng should of ryght be heard,
> He knoweth best to what ends he endyteth:
> Wordes sometymes beare more than the hart behiteth.
> Admit therefore the authors exposicion,
> If playne, for truth: if forst, for his submission.
>
> (ll. 211–27)

I take it that in this last antithesis, which matches that between rough, plain speech and touching "covertly in termes," "submission" is the word that defines the acceptance of encoding as the deference due to political authority.

As it happened, Collingbourne himself was guilty of inadequate submission. The "foolishe rime" that was his undoing was a beast fable about Richard III and his ministers, Catesby, Ratcliffe, and Lovell, of which the opening lines were apparently, "The Cat, the Rat, and Lovel our Dog / Do rule all England, under a Hog" (ll. 69–70); but, as Collingbourne ruefully admits, unlike Aesopian writing properly deployed, the meaning of his own fable "was so playne and true, / That every foole perceyved it at furst." Nevertheless, as Collingbourne struggles simultaneously with a rudimentary sense of English verse structure, with an early stage of English classical humanism and a nascent constitutional theory, the conviction that drives him forward in his own ungainly way is that poetry, or literature, has had from antiquity a unique role to play in mediating to the magistrates the thoughts of the governed.

The interest of the magistrates in this compromise is also explicit in the *Myrroure;* for after the ghost of Collingbourne has departed, the editorial committee of the *Myrroure* deliver their own critical responses to his message:

Gods blessing on his heart that made thys (sayd one) specially for revivinge our auncient liberties. And I pray god it may take suche place with the Magistrates, that they may ratifie our olde freedome, Amen (quoth another) For that shalbe a meane bothe to staye and upholde them selves from fallyng: and also to preserve many kinde, true, zealous and well meaning mindes from slaughter and infamie. If kyng Richard and his counsayloures had allowed, or at least but wynked at sum such wits, what greate commodities myght they have taken thereby. Fyrst, they should have knowen what the people myslyked and grudged at, (which no one of theyr flatterers eyther would or durst have tolde them) & so mought have found meane, eyther by amendment (whyche is best) or by some other pollicie to have stayed the peoples grudge . . . [and second] they should also have bene warned of theyr owne sinnes. (p. 359)

This statement is more than a timely warning to the new young monarch of the disadvantages of a repressive regime. Even in its form—the interpretive *frame* of a tale which is to serve as a mirror for magistrates—it makes a crucial point about literature as political representation. Framed by its conventions—in this instance, the fantastic visitor from beyond the grave and the topical recycling of past history—literature "reflects" only by displacement. A wise ruler will see the value of such indirection, and either "allow" it, give it a privileged place in the sociopolitical system, or at least "wynk" at such "wits" whenever possible. In so doing, she would not only be providing her subjects with a safety valve for the airing of contentious issues, but also contriving for herself an early modern version of the public opinion poll.

In 1625, Sir Francis Bacon published the third edition of his *Essays,* an edition which incorporated his experience of politics under both Elizabeth and James, and which reads in part as a warning to the new reign which began in the fall of that year. One of the new essays included in this edition was "Of Seditions and Troubles," which opens with advice to the "Shepherds of people" as to how to interpret the symptoms of political tempests:

Libels and licentious discourses against the State, when they are frequent and open; And in like sort, false Newes, often running up and downe, to the disadvantage of the State, and hastily embraced; are amongst the Signes of *Troubles.* . . . Neither doth it follow,

that because these *Fames,* are a signe of *Troubles,* that the suppress-
ing of them with too much Severity should be a Remedy of *Troubles.*
For the Despising of them, many times checks them best; and the
Going about to stop them, doth but make a Wonder Long-lived.[23]

Bacon had taken this position, legitimately entitled "Wise and Moderate," much earlier, when advising Elizabeth how to handle the Martin
Marprelate controversy, where he had recalled the principle first expressed by Tacitus: "punitis ingeniis gliscit auctoritas" ["the authority
of genius [or wit] is enhanced by punishment"].[24] The occasion for
Tacitus's aphorism was the trial of the historian Cremutius Cordus, a
notorious instance of the repressive regime of Sejanus; and a series of
writers who themselves had trouble with censorship—Ben Jonson, John
Milton, Jean Racine—would cite this same classical authority in defense
of the liberal position.

But if rulers or governments were to behave wisely and moderately,
writers had to learn, in Collingbourne's phrase, to "touch covertly."
And what we can find everywhere apparent and widely understood, at
least from the middle of the sixteenth century in England onward, is a
system of communication ("literature") in which ambiguity becomes
a creative and necessary instrument, while at the same time the art (and
the theory) of interpretation was reinvented, expanded, and honed. I call
this phenomenon "the hermeneutics of censorship," and my second and
longest chapter is concerned with demonstrating its existence and defining some of its strategies. I offer, in other words, an account of *functional* ambiguity, in which the indeterminacy inveterate to language was
fully and knowingly exploited by authors and readers alike (and among
those readers, of course, were those who were most interested in control). Functional ambiguity, as a concept, frees us somewhat from more
absolutely skeptical conclusions about indeterminacy in language and
its consequences for the reader or critic; unlike other theories of ambiguity, it does not privilege either writer or reader, or eliminate either.
It is hospitable to, and indeed dependent upon, a belief in authorial intention; yet it is incapable of reduction to a positivistic belief in meanings that authors can fix. Indeed, what this study of the hermeneutics
of censorship shows happening over and over again is that authors who
build ambiguity into their works have no control over what happens to
them later. So Sidney's *Arcadia,* a text the history of whose reception
is woven in and out of this book from beginning to end, was constantly
rewritten by later readers (as well as by Sidney himself) in the light of

their own historical circumstances and ideological needs. So Jonson's *Sejanus,* published in 1605, became subsequently, and in ways that Jonson could not possibly have intended, a metaphor for the career of George Villiers, duke of Buckingham. So, at an early moment when the law was forced to take cognizance of a problem of literary interpretation, the 1633 trial for seditious libel of William Prynne, Prynne's judges asserted that authorial intention (the defense that Collingbourne had entered) lasted no longer than the book remained in manuscript in the author's own hands. And so, in 1977, "political use" would be made of Havel's request for release from prison, with appropriate "recasting" and "additions."

I say that the hermeneutics of censorship developed in England in the middle of the sixteenth century, although, I have also indicated, this was in effect a rediscovery of a classical system of rhetorical ingenuity, the "ancient freedoms." It seems clear that whenever the need for it arises, the same system is reinvented. According to Daniel Balmuth, Russian writers at the end of the nineteenth century "became expert at the use of elliptical language, at innuendo and allusion, at the art of saying explicitly what they meant and not meaning exactly what they said." This Aesopian language, which included "the art of knowing when to say nothing" was the medium of a quiet but sustained critique of their government. And Balmuth makes the important point that one should not overemphasize the imperception of censors, who, as university graduates, were "often as well equipped as other members of educated society to read 'between the lines' ":

> The censorship . . . did not consider itself to be at war with writers; or perhaps . . . the warfare . . . was a 'cold war' in which ultimate weapons, confiscation and stoppage, were sparingly used, as sparingly as the openly radical or harsh criticism of the government and society. Censors and writers . . . fought each other, carefully observing rules for limited warfare.[25]

This story was confirmed yet again, and closer still to our own time, by an interview with a former Polish censor, published May 8, 1981, in the weekly newspaper of Solidarity, *Tygodnik Solidarnosci,* which the Censor's Office wished to suppress but which was printed at the insistence of the paper's editor, Tadeusz Mazowiecki (today, like Havel, a leading member of his own government). The young ex-censor divided his colleagues into three groups: the ideologues, those who see it as a job, and those who see it as a battle of wits. Claiming to belong to the middle category (and claiming also to be a social democrat at heart, opposed to limiting the freedom of the press), he quickly revealed himself to be a gamesman of the first order. He described the training program, how the office would select not the trainee who deleted the most from a text but the one who "crossed off the cleverest."

> It is more like a game, where one party tries to get the better of the other. No, but seriously, there was a sort of admiration for the intelligent journalist who wrote his stuff and tried to be cleverer than we. . . . Kisielewski, for instance, would write a little note to the censor: "How about letting it through this time, pussy cat?"[26]

K-62, as the interviewee was known, also produced an interesting if cynical variant on the *Myrroure*'s thesis that a literature critical of government is a necessary corridor of public opinion; for in *his* system, those complaints reached the authorities in the form of *deleted* passages carefully compiled as a censor's report!

> The unit was like an appeal to our lords and masters to take interest in the stuff that was in the press [i.e., *not* in the press] . . . all those demands and problems that have now flooded our long-suffering country, all that stuff that you [the journalists] ferreted out and we took out again, went out neatly marked to the press department of the CC across the road. So it is an evident untruth that the authorities were not informed. (p. 106)

And he also proposed that, at the opposite end of the spectrum from the ideologue (like Sir Roger L'Estrange), there existed a superior censor of liberal tendencies. "Quite frequently, the higher you go, the more liberal they get. . . . My chief was very favorably inclined towards the outspoken papers, and he would save all he could" (p. 108).

One must suspect a strong component of self-justification in such an interview. But many of its claims are supported by a completely persuasive account of censorship from the inside, deriving from the period in Russia just prior to that described by Balmuth. The diary of Alexsandr Nikitenko, a censor under both the reactionary Nicholas I and the vacillating Alexander II, though ultimately intended for publication, is not a document of which one can be either suspicious or contemptuous. It illustrates both the fluctuations in censorship policy that result from changes in leadership, and the possibility that a censor could himself be an intellectual with a high regard for literature, and what he called "the literary idea."

> What is meant by the literary idea? In the main it means to arouse in the hearts of people a respect for intellectual and educational achievements. Let at least a few bright, noble ideas sweep through the foggy and lifeless field of our society![27]

Nikitenko was, in fact, a compromise between the ideal "magistrate" envisaged by the *Myrroure* and a writer-intellectual himself. He also exemplified some of the most resistant self-contradictions in the liberal tradition. Believing in reform, Nikitenko advocated gradualism;[28] himself an emancipated serf, he embraced the emancipation that was finally legislated in 1861, yet he remained (as an autodidact) determinedly elitist.[29] In 1848, he proclaimed his support for the revolutions taking place in Europe ("May God be with them as they stride toward their great future," pp. 115–16) while protesting the formation of the notorious Buturlin Committee which was to reorganize Russian censorship against radicalism at home. The accession of Alexander II in 1855 made possible a brief era of *glasnost* (Nikitenko actually uses the term, p. 171), but within a few years he reports that the emperor's "faith in literature has been shaken and he has turned against it" (p. 169). "One thing is clear," Nikitenko reflected in April 1858, "you cannot, by imposing restrictions, direct and control minds that have awakened from centuries of slumber":

> Yes, it is hard, very hard, to guarantee freedom of thought. We seek improvements and think we can attain them through that same bureaucracy which has so wallowed in thievery, rather than with the help of public opinion. For the government, meanwhile, it is obviously better and safer to join with the press than to war with it. If it tells the press which way it must go, it will begin to move in secretive ways and will become impossible to control. No force can keep track of an idea labored over in secret, an idea that has been frustrated and forced to resort to cunning. Indeed, we still do not know how that terrifying system of police persecution of thought and speech in France [under the Second Empire] will end. But, at least there, the system is well defined, while we vacillate between permitting and not permitting, between constraining and not constraining. (p. 170)

Note that Nikitenko was less afraid of the press than that, under tighter controls, "a handwritten literature would come into being that would be impossible to control" (p. 170), a position diametrically opposite to that of those who now argue that printing made censorship unfeasible; and that he hereby anticipated the development in the Soviet bloc before *glasnost II* of *samizdat* "printing," the surreptitious production and distribution of merely typescript materials.

Yet two years later, his disillusionment is directed instead at the writers, who have failed to develop a properly flexible system of their own:

> At the beginning of the present reign our writers were not sufficiently tactful to benefit from the increased freedom bestowed on the press. They could have done a great deal to strengthen certain principles of society and incline the government toward various liberal measures, but instead they went to extremes and spoiled everything. . . . Instead of using the printed word, they abused it. I tried in vain to be the mediator between literature and the government, but literature had gone so far that it suddenly found itself in open and bitter opposition to the government, while the government shuddered and began in earnest to tighten the reins. (p. 216)

Had we such a document for the trajectory of censorship in early modern England, it is more than likely that the story it could tell would resemble Nikitenko's. I do not, of course, by so dwelling on the case of a liberal censor, intend to suggest that censorship is a benign institution, a complaint that Christopher Hill has made about my general thesis of literature's collaboration.[30] My point is rather to complicate the argument, to preclude a naive, black-and-white version of the liberal position on censorship, without ever denying that, in certain circumstances, censorship can be extremely, perhaps disastrously, repressive. It is good for literature only in the sense that it sharpens the wits and raises the stakes, giving writers a real task and their work a definable social value, supplying a costly content to a sometimes merely notional intellectual freedom. As Mario Vargas Llosa wrote in 1977, with respect to the situation in Argentina, Chile, and Uruguay, where academic departments of sociology were closed indefinitely as subversive, and creative writers had to shoulder the burden of social and political commentary:

> We can say that there are some positive aspects in this kind of situation for literature. Because of that commitment, literature is . . .

prevented from becoming—as unfortunately has happened in some developed societies—an esoteric and ritualistic experimentation in new forms of expression almost entirely dissociated from real experience. . . . In this context, the printed word, the written word, the book, have a privileged position, deserve respect and encourage hope. They enjoy total credibility. The pressure put on the pen presupposes that it is capable of telling the truth.[31]

Moreover, Nikitenko's *Diary,* like Havel's *Letters,* confirms my theory of how the hermeneutics of censorship work in practice. In an episode early in the *Diary,* he reported a Moscow scandal which I shall quote at some length, partly because this is one of the few places where a woman's voice enters the story of censorship, its effect doubled, moreover, by double entendre:

> The city is in an uproar and buzzing with gossip. Several poems by Countess Rostopchina were printed in the December 17th issue of the *Northern Bee,* and among them appeared her ballad, "The Forced Marriage." A knight-baron complains that his wife doesn't love him and is unfaithful to him, and she replies that she cannot love him because he had taken her by force. What could appear more innocent in respect to censorship? At first, both the censorship department and the public thought that Countess Rostopchina was talking about her own relations with her husband, which everyone knows are most unfriendly. I am simply amazed by the boldness with which she aired her family affairs before the public. . . . But now it turns out that the baron represents Russia, and the wife taken by force, Poland. It is really amazing how the poem fits either possibility, and since it is well-written, everyone is memorizing it. For example, the baron says:

> I sheltered her as an orphan
> Brought her here impoverished,
> And gave her my protection
> With a sovereign hand;
> ....
> But sad and unhappy
> Is my unappreciative wife,
> I know—with complaint, with slander
> She brands me everywhere.
> ....

> To this the wife replies:
> He forbids me to speak
> In my native tongue.
>
> ....
>
> He sent into exile, into prison
> All my loyal, true servants;
> And surrendered me to the oppression
> Of his slaves, his spies. . . . (pp. 109–10)

"There can be no doubt," Nikitenko continued (although he himself was initially deceived) "about the real meaning and significance of this poem. Bulgarin [the licenser] has already been summoned to Count Orlov. The censorship department awaits the storm." It is only one of the delicious ironies of this tale that the "outrage aux bonnes moeurs" (the standard invoked against *Madame Bovary*) which the countess would have committed had she been writing literally is of no concern to the emperor.

At this point a reader might perhaps inquire what relationship this argument holds to the theories of Leo Strauss, as set out in *Persecution and the Art of Writing*.[32] It differs absolutely. That is to say, Strauss was concerned solely with what he called the esoteric text, a concealed and heterodox subtext directed only to the privileged few and discernible between the lines of the exoteric text, some treatise of a moral or philosophical nature; for example, the *Laws* of Plato and the commentaries on Plato of Al Farabi, the philosophical works of Spinoza and Moses Maimonides. He was not interested in the vast territory of written discourse that was not philosophical, but in which, I argue, encoding did take place, along with discussions of ambiguity and interpretive practice. This territory includes political pamphlets, royal proclamations, published speeches or other records of parliamentary proceedings, sermons (both as delivered and as published), plays (both as performed and as printed), histories, editions and translations of classical authors, familiar letters, the pastoral romance, and the Pindaric ode.

When I initially made this distinction between what I call the hermeneutics of censorship and Leo Strauss's theory of "reading between the lines," I did not fully realize, as I now do, the vital importance of making the distinction clear. I now believe that the source of Strauss's contrast between the esoteric and the exoteric text, and indeed the basic principle of Straussianism itself, was John Toland, the Whig editor of Milton and John Harrington, who in 1720 published a brief pamphlet with the following remarkable title: *Clidophorus, or, Of the Exoteric and Esoteric Philosophy; That is, Of the External and Internal Doctrine of the Ancients: The one open and public, accommodated to popular prejudices and the Religions establish'd by Law; and the other private and secret, wherein, to the few capable and discrete, was taught the real Truth script of all disguises.* Toland himself claims to have derived the distinction between exoteric and esoteric texts from Cicero, *De Finibus* (5:5). In fact, although Cicero does there distinguish between exoteric works, defined as "popular in style" ["populariter scriptum"] and those "more carefully wrought" ["limatius"], this passage implies no secret agenda in the nonpopular text, nor the existence of any subtext.

There is heavy irony involved in this debt of Strauss to Toland, if it is one, since Toland's theory of reading between the lines was a response to English political censorship at the end of the seventeenth century, and was clearly presented as only a temporary recourse. The goal is the open society. If I now quote at some length from this lively and enterprising, if somewhat disreputable writer,[33] it is in order to clarify the tradition I myself choose to inherit, intellectual and political liberalism of an egalitarian bent, the diametrical opposite of Straussianism as properly understood. Toland inserted into *Clidophorus* a superb anecdote resonant with the political, religious, and indeed sexual politics of the preceding century:

> I have more than once hinted, that the External and Internal Doctrine, are as much now in use as ever, tho the distinction is not so openly and professedly approv'd, as among the Antients. This puts me in mind of what I was told by a near relation to the old Lord Shaftesbury. The latter conferring one day with Major Wildman about the many sects of Religion in the world, they came to this conclusion at last; that, notwithstanding those infinite divisions caus'd by the interests of the Priests and the ignorance of the People, ALL WISE MEN ARE OF THE SAME RELIGION; whereupon a Lady in the room, who seem'd to mind her needle more than their discourse, demanded with some concern what that Religion was? to whom the Lord Shaftesbury straight reply'd, Madam, *wise men never tell.* (pp. 94–95)

The point of this anecdote, for Toland, is not to imply the desirability of wisdom's continuing to preserve its silence (in a community from which women are excluded); on the contrary:

> if it be a desirable thing to have the Truth told without disguize, there's but one method to produce such a blessing. Let all men freely speak what they think, without being ever branded or punish't but for wicked practises, and leaving their speculative opinions to be confuted or approv'd by whoever pleases: then you are sure to hear the whole truth, and till then, but very scantily, or obscurely, if at all. (pp. 95–96)

Toland, however, two decades into the eighteenth century, and despite the fact that in 1695 precensorship by licensing was formally abolished, had no illusions about the constraints on freedom of expression that governed the age of Swift and Defoe. "In this state of things," he continued:

> while liberty in its full extent is more to be wish'd than expected, and thro human weakness people will preferr their repose, fame, or preferments, before speaking of Truth, there is nevertheless one observation left us, whereby to make a probable judgement of the sincerity of others in declaring their opinion. 'Tis this. When a man maintains what's commonly believ'd, or professes that's publicly injoin'd, it is not always a sure rule that he speaks what he thinks: but when he seriously maintains the contrary of what's by law establish'd, and openly declares for what most others oppose, then there's a strong presumption that he utters his mind. (p. 96)

In other words, while alert to the less-admirable human impulses which promote self-censorship (a point to which we shall return), Toland was unambiguous as to the ethical superiority of those who dare to express minority or heterodox opinion.

Strauss, on the contrary, created a hermeneutics or reading the ancients between the lines in order to find, beneath their surface idealism or piety, a message of such deep cynicism that it should *never* be made public except to a chosen group of acolytes; a deeply hypocritical system of communication which uses the "noble lie" of religion and morality to preserve social order and enterprise against an essentially Hobbesian human nature.[34] Strauss believed that philosophy is only for the few. The key text here is "On a Forgotten Kind of Writing," in which Strauss repeated his distinction between exoteric and esoteric writing and related it directly to his own profession:

Philosophy or science, the highest activity of man, is the attempt
to replace opinion about "all things" by knowledge of "all things";
but opinion is the element of society; philosophy or science is
therefore the attempt to dissolve the element in which society
breathes, and thus it endangers society. Hence philosophy or science
must remain the preserve of a small minority, and philosophers or
scientists must respect the opinions on which society rests. To respect
opinions is something entirely different from accepting them as true.
Philosophers or scientists who hold this view . . . are driven to
employ a peculiar manner of writing which would enable them to
reveal what they regard as the truth to the few, without endanger-
ing the unqualified commitment of the many to the opinions on which
society rests. They will distinguish between the true teaching as the
esoteric teaching, and the socially useful teaching as the exoteric
teaching; whereas the exoteric teaching is meant to be easily accessible to every reader, the esoteric teaching discloses itself only
to the very careful and well-trained readers after long and concen-
trated study.[35]

Strauss's own emphasis on the term "persecution" in *Persecution and
the Art of Writing* is therefore highly misleading. Despite his own Jewish
heritage (and departure from Germany in 1932),[36] Strauss aligned himself *not* with those heterodox philosophers of the early modern period
who, having themselves suffered from persecution, "desired to contribute
to the abolition of persecution as such,"[37] but rather with the ancients
(especially the Plato of the *Laws*), who believed "that the gulf separating
the 'wise' and the 'vulgar' was a basic fact of human nature" that dic-
tated not only the failure but the positive danger of popular education:

Even if they had nothing to fear from any political quarter, those
who started from that assumption would have been driven to the
conclusion that public communication of the philosophic truth was
impossible or undesirable, not only for the time being but for all
times. (p. 34; italics added)

For Strauss and some of his followers, it would be better if we still lived
in a society like the one Toland inhabited, before the Enlightenment,
the American Revolution, the French Revolution, and the dominance
of American democratic principles in the "Free World" all helped to

weaken the control of the many by the few. Despite the fact, then, that some of the *strategies* for evading censorship that I shall describe in what follows resemble features of Straussian esotericism, there is an absolute difference between us on what such codes were intended to accomplish, and what their redescription can accomplish today.

We share, however, one procedural or theoretical difficulty. As Hans-Georg Gadamer protested in relation to *Persecution and the Art of Writing,* any theory of encoded writing must today compete with several theories of self-censorship. "Is not conscious distortion, comouflage and concealment of the proper meaning," wrote Gadamer in *Truth and Method,* "in fact the rare extreme case of a frequent, even normal situation?—just as persecution (whether by civil authority or the church, the inquisition, etc.) is only an extreme case when compared with the intentional or unintentional pressure that society and public opinion exercise on human thought. Only if we are conscious of the uninterrupted transition from one to the other are we able to estimate the hermeneutical difficulty of [the] problem."[38] What Gadamer here raises (with respect to Strauss, mistakenly) is essentially a quantitative problem. How *much* importance should censorship in the older sense, as a set of constraints against freedom of expression, legislated or otherwise known to exist, be given in any contemporary theory of interpretation? By the time of John Stuart Mill, he at least believed that the primary tyranny was that of social opinion and its primary territory sexual relations. From the mid-nineteenth century onward, the major cases of literary censorship in the West (*Madame Bovary, Ulysses, Lady Chatterley's Lover*) have supported this premise.

Alternatively, a Marxist critic, especially since Louis Althusser, might (in defiance of the events of late 1989) continue to claim that the problem of political or religious censorship was insignificant compared with the ideological control that all public institutions—the church, the law, education—promote in a given society, and against which the individual has no defense because he or she is inside ideology. Indeed, the very category of the individual, with its liberal connotations, is but another trick of the system to make us, believing we are free, content to be slaves.[39] Michel Foucault, extending this notion still further, argued not only that the regulatory modern society is more tyrannical than the early modern one (hospitals are but another version of prisons) but that all professional discourses are forms of control of speech, since if we wish to have power and influence, to participate in "le vrai," we must learn to fit our speech to what is expected of us.[40] And, of course, Freud's concept of repression was also, in *The Interpretation of Dreams*, denoted censorship, a point which Jacques Lacan incorporated into his own linguistic rewriting of Freud.[41]

There are several ways of answering Gadamer's objection, or those of my own critics who have claimed that I overemphasize either the extent of actual censorship or its conscious resistance. First, however much we have learned about the modern tyranny of opinion, about hegemony, or the workings of the unconscious, this does not permit us to forget that there have been and continue to be times and places, historical periods and geopolitical arenas, in which only one kind of censorship really counts; in which political censorship is so pervasive that it rises to the forefront, at least among intellectuals and to some extent all literate people, as the central problem of consciousness and communication. Conditions in nineteenth-century Russia under the emperors, in the Soviet Union until 1989, in South Africa, in the unstable regimes of Latin America, and above all the case of Salman Rushdie, substantiate with considerable precision the claims I make about England in the early modern period, including the claim that literature was the territory in which ideas of individual freedom were transmitted and consolidated.

Second, I question the premise that persecution was indeed the "rare extreme case." Apart from Soman's argument that early modern censorship had, for practical necessity, to be frugal with its punishments, especially if they were to be exemplary, there is also the strong presumption that we overlook hundreds of cases where anonymous, socially insignificant persons were punished (under the broader definition of censorship that includes spoken offenses, heresy, etc.).[42] As Soman points out, "it was the highest placed author who was capable of giving the greatest offense, but who was at the same time the least vulnerable" to a government that preferred not to make highly visible martyrs, religious or secular;[43] with the result that major intellectual figures, aristocrats and courtiers, or "canonical" authors were either exempted, or had only minor difficulties. The "rare extreme case," then, is the case of Bruno or Galileo or Sir John Hayward or William Prynne, whose names have entered history at large; though if one reads the annals of censorship this list rapidly becomes so long as to put their exceptionality in question.[44] But even without adjusting the statistics, Gadamer's logic can be simply inverted. The more successfully a society impressed on its writers that it was dangerous for them to speak their minds without inhibition, the more they were likely to encode their opinions. The more successfully writers encoded their opinions, the less evidence of "persecution" we have.

Finally, a constant stress on intentionality (perhaps less under embargo today than it was even in 1984) does not rule out an equal interest in and respect for the psyche, for the subtle intersections of state censorship with self-censorship, as fear shades into caution, caution into prudence, and prudence into more self-serving emotions and motives. As Toland put it, "thro human weakness people will preferr their repose, fame, or preferments, before speaking of Truth." This book is full of evidence of complex psyches at work, in Sidney, Jonson, Donne, Cowley, Marvell; and it is because of my respect for the psychological component in interpretation, for the value of the devious traces real authors leave of themselves in their writing, that I have wished to tell a more intricate story about censorship than is still, I believe, the norm. That story is properly introduced and substantiated by what we have seen, from the inside, of Nikitenko, the mid-nineteenth-century censor, and Václav Havel, contemporary victim and hero.

My book, I now realize even more strongly, only scrapes the surface of the topic.[45] It begins with Sir Philip Sidney and what the revision of his *Arcadia* can tell us about authorial intention, a problem on which, in the interval, I have had the opportunity to clarify my own position.[46] The second, and the most important, chapter describes the workings and some of the most recognizable components of the hermeneutics of censorship; and the remaining three chapters explore the creation of new genres, or the adaptation of already existent ones to new purposes, specifically the lyric, the romance, and the familiar letter. In each of these, one of the conditions which reactivated generic thinking was the widely perceived contradiction between censorship, as a set of rules and sanctions devised by society to limit individual freedom, and writing, the ultimate expression of the old proverb, "Thought is free."

In my first version of this introduction, I ended with an indictment, which some reviewers applauded, of the self-censorship imposed on itself by the academy, its habit in this century of restricting itself to a narrow definition of what constitutes, in Nikitenko's phrase, "the literary idea," a wrong solution to the parodox recognized by Howell and many of his contemporaries. "By discarding the time-honored tradition of literature as a privileged medium by which matters of grave public concern could be debated," I wrote then, "by allowing the logic of a philosophical enquiry into the indeterminacy of language to erase the social function that indeterminacy once had, we have handed over to others the absolute control of the public discourse of our time. We have made our writing and reading irrelevant, not merely to the awesome policies that threaten our physical survival, but even to the question with which this book directly deals—the role of the intellectual in the national and international consciousness.'' Fortunately, since I wrote those words, unforeseeable and great changes have made the world less dangerous, and demonstrated that indeed intellectuals, especially those who have tested their wits and endurance against censorship, can move with authority (''the authority of genius is enhanced by punishment'') into the public sphere. There are ways of being out of date that are better than being avant-garde; and this is a form of obsolescence I find particularly satisfying.

But because there are some things that never change, I want to end this new introduction by going back to the first writer to whom I made a major commitment: Andrew Marvell. This reprise also invokes Salman Rushdie and the role of humor (''pitting levity against gravity'') in the writer's battle with censorship. In the case of *The Satanic Verses,* levity seems not yet to have offered its conventional protection; but in the case of *The Rehearsal Transpros'd* and its sequel, it did. In 1672, Sir Roger L'Estrange, attempting to track down the author of this anonymous defense of toleration against Samuel Parker, was summoned to the house of Arthur Annesley, earl of Anglesey, to hear the following:

> Look you, Mr. Lestrange, there is a Book come out (*The Rehearsal Transpros'd*) I presume you have seen it. I have spoken to his Majesty about it, and the King says he will not have it suppressed . . . and since the King will have the book to pass, pray give Mr. Pinder your license to it.[47]

And Marvell's opponent Parker subsequently went down in history as he who ''gave occasion to the wittiest books that have appeared in this age.'' ''One may judge,'' wrote Bishop Gilbert Burnet, ''how pleasant these books were; for the last King, that was not a great reader of books, read them over and over again.''[48]

1   "Under . . . pretty tales"
Intention in Sidney's *Arcadia*

Sir Philip Sidney's *Arcadia* is a natural introduction to the joint study of interpretation and culture. Defined by C. S. Lewis as the paradigmatic literary representation of Elizabethanism,[1] the *Arcadia* is also, in more ways than one, a central Caroline and civil war text. It achieved extraordinary significance as a cultural symbol in the court and even the life of Charles I; it featured in the political debates over his execution; it became not only a model for later-seventeenth-century fiction but a symbol of a certain type of fiction — the romance — fiction with ideological content, whose very fictionality held an interesting and provocative relation to its engagement with history. As such, the *Arcadia* was crucial to the evolution of seventeenth-century genre theory.

But these facts (to be detailed in Chapter 4) also imply that the *Arcadia* was constantly being reread during the seventeenth century; that is, reinterpreted, as the historical context and needs of the audience changed. Sidney's friend and editor, Fulke Greville, provided one interpretation in his *Life of Sidney,* written between 1610 and 1612. In so doing, he raised explicitly the question of authorial intention. According to Greville, Sidney's "intent and scope" in the *Arcadia* was "lively to represent the growth, state and declination of Princes, change of Government, and lawes; vicissitudes of sedition, faction, succession."[2] Greville was clearly unbothered by fears or even fine distinctions about representationalism in art, accepting without difficulty a principle of fictional displacement, along with belief, common to his age, that literature could and should carry messages. The message of the *Arcadia* was, Greville asserted, particularly directed at "Sov-

32

eraign Princes," especially those who, like Sidney's Basilius, "put off publique action" in order to "play with their own visions." Such rulers should recognize themselves in Sidney's text, and understand that they "bury themselves, and their Estates in a cloud of contempt" (pp. 13–14).

Greville might be supposed to have known something about Sidney's intentions; but if his reading were "correct," how was it possible for Charles I so to "misread" the *Arcadia* as to incorporate it into his own visions, his own program of English arcadianism, the halcyon days of the 1630s? Greville's *Life of Sidney* was not published until 1652, when someone perceived its potential appeal to a Puritan and republican audience, the relevance of its message to the monarchy that had just been abolished; yet by 1658 the *Arcadia* had been reclaimed, as it were, by the royalists, who discovered in the romance a key to class solidarity, a language in which to express and assess their own recent history.

These facts make Sidney's *Arcadia* an unusually elegant test case for theories of interpretation, particularly those of authorial intention and reception. By authorial intention I choose to mean conscious intention, Sidney's motives in embarking on the work, his changes of intention (for which the many revisions of the *Arcadia* provide a potent source of evidence), his concept of its function and audience. By reception I choose to mean the *Arcadia*'s history of publication, adoption (by certain groups of readers), adaptation (for certain ends), any evidence that we can recover of the way it has been understood at different moments after it passed beyond Sidney's control.

Questions of interpretation and authorial intention lead directly to the third reason for beginning with the *Arcadia:* its status as disguised discourse. It is well known that Sidney felt himself to have serious problems of communication in the Elizabethan court, that his known advocacy of a militant international Protestantism deprived him of effective address to the queen. It is also known (though not so widely) that Sidney was directly involved in parliamentary debates about political censorship. In 1581 the House of Lords had introduced a harsh bill designed to repress any further public comment on the notorious French marriage controversy: Elizabeth's hopes, from late 1578 through early 1581, of marrying the duc d'Alençon. This project raised a storm of national and Protestant outrage involving, among others, John Stubbs, author of *The Discoverie of a Gaping Gulf, whereinunto England is like to be swallowed by another French mar-*

riage, if the Lord forbid not the banes (1579). The punishment for
Stubbs was the old punishment for seditious libel, loss of the right
hand. Sidney, who had written a private letter to Elizabeth arguing against the marriage, suffered temporary disgrace and exclusion
from court.[3] The *Act against seditious words and rumours* (23 Eliz.
Cap. II), sometimes referred to as the "Statute of Silence," was introduced by the Lords in January 1581. It began with the premise that
in previous censorship laws there had not been specified "sufficient
and condign punishment" for those who spoke or published what
the queen did not wish to hear; and it proceeded to specify a scale
of increasingly gruesome penalties, from loss of one ear for spread-
ing rumors, to capital punishment for seditious *publication*. Sidney
was not only a member of this parliament, as was Stubbs, but also
sat on the Commons committee that amended the bill and softened
its rigor. In particular, they managed to write in a saving clause, "with
malicious intent," to govern all offences.[4] The effect of this amendment was not only to complicate the business of proof in charges
of sedition, but to bring explicitly into the political area a form of
literary inquiry. The state had formally entered the business of textual interpretation, and had been forced to declare a respect for authorial intention.

In the light of these facts, it is reasonable to ask what relation the
Arcadia held to Sidney's known concerns and recent experience; and
particularly in the light of political censorship, to what extent its fictionality, its generic affiliations, its plot and other textual procedures
may relate to the problem of restricted or proscribed communication.
Such an inquiry will, inevitably, set up the key terms and methodological premises for subsequent chapters.

We should start, then, with what is known of the *Arcadia*'s genesis and production, something that the best editorial minds have had
difficulty in reconstructing, and in which authorial intention and reception are already confused. Even here, there are signs that genetic
mystery may be actually mystification. The text exists in three major
versions, none of which was published by Sidney himself. The first
version, that we now call the *Old Arcadia,* may have been begun soon
after Sidney's return from his German embassy in June 1577 and completed in the spring of 1581.[5] On the other hand, it may have been
entirely conceived and executed while Sidney was in rustication from
the Elizabethan court during 1580. The difference is not small if we
are considering Sidney's motives in writing, and to that end investi-

gating the *exact* historical context of his work. In any case, Sidney apparently abandoned the *Old Arcadia* sometime in 1582, and either then or in 1584 embarked on a massively expanded and substantially revised version, the *New Arcadia,* that he never finished. It breaks off in mid sentence, partway through its third book. We do not know whether this was because of reasons internal to the text, or Sidney's own dissatisfaction with it, or whether its composition was simply interrupted when he left to take up his military commission in the Netherlands, where he died of gangrene. Nor do we know how much authorial instruction Sidney's friend Greville was working with when he published the revised version, in its incomplete state, in 1590.[6] Finally, we do not know why, in 1593, Greville and Sidney's sister, Mary, countess of Pembroke, apparently agreed to bring out a composite text, under the nominal editorship of Hugh Sanford, the Pembrokes' secretary. In the 1593 text, the last two and a half books of the *Old Arcadia* were grafted upon the *New,* with predictable effects of disproportion and incongruity. It was this version that became "the" *Arcadia,* for the seventeenth century and for all readers, until manuscripts of the *Old Arcadia* were discovered and a text was published at the beginning of this century.

The hints of authorial intention that survive seem to confuse the issue still further. They are, first, Sidney's mention of an unspecified "toyfull booke" or "books" in an October 1580 letter to his brother; second, an undated letter to his sister, entrusting her with the manuscript of an "idle worke . . . done onelie for you, onely to you," a work whose "chiefe safetie, shalbe the notwalking abroad."[7] This letter was published by Greville as a preface to the *New Arcadia* in 1590. It suggests a recreative exercise, a pastime, intended at most for a small private audience. We do not know, however, which version of the *Arcadia* it originally referred to. Some critics have felt that it fits the *Old Arcadia* better than the *New,* some that it fits neither. Few have remarked the obvious conflict between the discretion invoked in the letter, the emphasis on the text's "safetie" in "not walking abroad," and its appearance as the preface to a *published* work. It may be that the letter is only a clever and specious disclaimer, either written by Sidney himself, or constructed by Greville, who (as we shall see later) was quite capable of such disingenuousness.

Third, there is the preface to the 1593 composite text, which sets the problem of intention squarely before the audience, without making any gestures toward solving it:

> Though they finde not here what might be expected, they may
> finde nevertheless as much as was intended, the conclusion, not
> the perfection of Arcadia: and that no further then the Authours
> own writings, or knowen determinations could direct. Whereof
> who sees not the reason, must consider there may be a reason
> which he sees not. [8]

This certainly sounds like intentional mystification, the kind of statement frequently found in the prefaces to seventeenth-century texts
that provoke the suspicions or curiosity of the reader, inviting him
to look closely.

Such a reader, denied explicit guidance, would probably look for
authorial intention in the genre of the work before him. Now, the
obfuscating textual history of the *Arcadia* has caused perhaps less
dispute than its genre, not only because Sidney's recognizable models imply generic mixture, but also because he seems to have changed
the generic emphasis of the work in revision. Without discussing for
the moment the *Arcadia's* romance and epic affiliations, we must
surely agree that its first generic signal—its title—foregrounded a pastoral tradition, the kinship of the work to Sannazaro's *Arcadia*, and
behind that to Vergil's *Eclogues*. In his *Defence of Poesie,* Sidney had
articulated the standard Renaissance reading of Vergilian pastoral:

> Is the poor pipe disdained, which sometime out of Meliboeus'
> mouth can show the misery of people under hard lords or raven-
> ing soldiers? And again, by Tityrus, what blessedness is derived
> to them that lie lowest from the goodness of them that sit high-
> est; sometimes, under the pretty tales of wolves and sheep, can
> include the whole considerations of wrongdoing and patience. [9]

It is easy to assume that this passage could have very little bearing
on a work as generically complex as the *Arcadia;* but the pastoral
theory of the *Defence* is, if read carefully, both more complex itself
and more germane to the *Arcadia* than it might seem. Lexical connections between it and crucial statements in the *Arcadia* suggest that
Sidney himself not only connected the two, but intended the echoes
to serve as a two-way gloss.

The passage from the *Defence* is distinctly cunning, both syntac-
tically and semantically. It contains a condensed argument about the
relationship between literature and sociopolitical experience. If you
live "under hard lords or ravening soldiers," you may have to com-

municate "under the pretty tales of wolves and sheep." The prepo-
sitional symmetry ("under . . . under") supports the propositional
irony of seeing pastoral as the genre in which writers "lie lowest" in
more senses than one. The central allusion is, of course, to Vergil's
First Eclogue, in which the sad shepherd, Meliboeus, converses for a
moment, before heading out into exile, with his more fortunate neigh-
bor, Tityrus. The historical context of the poem was the last phase
of the civil war and the expropriation of farm lands in Italy by Octavius, who wished both to reward his own soldiers and to punish
those who had supported Brutus and Cassius. According to the ancient commentary of Servius, widely accepted during the Renaissance,
Vergil's point was that the expropriated farmers were innocent victims. By representing himself as the fortunate shepherd exempted
from their fate, he was able, however indirectly, to indicate the severity of Octavius's policy. The dominance of the First Eclogue over the
Eclogues as a whole had the effect, also, of causing the other pastoral subjects — song contest and especially love complaint — to be
measured by those larger standards of responsibility. This was something that Sidney's contemporary, George Puttenham, felt his audience needed to remember:

> The Poet devised the Eglogue . . . not of purpose to counter-
> fait or represent the rusticall manner of loves and communica-
> tion; but under the vaile of homely persons, and in rude speeches
> to insinuate and glaunce at greater matters, and such as per-
> chance had not bene safe to have beene disclosed in any other
> sort, which may be perceived in the Eglogues of Virgill, in which
> are treated by figure matters of greater importance then the loves
> of Titirus and Corydon.[10]

The connection between this theory and the *Arcadia* is made at
the point where Sidney describes Arcadian mores. This point is differently located in the *Old* and *New* versions of the text. In the *Old Arcadia,* the description immediately precedes the First Eclogues, the
first group of poems that interrupts the romantic narrative of Basilius and his daughters. "The manner of the Arcadian shepherds," Sidney wrote, "was . . . to pass their time," either in music or sports:

> But, of all other things, they did especially delight in eclogues,
> wherein sometimes they would contend for a prize of well sing-
> ing, sometimes lament the unhappy pursuit of their affections,

sometimes, again, under hidden forms utter such matters as
otherwise were not fit for their delivery. (p. 56)

In the *New Arcadia,* this passage was moved back to the opening description by Kalander of the unhappy state of affairs in Arcadia. The
context is the news that Basilius has abandoned his responsibilities
and gone into retreat on his country estate. The last phrase of the
relocated passage was, moreover, significantly altered. Instead of "under hidden forms utter such matters as otherwise were not fit for their
delivery," Sidney wrote, "under hidden forms uttering such matters,
as otherwise they durst not deale with" (p. 28). By making the textual alteration, Sidney removed the possibility that he might have been
referring merely to a theory of pastoral decorum, in which any kind
of high subject or deep thought was out of bounds. By relocating
the passage to Kalander's account, he placed it in a context that was
already critical of Basilius, so that the theory of "hidden forms" was
connected to the problem of political expression, when a ruler is at
fault. Further, to glance back at the passage from the *Defence* is to
see that the crucial phrase — "under hidden forms" — is an extension
of the series "under hard lords" and "under the pretty tales"; while
an intentional connection between the two passages is further assumed
by the "sometimes . . . sometimes" formula in both.

But aligning the two passages also shows up the distinction between them. In the *Arcadia,* the triple set of "sometimes" introduces
not, as in the *Defence,* a series of examples of arcane political comment, but a series of competing propositions about the function of
pastoral. Writing "under hidden forms" is distinguished both from
song contest, i.e., "wel singing" for its own sake or for fame, which
we might call formalism, and from love complaint, i.e., "lamenting
their affections," in which we would recognize a poetry of self-
expression. Moreover, all three possibilities are governed by the assumption that the Arcadians engage in the making of eclogues in order
"to pass their time," a phrase that creates a distinctly undermining,
recreative context. It reminds us of those deprecatory references to
a "toyfull booke" and an "idle worke"; and it suggests that the questions critics have asked about the *Arcadia* are questions Sidney was
asking by means of it. Given that pastoral song is here, as it was in
Vergil's *Eclogues,* a metaphor for literature both in the largest sense
and specifically as its function was brought into question by events
in Vergil's Rome, Sidney's analysis is recognizable as a poetics, its

ostensible subject Arcadian culture, its real subject Elizabethan culture. The alternative theories of literature's function that he suggests — indirect didacticism, formalism, and expressivism — are, of course, still in competition today; but we do not easily credit Sidney and his contemporaries with such perception.

In fact, the history of Sidney criticism during this century shows a marked tendency to argue from one of these positions at the expense of the others; and the alternation of those preferences is itself not without significance as part of the *Arcadia*'s history of reception. At the beginning of the century it was still possible to assume, as Greville had done, that literary texts could carry messages, and that those messages were determined by the original historical context of the work. In 1913 Edwin Greenlaw proposed a reading of the *Arcadia* as a sustained account "under hidden forms" of Elizabethan politics. Basilius's defection from government, he suggested, was a metaphor for Elizabeth's foreign policy, whereby peace was purchased at the expense of the Protestant activism to which Sidney, Leicester, and Walsingham were dedicated. Similarly, the romantic misbehavior in *Arcadia* was a figurative account, according to Greenlaw, of the French marriage controversy, which he saw as the historical origin of the *Arcadia*'s focus on romantic self-indulgence and excess. [11]

Greenlaw based his case on contemporary documents. One was Sidney's own letter to Elizabeth advising against the marriage. Then there was Sidney's correspondence with his mentor, Hubert Languet, a Huguenot refugee and ardent promoter of the Protestant cause in Europe. In their correspondence, both sides complained of a dangerous passivity among Protestant princes in the face of Spanish imperialism. That Sidney referred to this passivity as "sleep" was, at the very least, suggestive in view of the *Arcadia*'s use of sleep — the extreme *otium* of Basilius's deathlike trance — as a central narrative device and moral emblem. [12] The third document, and the one on which Greenlaw relied most heavily, was Greville's *Life of Sidney,* with its assertions that the work was intended as a textbook for rulers, a taxonomy of political and ethical thought.

Greenlaw's argument was an interesting case of the old historical criticism at its intuitive best and with its methodological inadequacies plain. He drew attention to Sidney's demonstrable concerns, and suggested a plausible system for their displacement into fiction — that is, by broad analogy and symbolic transfer, rather than the tight system of equivalences we call allegory. At the same time, he made two serious mistakes. One was to invoke the historical context of the *Old Arcadia,* whereas Greville's *Life* refers unmistakably to the *New,* not begun until the French marriage crisis was clearly over. The other was to ignore the fact that Greville's *Life* was itself a "text," with its own motives and strategies, rather than an authoritative account of Sidney's intentions. Writing not under Elizabeth, but under James, Greville held a view of Elizabethan foreign policy that was entirely different from that of Sidney in 1580. Much of the *Life* is devoted to a eulogy of Elizabeth, from a post-Armada perspective. Its moralism is therefore addressed to Jacobean "visions" and failures, particularly the pro-Spanish policies and pacificism of James himself;[13] and for Greville, Sidney's own career illustrated the "*differences,* between the reall and large complexions of *those* active times, and the narrow salves of *this* effeminate age" (p. 11; italics added). Greville also makes it clear that the *Life* is his substitute for the history of Elizabeth's reign that he had wished to write, and that he was prevented from writing by Cecil's refusal to release the historical records to him, on the grounds that he might "deliver many things done in that time, which might perchance be construed to the prejudice of this" (p. 239). The *Life,* then, has its own obliqueness, necessitated by the restraints against open historical reporting that Greville himself experienced. Its value as a guide to Sidney's intentions lies more in this, perhaps — their equally restrictive cultural environments — than in Greville's account of the *Arcadia.*

Greenlaw's arguments quickly disappeared from sight, as criticism since the 1920s became increasingly antihistorical. One could say that the latest phases of the *Arcadia*'s reception illustrated the rise and decline of formalism. Ringler's edition of the poems, with its elaborate stemma, emphasized the significance of textuality, while detaching the poems from their narrative, or any other, context. Rudenstine's teleological account of Sidney's career used metrical analyses of the Arcadian poems to prove their significance as apprentice work, a technical stage on the way to *Astrophil and Stella.*[14] Walter Davis and Richard Lanham transferred the formalist impulse from metrics to genre, a matter still of narrative and tonal relationships internal to the work; and Lanham explicitly declared that Sidney's intentions "can reasonably be inferred from the text," and the text alone: "We need not flee to biography."[15]

In the 1970s, however, there began to be signs that formalism was proving too limited an approach to the *Arcadia.* In effect, the Greenlaw hypothesis was disinterred, though with important differences. Dorothy Connell, for example, applied the French marriage question, appropriately, to the *Old Arcadia*. She compared Sidney's letter to Elizabeth to Philanax's opening advice to Basilius, and concluded that Philanax was a figure of Sidney's own role "in trying to advise the Queen."[16] Connell, however, resisted any implication that Sidney could have been opposed to Elizabeth's policies, as too subversive a notion; and she even more strenuously resisted the dreaded term "allegory." Yet she argued that the *Old Arcadia* carried an implied political message, and that its primary audience was intended to be the queen herself.

Richard McCoy, on the other hand, attempted to combine a sociopolitical reading of the *Arcadia* with a psychological one. The text reflects, he argued, the "social and personal predicament of an Elizabethan aristocrat, caught up in a tangle of diminishing feudal power . . . courtly dependence and intrigue, and a cult of devotion to a formidable, emasculating queen."[17] In this reading, the dialectical tensions in the *Arcadia* are explained in terms of Sidney's own *ambivalences,* and McCoy's language implies an expressive theory of function, rather than a calculated act of persuasion. The text is described as "an engaging diversion," a "fictive exploration of the problems of sovereignty," "an outlet," something that "reflects" or "illuminates" Sidney's personal conflicts which were also those of his class. That the illumination might have been intended for others was not, apparently, considered. For McCoy, Sidney was engaged in literary self-help, displacing his frustrations into fiction in order to acquire some emotional distance from them.

It is of course possible to argue, both from the dialectical nature of the *Arcadia* and from the diversity of critical opinion about it, that the work itself remains multivalent. There is a difference, however, between arguing that Sidney was himself responsible for the divisions among his readers, and that he had not himself made up his mind. The debate on the function of poetry is not, I think, left unsettled in the *Arcadia.* The early description of Arcadian culture, with its competing propositions, functions as a hypothesis to be complicated by later arguments. Any complete statement about what the *Arcadia* contributes to poetics or cultural analysis must certainly include a discussion of the role of Philisides in the text, Philisides who is clearly a figure for Sidney himself.[18]

If Philanax (king lover, monarchist) stands for Sidney in his role of would-be counsellor to Elizabeth, Philisides (star lover, idealist) stands for him in his role as a literary man, a maker of texts. Yet there is reason to think that the roles of Philanax and Philisides are not so far apart. Behind Philisides is Sannazaro's Sincero, a figure for Sannazaro as a member of the Neopolitan Academy; and behind Sincero, Tityrus, as Vergil's persona in the *Eclogues,* and the figure who brings into question the function of poetry in Rome.

Philisides first appears in the *Old Arcadia* during the First Eclogues, as a lovesick youth in dispute with Geron (old man). Geron's arguments are not only against lovesickness, arguments which go back to, among other classical sources, the reproach of Gallus in Vergil's tenth Eclogue, but also against love complaint, as something that makes matters worse: "Up, up, Philisides, let sorrows go," cries Geron, "who yields to woe doth but increase his smart" (p. 72). Love complaint, in other words, represents an abuse of poetry. In the next poem, formally connected to "Up, up, Philisides" by its opening line, "Down, down, Melampus," Geron's anger at Philisides leads into another debate on appropriate discourse, this time with the satirist Mastix (scourge). As Mastix sees it, the behavior of Philisides is symptomatic of a crisis in Arcadia. Like the sheep dog Melampus, who is supposed to govern and protect the sheep, not fight with his fellow canines, the greatest shepherds in Arcadia are misusing their position by quarreling with each other; and if not infighting, they are "asleep," lulled by a false sense of security. Small wonder then that the younger men waste their days in trivial occupations:

> At blow point, hot cockles, or else at keels,
> While, "Let us pass our time," each shepherd says.
>
> (p. 77)

This return of the concept of pastime is significant, as is the use of "sleep" as a metaphor for irresponsibility, echoing as it does Sidney's correspondence with Languet and foreshadowing the long sleep of Basilius. In the mind of Mastix the satirist, Arcadian culture, with its emphasis on *otium* and on pastime, is clearly decadent:

> . . . "Let us pass our time" each shepherd says.
> So small account of time the shepherd feels,
> And doth not feel that life is naught but time,
> And when that time is past, death holds his heels.
>
> (pp. 77–78)

For Geron, however, a recourse to satire in this situation is not only
too negative, but dangerous to the satirist. He proceeds to warn Mastix to keep quiet for his own good, producing as evidence a beast fable,
the tale of a swan who lost his voice for excessive social criticism.
The swan having unwisely attacked all the other birds for various vices,
they join ranks against him, summon a parliament, and mute him:

> There was the swan of dignity deprived,
> And statute made he never should have voice,
> Since when, I think, he hath in silence lived.
>
> (pp. 78–79)

Now, the word *silence* had, in the *Old Arcadia,* clearly been given
political connotations. In the last of the First Eclogues, Musidorus
(as Dorus) had extended his complaints about unrequited love into
a general discussion of failed communication; and however deeply
he deplored the ineffectuality of love complaint, that form of frustration is to be preferred, he declared, to the absolute restriction of
discourse experienced at court:

> Then do I think, indeed, that better it is to be private
> In sorrow's torments than, tied to the pomps of a palace,
> Nurse inward maladies, which have not scope to be breathed out,
> But perforce digest all bitter juices of horror
> *In silence,* from a man's own self with company robbed.
> Better yet do I live, that though by my thoughts I be plunged
> Into my life's bondage, yet may disburden a passion
> (Oppressed with ruinous conceits) by the help of an outcry;
> *Not limited to a whisp'ring note, the lament of a courtier.*
>
> (p. 86; italics added)

In the light of Sidney's own political experience, these lines provide
both an intertextual and a contextual gloss on Geron's fable. Both
poems derive their emotional force and point from the foreground-
ing of political censorship in 1579 through 1581, especially the case
of John Stubbs; and the mention of both "parliament" and "statute"
in Geron's beast fable made inevitable, one would think, a connection with the notorious "statute of silence."

This reading must affect our dating of the *Old Arcadia,* since the
Geron-Mastix debate would seem to have been partly motivated by
the events of January 1581. But it is also important to note what happened to this poem in the *New Arcadia,* conceived and executed in

a less confrontational political atmosphere. The Geron-Mastix debate, along with its companion piece ("Up, up, Philisides"), disappeared from the First Eclogues, and there seems to have been no plan for their relocation. If one believes, as I do, that Sidney remained deeply interested in the function of the eclogues in his revised conception of the work, then it follows that these poems were not simply lost in the shuffling of papers, but deemed no longer necessary. This was not, however, a gesture of conciliation. Mastix the satirist ("saying still the world was amiss, but how it should be amended he knew not") disappeared; but if we look closely at the *New Arcadia* we find that his critique of society, his outspokenness, survived him, that the echo even of his words has been carefully retained, and cunningly reconstructed.

In an important passage describing the state of Macedon before Evarchus took over, Sidney provided an indictment of a badly governed state. There was

> a very dissolution of all estates, while the great men . . . grew factious among themselves; . . . old men long nusled in corruption, scorning them that would seeke reformation; yong men very fault-finding, but very faultie . . . townes decayed for want of a just and naturall libertie; offices, even of judging soules, solde; publique defences neglected; and in summe . . . witte abused, *rather to faine reason why it should be amisse, then how it should be amended.* (p. 186; italics added).

The explicit echo, with corrections, of Mastix's position is vitally important here. Sidney's indictment of Arcadian government is not now contained within the point of view of one destructive personality, but generalized and aligned with the politically normative figure of Evarchus, antitype to Basilius. Still more to the point, its emphasis is cultural as well as political, its focus the role of the intellectual, the possessor of "witte." "Witte [is] abused," or cultural energy dissipated, in a realm deprived of authority. It cannot be an accident, either, that this passage sets up another echo, with Sidney's own *Defence of Poesie,* and specifically with that moment where he admits that all is not well with Elizabethan literature:

> Say not that poetrie abuseth man's wit, but that man's wit abuseth poetrie.

We can follow Sidney's intentions here as they become clearer to himself. Philisides (irresponsible expressivism) has been corrected by

Geron (moral didacticism) and so has Mastix, the would-be conveyor of political messages, though not, perhaps, in a sufficiently covert form; but in the final version the impulse to sociopolitical commentary is released from its dialectical subordination. More or less objectified, it becomes the dominant position.

Philisides, however, was to come into his own again, and in a way that was compatible with the process just described. In the middle of the *Old Arcadia,* during the Third Eclogues which celebrate a rural marriage, Philisides reappears, having now acquired a mysterious presence and authority. Upon request, he sings to the shepherds attending the wedding a song "old Languet had [him] taught," a statement that certainly encourages his readers to supply a historical or autobiographical context. The song he sings is an enigmatic beast fable, whose subject has nothing whatever to do with the concept of marriage that dominates the rest of the Third Eclogues.

In Sidney's fable, all the animals appeal to Jove for a king. After warning them that monarchy leads to tyranny, he grants their request, on certain conditions:

> . . . beasts, take heed what you of me desire.
> Rulers will think all things made them to please,
> .   .   .   .
> But since you will, part of my heav'nly fire
> I will you lend; the rest yourselves must give.
>
> (p. 257)

When the divine spark is incarnate, and endowed with characteristics derived from each of the animals, the result is Man, the superbeast. As Jove predicted, the new king quickly becomes a tyrant over those who made him what he is. He foments hostility between the great wild beasts and the lesser animals, driving the former into exile and then preying himself on the meeker animals left without protection. The fable ends with a double message:

> O man, rage not beyond thy need;
> Deem it no gloire to swell in tyranny.
> .   .   .   .
> And you, poor beasts, in patience bide your hell,
> *Or know your strengths,* and then you shall do well.
>
> (p. 259; italics added)

Whatever this means, it is clearly not the appeal of an early ecologist. Modern critical opinion has attempted to decode the poem, using the reference to Languet as a key, but with various results. The fable has been read as an incitement to rebellion, in the line of Huguenot pamphlets like *Vindiciae contra Tyrannos;*[19] as an expression of orthodox Tudor absolutism designed to ingratiate Sidney with the queen;[20] as an assertion of the importance of a powerful aristocracy in maintaining the balance of power;[21] and as a Calvinist allegory on the fall of man.[22] While the last suggestion seems to have little merit, the text of the fable *is* capable of supporting any, or rather all, of the other three readings, and in ways that invite our careful scrutiny.

The story itself is, of course, a reworking of Aesop's fable of the frogs desiring a king.[23] As John Ogilby pointed out in his 1651 paraphrase of Aesop, the fable of the frogs had an ancient history of political meaning:

> Phaedrus will have this Fable to have been made by Aesop, upon occasion of Pisistratus his seising of the Port of Athens, and taking the Supreme Power into his own hands, as Tyrant.[24]

But Ogilby also noted that in Phaedrus's application of the fable the concluding moral reads:

> You, O Citizens, bear this, he said,
> Lest you a greater mischief do invade.
>
> (p. 32)

Clearly this is the source of Sidney's conclusion, but with a significant variant; the insertion of an alternative to patient forbearance. "*Or* know your strengths," wrote Sidney; and for those who could recognize the original, he thereby signaled his desire for less stoical advice. Also, he ambiguated his message by addressing himself both to sovereign ("O man") and people ("poor beasts"); while in its entirety his version of the fable implies a more subtle analysis of political tyranny than that available in Aesop. A ruler who combines Jove's "heavenly fire" with a full set of animal characteristics is perceived both in ideal terms, kingship by divine right, and with a Machiavellian realism. Yet both these forms of absolutism are modified by hints of contract theory, since the animals agreed to what they got. Contract theory is also implied in these lines, crucial to the meaning and status of the poem:

To their own work this privilege they grant:
That from thenceforth to all eternity
No beast should freely speak, but only he.

(p. 257)

The price they have to pay for a monarchy is their freedom of speech.

It seems clear that this fable is, like Geron's tale of the silenced swan, not only about repression and the restriction of free political commentary, but about itself, about fabling, and about equivocation in the interests of safety. It is worth remembering Sidney's point in the *Defence,* that living "under hard lords" leads to writing "under the pretty tales of wolves and sheep," a phrase that conflates pastoral and beast fable as those forms which can imply "the whole considerations of wrongdoing and patience." While Sidney's fable seems to remain ambivalent on these subjects (and hence, as we have seen, provocative of different interpretations), it does not remain ambiguous; for by pointing out the *need* for ambiguity, in a system where noone may "freely speak" except the ruler, Sidney, in effect, makes plain his desire for reform.

Yet even this is not the end of the matter, and the note of certainty I have just sounded, the sense of superiority in having delivered the consummate reading, is immediately challenged by the text. For as soon as Philisides' song is over, the Arcadians themselves take to criticism:

> *According to the nature of diverse ears, diverse judgements straight followed:* Some praising his voice; others the words, fit to frame a pastoral style; others *the strangeness of the tale, and scanning what he should mean by it.* But old Geron . . . took hold of this occasion to make his revenge and said he never saw thing worse proportioned than to bring in *a tale of he knew not what* beasts at such a banquet when rather some song of love, or matter for joyful melody, was to be brought forth. "But," said he, "this is the right conceit of *young men who think they speak wiseliest when they cannot understand themselves."* (pp. 259–60; italics added)

Everything in this passage dramatizes the problems of reception and interpretation that we, three hundred years later, continue to wrestle with.

Now, the source of this passage is Sannazaro's *Arcadia.* In Sanna-

zaro's Tenth Eclogue, the Neapolitan poet Caracciolo sings a mysterious poem, with sharp echoes of Vergil's First Eclogue, that is obviously a lament for Naples under the oppression of France and Spain,
in allusive, metaphorical terms. Caracciolo warns his audience: "Great
matter today I wrap in a thin veil." After the song is finished, Sincero
describes its reception. It was "by divers men in divers manners interpreted" ("*da diversi in diversi modi interpretato*"), and "even if by
reason of the covert language it was little understood by us, nevertheless it did not follow that it was not heard by each man with the
closest attention."[25] The overt latency here, the well-advertised secrecy,
is designed to provoke interpretive effort. But Sidney's quotation of
this passage ("According to the nature of diverse ears, diverse judgements straight followed") seems to lead in a different, sadder direction. In his *Arcadia*, the inscrutability of the text is exaggerated by
the audience, whose limitations—a formalist preoccupation with voice
and style, a moralist concern with decorum—prohibit most of them
from even considering "what he should mean by it." There may also
be some irony directed at himself in Sidney's reference, even if it comes
through Geron, to young men who "cannot understand themselves."
It seems to me that Sidney was fully and tragically aware, as the *Arcadia* evolved, that he ran the danger finally of not being understood,
because he had chosen the wrong medium. If he chose to write in
a pastoral form because in Elizabeth's culture that form was privileged and so might get access to the queen where direct address had
failed, he ran the danger that she would choose to read it, if at all,
only as pastime, as entertainment. If he chose covert discourse because ambiguity gave him some protection, he ran the risk of going
safe but unheard or misinterpreted. The hermeneutics of censorship
create their own paradoxes. It may be that in them lies the best explanation we are likely to produce for the abandonment of the *Old
Arcadia* and the beginning of the *New*.

The *Old Arcadia*, then, offers to anyone who would listen carefully an analysis of Elizabethan culture, finding it wanting. It also
presents (in the fable) conflicting theories and arguments about the
nature of monarchy and the rights and duties of subjects, but leaves
their consequences unspoken. The entire narrative offers both the
queen and her leading courtiers advice which could, if taken, transform Basilius into Evarchus, combining the best of the Arcadian ideals
with public reforms and international imperatives. By choosing to
work within the system, Sidney, in the *Old Arcadia*, still maintained

his commitment to a principle of moderate reformism. The consequences of being understood would have been either success, in the sense of influence, or an enforced and total silence.

Instead, we have the *New Arcadia*. For it, Sidney (or Greville) dismantled the Eclogues, and we may speculate on what, if anything, the changes meant. Most important, the presence of Philisides in the work was much reduced. In particular, the two love complaints for which he was responsible in the Fourth Eclogues were reassigned respectively to Amphialus (pp. 394–99) and Musidorus (pp. 357–59). Philisides was also no longer said to be the original composer of Pyrocles' erotic blazon. He becomes throughout an anonymous young shepherd, though recognizable still, for anyone who knew what to look for, in the allusion to Languet which introduces his beast fable on monarchy. That poem was transferred to the First Eclogues, a move consistent with the more frontal emphasis on politics throughout, and the dissociation of Sidney himself from the erotic or amorous impulses of the work. All of the other developments—the generic shift from pastoral to chivalric romance, the massive expansion of the narrative to broaden the political perspective of the work and create the taxonomy of political theory and example recognized by Greville—are consistent with a loss of confidence in indirect or covert discourse, or in messages accommodated to the forms of Elizabethan courtship. Only two of Sidney's additions will have to suffice here as evidence. In Chapter 16 there appears the Knight of the Tomb, at a moment when the rebellious forces of Amphialus confront the loyalists, and when "the horrour of Mars—his game" displaces the play world of romantic tournament. The Knight of the Tomb represents metaphor, figuration, and mystery, "straunge not onely by the unlookedfornesse of his comming, but by the straunge maner of his comming" (p. 445), and "himselfe in an armour, all painted over with such a cunning of shadow, that it represented a gaping sepulchre" (p. 445). But unlike the artful emblematical entries in the earlier Tournament of Beauty, the Knight of the Tomb is a victim of his own metaphors. For him, interpretation is both necessary and fatal. Mortally wounded by Amphialus and uncased, he becomes Parthenia, following her husband to the grave.

If arcane representation in the *New Arcadia* leads to tragedy, direct counsel fares little better. Sidney's shift toward it, however, is expressed through his revision of the role of Philanax, a role scarcely compatible with that of the zealous prosecutor of the last two books of the *Old Arcadia*. Now Philanax both leads the loyalist forces against Amphialus, and, after the bloody battle, counsels Basilius against raising the seige, an act that would effectively render those already killed a useless sacrifice, merely in response to a threat against his daughters' lives. Philanax's speech here is notable for its advocacy, not only of a public code of conduct, but also of force and resolution; and it is delivered with manifest reluctance, in the certain knowledge that its message will be unacceptable: "If ever I could wish my faith untried," he begins, "& my counsell untrusted, it should be at this time, when in truth *I must confesse I would be content to purchase silence with discredit*" (p. 467; italics added). It is a sad coincidence that Sidney's letters home from the Low Countries, after he had finally achieved his goal of a military commission, are burdened with allusions to the queen's failure to support her own soldiers and commanders, and haunted by a conviction that nothing he or his friends at court may do will ever be correctly interpreted. In March 1586, for example, he wrote to Walsingham (now his father-in-law) a letter which alternates between religious dedication to the cause ("If her Majesty wear the fowntain I woold fear considring what I daily fynd that we shold wax dry, but she is a means whom God useth and . . . I am faithfully persuaded that if she shold withdraw her self other springes woold ryse to help this action"); practical cynicism ("If the queen pai not her souldiours she must loos her garrisons"); and personal irony ("How apt the Queen is to interpret every thing to my disadvantage.")

In the local failure of hermeneutics, then, Sidney abandoned the *Arcadia* but stuck (literally) to his guns. He left the manuscript of the *New Arcadia* with Fulke Greville who, when he published it in 1590, attached to it the notorious prefatory allusion to "idle worke."

I trust that enough has been said by now to suggest how that phrase was intended to be read. But if there are any remaining doubts, it might be possible to remove them by referring one last time to Greville's *Life of Sidney*. In the *Life*, Greville describes the evolution of his own tragedies as media of political analysis, as another substitute, in effect, for the repressed history he was prevented from writing by Cecil. Greville contrasts his plans to Sidney's more radically fictional or poetic strategies of displacement; but the authorial anxieties he describes, the process by which restraint becomes a source of literary energy and motive, were equally applicable to Sidney. In particular, we should note the language in which he talks about the question of seriousness in literature and how an author may choose to conceal, or partly conceal, the seriousness of his intentions:

> When I had in mine own case well weigh'd the tendernesse of that great subject; and consequently, the nice path I was to walke in betweene two extremities; but especially the danger, by treading aside, to cast scandall upon the sacred foundations of Monarchy . . . a new counsell rose up in me, to take away all opinion of seriousnesse from these perplexed pedigrees; and to this end carelessly cast them into that hypocriticall figure Ironia, wherein men commonly (to keep above their workes) seeme to make toies of the utmost they can doe. (pp. 175–6)

Greville's "toies" and Sidney's "pretty tales" have the same function: to allow their authors to keep faith with themselves, while creating a medium of expression that may, with luck, break through the political restraints and cultural assumptions.

2 Prynne's Ears; or, The Hermeneutics of Censorship

On 1 March 1599, John Chamberlain wrote to Dudley Carleton about the appearance of Sir John Hayward's *Life of Henry IV*,[1] which resulted in the temporary disgrace and imprisonment of the historian:

> Here hath ben much descanting about yt, why such a storie shold come out at this time, and many exceptions taken, especially to the epistle which was a short thing in Latin dedicated to the erle of Essex . . . there was commaundement yt shold be cut out of the booke, yet I have got you a transcript of yt that you may picke out the offence yf you can; for my part I can finde no such buggeswordes, but that every thinge is as yt is taken.[2]

In this delightfully personal and slightly comic message we have in effect a sketch of a hermeneutics. What I shall suggest in this chapter is that Chamberlain and his contemporaries were far more sophisticated about the problems of interpretation than we might suppose; that their sensitivity to both the difficulties and the interest of interpretation is remarkably well documented; and that we can from these documents reconstruct the cultural code, for that is what developed, by which matters of intense social and political concern continued to be discussed in the face of extensive political censorship.

I group together here a range of very different types of texts or documents, the majority of which could be said to have had an essentially public presence, and therefore to raise in the most exacting form how it could be that tendentious subjects could find a form against which, to use Chamberlain's phrase, exceptions could not be taken.

52

In the plays of Ben Jonson and Philip Massinger, in Shakespeare's *King Lear,* in a court masque by Thomas Carew, in the sermons of John Donne, there is evidence, if we look carefully, of a highly sophisticated system of oblique communication, of unwritten rules whereby writers could communicate with readers or audiences (among whom were the very same authorities who were responsible for state censorship) without producing a direct confrontation. The official recognition of the public theater as both, up to a point, a privileged domain with laws of its own, and a useful safety valve or even a source of intelligence, has been well established. Elizabeth's famous recognition of herself in a 1601 revival of *Richard II* and James's equally famous decision to let Middleton's *Game at Chess* play for twelve days tell the same story, and show that they recognized the wisdom of the message brought from the grave by the poet Collingbourne. One of the least oblique critics of Jacobean policy, the pamphleteer Thomas Scott, remarked in the significantly entitled *Vox Regis* that "sometimes Kings are content in Playes and Maskes to be admonished of divers things."[3] But although the whole area of the political drama has become of increased interest in the past few years,[4] there is as yet no systematic account of the strategies of indirection, one that would apply equally to other public modes such as the sermon or the speech in Parliament, for example. At the end of this chapter I turn to a text which pretended to be a speech delivered in Parliament, and one without which no discussion of the effects of censorship on thought would be complete — Milton's *Areopagitica* — and show how much of its language and structure both conforms to and further develops the hermeneutics of censorship and the rhetoric that it demanded.

This chapter also deals with a different kind of theater: the whole ghastly area of the sensational public trial and dismemberment, of which the case of Prynne's ears, as registered in my title, stands as the symbol. Such trials were indeed the exceptions in England in the period under review, for they were the signs that the codes governing sociopolitical communication had broken down, that one side or the other had broken the rules. And because this was so evidently the case, they gathered to themselves a whole range of signification; they became part of the code. In 1579, John Stubbs lost his right hand, the hand that had actually produced *The Discoverie of a Gaping Gulf, whereinto England is like to be swallowed by another French marriage, if the Lord forbid not the banes, by letting her Majestie see*

the sin and punishment thereof. The punishment was hideously appropriate, both to his name and to his method, which was, as Collingbourne had remarked of his own case, "so playne and true / That
every foole perceyved it at furst." In 1630, as one of the first symbols
of Charles's decision to rule without Parliament, and to brook no
interference with his foreign policy, Alexander Leighton was fined by
the Star Chamber ten thousand pounds for his authorship of *Sion's
Plea,* in which he had incited the already rebellious members of the
1628 Parliament against the bishops:

> He was then transferred to the High Commission Court, to be
> deprived of his ministry, then to be whipped, pilloried, to lose
> his ears, his nose slit, his face branded with a double SS for sower
> of sedition, and lastly sent to the Fleet for life. This horrid sen-
> tence was executed in November 1630, in the midst of frost and
> snow; as according to the terms of the sentence *he was to be
> publicly exposed* and punished twice, the second part of it, after
> the short interval of seven days, (his back and face being yet
> excoriated and disfigured,) was inflicted with unrelenting severity.
> (italics added)[5]

Yet even the ritualism of this case is surpassed by that of William
Prynne, which lies at the very center of everything we could possibly
mean by the theater of state. The brutality of Prynne's sentence is
better known than that of Leighton; but what has not been previously
considered is the significance of the records of his trial in the Star
Chamber, which survive in unusual detail, and which make it clear
that explicitly at issue was a test case in the hermeneutics of censorship. In this case both sides broke the rules; Prynne, by attacking one
of his culture's main media of indirection, the public (and private)
drama; Charles I and Laud, by disallowing Prynne's own use, however scanty, of the time-honored protective devices of analogy and
"authority." It is tempting, though anachronistic, to see a symbolic
value also in the shift in the particular form of mutilation (expurgation) preferred by Elizabeth and Charles, a change that one could
imagine reflected an evolution in the code. In the distinction between
the lopped right hand and the sheared ears the focus is changed from
a concept of agency to one of audience, the writer's own sensitivity
or insensitivity to his audience determining his ability to survive.

To return, then, to Chamberlain's letter about Sir John Hayward,
it is evident that we are looking at a comparatively minor breach of

decorum, and a punishment to suit. Yet the letter is no less important as a key to the cultural assumptions of this system, in which the meanings of texts, and the procedures by which meanings are signified, had acquired such a formidable centrality. We can detect in Chamberlain's letter four hermeneutical principles, whose general acceptance throughout the period will eventually be demonstrated:

1. "Why such a storie shold come out at this time." That is, the importance of an exact chronology in determining what any given text was likely to mean to its audience at the time of its appearance. Chamberlain obviously recognized that Hayward's history had acquired its dangerous significance by appearing at a particularly tense moment toward the end of Elizabeth's life, that the significance resided precisely in the connection between "this time" and "such a storie." In other words, to retell the story of Richard's deposition by Henry Bolingbroke at a time when Elizabeth's authority was being challenged by the earl of Essex was inevitably to suggest an analogy — the same analogy that Elizabeth admitted to William Lambarde in 1601 when she saw herself in Shakespeare's play. The importance of implied analogy of all kinds, but especially between "this time" and episodes from past history, cannot be overstressed; and it is important to notice that Chamberlain takes this possibility for granted, without being at all bothered by the inexactness or the incompleteness of the parallel. It was for this reason, among others, that the writing of history was specifically included in the province of official censorship by the Bishops' Order of 1599, which included, along with its prohibition of satire, the direction that "noe English historyes be printed excepte they bee allowed by some of her maiesties privie Counsell." But there were multiple ways in which history — English, European, and especially ancient — could be introduced as a text for which local history stood, in whole or in part, as the subtext. Chamberlain's contemporaries were far more flexible on this issue than many modern critics, who have argued against the presence of topical allusion on the grounds that one-to-one correspondences cannot be found. Often, it was the very inexactness of the analogies so produced that made them useful, by providing writers with an escape route if, as in Hayward's case, "exceptions were taken."

2. Exceptions were taken "especially to the epistle which was a short thing in Latin dedicated to the erle of Essex." In this way Chamberlain suggests that provocation is given, or signification promoted, by some kind of signal in the text itself, especially in those preliminary

features that addressed themselves to reader expectations. In general, late modern criticism has not paid enough attention to the interpretive status of introductory materials in early modern texts. All too often given over to the province of bibliographers, or even omitted from standard editions, dedications, engraved title pages, commendatory poems and epigraphs are lost to sight. Yet often their function is to alert the reader to his special responsibilities. In the case of Hayward's dedication to Essex, the notoriety of the dedicatee would perhaps have been signal enough; but the language of the dedication also seems to emphasize the concept of safety and self-protection, in such a way as to promote questions. Latin was itself a kind of latency; and when Hayward hoped in Latin that his work would "lie hidden in utmost safety under the shadow of Essex's name, as Homer's Trojan under the shield of Ajax,"[6] he surely alerted an educated audience to the possibility of hidden meaning. Later in the century, the provocative semantics of the pre-text was recognized by law, when the Printing Act of 1662 required that all "Titles, Epistles, Prefaces, Proems, Preambles, Introductions, Tables, Dedications," be brought to the licenser for scrutiny along with the main body of the text.

3. "There was commaundement yt shold be cut out of the booke, yet I have got you a transcript of yt that you may picke out the offence yf you can." In this entertaining way Chamberlain points to the central predicament of censorship, in his day and thereafter. Not only is it ineffective in preventing the dissemination of prohibited views, it also confers on them a greater importance than they would otherwise have had, promoting the search, as Chamberlain puts it, for "buggeswordes."

4. Finally, and perhaps most important, there is Chamberlain's wry recognition of the resistance of the text to his own readership, a recognition that topical (and hence exciting) meaning may be present but cannot be proven to be so. This indeterminacy is central to the hermeneutics of censorship. "Every thinge is as yt is taken." What better motto could we find for the adherents of interpretive relativism? The difference is, however, that Chamberlain and his contemporaries could *combine* a practical recognition of the indeterminacy of the text in a culture governed by censorship with an equally pragmatic recognition that behind each text stood an author, whose intentions it was the reader's responsibility to try to discern. If this was an inconsistency, it was one which his own historical experience daily imposed on him.

Reading *Sejanus:* ciphers and forbidden books

We can expand on the principles of the hermeneutics of censorship by turning to another famous case, Ben Jonson's *Sejanus.* Jonson, as his editors have pointed out, had a long history of trouble with the authorities. He was at various times, and not only in his rambunctious youth, subjected to various degrees of harassment for his work in the public theater:

> Imprisoned for his share in *The Isle of Dogs,* 1597, cited before Lord Chief Justice Popham for *Poetaster,* 1601; summoned before the Privy Council . . . for *Sejanus,* 1603; imprisoned for his share in *Eastward Ho,* 1605; "accused" for *The Devil Is an Ass,* 1616; examined by the Privy Council for alleged verses of his on Buckingham's death [an event connected, as we shall see, to the reception history of *Sejanus*]; and cited before the Court of High Commission for *The Magnetic Lady,* 1632.[7]

In addition, there is evidence that throughout his life Jonson meditated on these facts, and incorporated them into a political and social theory of literature, a poetics of censorship. In his *Epigrammes* he complained frequently about different aspects of Jacobean censorship. No. 44 attacks a personal enemy who "cryes out, my verses libells are; / And threatens the starre-chamber, and the barre." The subject of No. 59, "On Spies," needs no comment. No. 68, "On Playwright," deals, in a powerfully squeezed form, with repression of the public theater:

> Play-wright convict of publike wrongs to men,
> Takes private beatings, and begins againe.
> Two kindes of valour he doth shew, at ones;
> Active in's braine, and passive in his bones.
>
> (8:49)

In the next chapter, I will argue that Jonson's interrogation of the tension between private opinion and public behavior caused him late in life to re-collect his previously unpublished poems of both the Jacobean and Caroline eras, and to transform them in the process into a new literary form. If we read *Underwood,* a posthumously published volume, in the sequence that Jonson provided, we can discover in it a lyric narrative, a sociopolitical autobiography. And at approximately the same stage in his development, Jonson inserted into

Timber, a collection of a different kind, a reflection on a long life of insecurity, of being misunderstood:

> I have been accus'd to the Lords, to the King; and by great ones.
> . . . They objected, making of verses to me, when I could object to most of them, their not being able to reade them, but as worthy of scorne. Nay, they would offer to urge mine owne Writings against me; but by pieces, (which was an excellent way of malice) as if any mans Context, might not seeme dangerous, and offensive, if that which was knit, to what went before, were defrauded of his beginning; or that things, by themselves utter'd, might not seeme subject to Calumnie, which read entire, would appeare most free. (8:604–5)

He thereby articulated another central principle of the hermeneutics of censorship, that interpretations could be radically different depending on what one selected as the context of the utterance.

This issue is raised, in reverse, by *Sejanus,* a play which becomes more "dangerous," in the sense that Jonson used that word in *Timber,* the more widely it is contextualized. In 1603 Jonson was accused of writing treason in *Sejanus;* but no records survive of the specifics of the charge, of what form the treason was supposed to have taken. Modern critics have assumed either that he was suspected of alluding to the fall of Essex two years earlier, as the most obvious recent case of an ambitious favorite who came to grief, in which case the offence would have been to imply that Elizabeth had been a Tiberius; or that he was responding positively to the moment of James's accession by advising moderation and a liberal climate for the expression of political opinion.[8] At any rate, whatever exceptions were taken to the text or the timing of the 1603 *Sejanus* as actually performed (and we of course have no knowledge of what was actually spoken on the stage), Jonson was apparently able to answer them to his accusers' satisfaction. No further action was taken against him at that time.

But he then, in 1605, proceeded to publish a text of the play, a text that seems designed to provoke the same kind of curiosity as that aroused by Hayward's history, while at the same time giving Jonson better protection. The very fact that his plot is drawn from Roman and not from English history suggested a scholarly enterprise, rather than a topical one. But the particular section of Roman history selected, and indeed the reputation of Tacitus, the historian upon whom Jonson primarily depended, would have indicated to his audience that his motives were not entirely archeological.[9]

Jonson's preface both stresses his loyalty to the crown and his scholarly dependence on historical sources. In his preliminary address to the readers of the play, he asserts that the use of classical reference and quotation is not for show, but to prove his "integrity in the story [history]" and to protect himself from "those common torturers, that bring all wit to the rack." He even cites editions and page references to facilitate a check on his sources. His own responsibility for the text is thereby minimized. On the other hand, some of the commendatory verses reminded the original reader that the play was ambiguous, and had had problems of reception previously. Hugh Holland closed his sonnet by alluding to Jonson's arrest, but in language derived from the play:

> Ne of such crimes accuse him, which I dare
> By all his Muses sweare, be none of his.
> The Men are not, some Faults may be these Times.

Another contributor, identified merely as "Friend" ("φιλος"), made his poem a riddle on the problem of understanding:

> Thy Poeme (pardon mee) is meere deceat.
> Yet such deceate, as thou that doest beguile,
> Art juster farre then they who use no wile:
> And they who are deceaved by this feat
> More wise, then such who can eschewe thy cheat.
> For thou hast given each parte so just a stile,
> That Men suppose the Action now on file;
> (And Men suppose, who are of best conceat.)
> Yet some there be, that are not moov'd hereby,
> And others are so quick, that they will spy
> Where later Times are in some speech enweav'd;
> . . . .
> [Those] are so dull, they cannot be deceav'd,
> These so unjust, they will deceave themselves.[10]

The seventeenth-century reader was encouraged, as Carleton by Chamberlain, to see what he could find; but at the same time he was warned that most readings are either oversimple or oversubtle. Close study of the text is required; but that there is a "right" interpretation cannot be guaranteed. (It is typical of the conditions under which the modern reader must operate that these verses have been effaced from the text they were intended to introduce, either by complete omission, in texts designed for students, or, as in Herford and Simpson's edition of Jonson's works, by being banished to a separate volume.)

More important, the play actually dramatizes the hermeneutics of censorship. In a central scene, the historian Cremutius Cordus is tried in the Senate for an "oblique" attack on Tiberius in his annals, on the grounds that he has implied "parallels," or rather contrasts, between present tyranny and the old republican era. The charge seems patently unjust, and Cordus's famous speech of defense, translated entirely from Tacitus, disclaims any such intention. The effect, according to Jonas Barish in his edition of the play, was to provide a symbolic statement of the nature and function of *Sejanus*, and to disclaim any topical intention there also, on the grounds that history is, or should be, nonpartisan, a neutral mediator of fact.

What Barish did not perceive, however, is that the disclaimer, as extended to Jonson, must be disingenuous. The play speaks, it is true, to a climate of excessive, even perverse, interpretive ability by the government and its agents.[11] As another of Sejanus's victims puts it:

> . . . our writings are,
> By any envious instruments (that dare
> Apply them . . . made to speake
> What they will have.
>
> (4:423)

But this same character also delivers a comment on the indictment of Cordus, and the public burning of his annals, that leads in another direction. Still following Tacitus closely, he remarks that "the punishment / of wit doth make [its] authority increase":

> Nor doe they ought, that use this crueltie
> Of interdiction, and this rage of burning;
> But purchase to themselves rebuke, and shame,
> And to the writers an eternall name.
>
> (4:408)[12]

Now, this was already one of the loci classici for discussions of freedom of speech, or of intellectual freedom in a broader sense. Sir Francis Bacon had alluded to it in a pamphlet intended to advise Elizabeth on how to handle the theological pamphlet wars of the 1580s.[13] Milton would apply it in 1644, when he turned the whole force of his classical eloquence against the licensing act of the Long Parliament; and Jonson is here clearly using Tacitus to deliver a warning to the instruments of censorship in his own day. The very survival of Cordus's story, in fact, proves his point about the inefficacy of censorship, while the fate of Sejanus argues its unwisdom.

Jonson's play, therefore, allows Cordus to protest a political climate of overdetermination, and to argue the wisdom of rulers who permit historians their natural and necessary privileges. Augustus set the example by allowing Livy such eulogies of Pompey "as oft Augustus called him a Pompeian: / Yet this hurt not their friendship" (4:406). But Jonson's position must be more complex, as his perspective is longer. To *retell* Tacitus's historical account of Cordus's historiography in 1605 is itself both a historiographical and a historical act, one which inevitably provokes John Chamberlain's question, "Why such a storie shold come out at this time?" Men of "best conceat" would "suppose the Action now on file," and Jonson's emphasis on censorship would encourage such curiosity and indeed sanction it. Suspicious readers need not identify themselves with Sejanus or Tiberius. As suppression ensures the survival of censored texts, so it justifies authorial suppressions, or obliquities. As Jonson explained in *Timber, or Discoveries,* those jottings that blend politics with poetics, only a candid government deserves a transparent culture:

> The mercifull Prince is safe in love, not feare. Hee needs no Emissaries, spies, Intelligencers, to intrap true Subjects. Hee feares no Libels, no Treasons. His people speake, what they thinke; and talke openly, what they doe in secret. They have nothing in their brests, that they need a Cipher for. (8:600)

Jonson's interest in Tacitus was not, however, restricted to the story of Sejanus, or solely explicable by the temporary need for a cipher. Nor was the "meaning" for him of Tacitus, as a name and model, restricted to the confrontation between Sejanus and Cordus, a confrontation in which the rights and wrongs of the issue were expressed in chiaroscuro. The lighting in which Tacitus appeared to European writers and readers in the sixteenth and seventeenth centuries was in general far more diffused, if not confusing. The picture of Tacitus as a republican thinker and champion of free speech was certainly available. In 1656, for example, as Orest Ranum has shown in his study of French historiography in the age of absolutism, Racine could compile a commonplace book of excerpts from the *Annals* which gave special emphasis to the thematization of cultural repression, to the relationship between political life and literary creativity, of which a vital historiography was a central aspect; and when he came to the *moralitas* by which Tacitus had summed up the trial of Cordus, "punitis ingeniis gliscit auctoritas," Racine added his own gloss, "livres défendus."[14] But for other readers, Tacitus was far less transparent; indeed his text became a celebrated instance of difficulty and obscurity, qualities to be valued or devalued according to the reader's frame of reference. For Sir Richard Baker, one of the bright young men associated with the circle of John Donne at the beginning of the seventeenth century, obscurity had its own attraction. The darkness of Tacitus

> is pleasing to whosoever by labouring about it, findes out the true meaning; for then he counts it an issue of his owne braine, and taking occasion from these sentences to goe further than the thing he reads, and that without being deceived, he takes the like pleasure as men are wont to take from hearing metaphors, finding the meaning of him that useth them.[15]

Such thinking is surely connected to the interpretive challenges with which Jonson surrounded his first major essay into the transmission of Taciteanism.

And beyond such epistemological darkness lay the more sinister reputation that the historian had acquired in some quarters, the "black Taciteanism" that resulted from his influence on Machiavelli and Guicciardini as historians, or more generally from his association with a cynical view of politics, so different from the republican idealism of Livy, so readily associated with those elements in any state that were malcontent, even seditious. There is reason to believe that all these views of Tacitus were in some complicated way present in Jonson's consciousness, and at different stages of his experience arranged themselves in different patterns of preference. In order to give a balanced account of how the hermeneutics of censorship developed in this most complex of authors, we need to follow this pattern a little further.

At some comparatively early stage in his development, Jonson wrote (and published in the 1616 folio) a poem on the subject of Sir Henry Savile's translation of Tacitus.[16] The epigram did not appear in the 1591 edition of Savile's translation, or in any subsequent edition, despite its formal resemblance to a commendatory poem. Its theme is unquestionably similar to that of *Sejanus,* in that Jonson praises Savile especially for his honesty as a translator, which in turn reflects the honesty of the original; and he urges Savile, now that

Roman history has been treated with such fidelity, to turn his talents to the service of a national historiography "We need a man," Jonson wrote:

> . . . can speake of the intents,
> The councells, actions, orders, and events
> Of state, and censure them: we need his pen
> Can write the things, the causes, and the men.
> But most we need his faith (and all have you)
> That dares nor write things false, nor hide things true.
>
> (8:62)

These lines were themselves a translation of the great definition of *historia* in Cicero's *De oratore* (II.xv.62–63).

In 1605 Jonson, as we have seen, presented his own exemplum of the true Tacitean historian in the figure of Tacitus's Cordus; but he also did something else rather peculiar. He reworked his definition of the true historian from that presumably earlier epigram, and had it delivered, ironically, by Sejanus, as the very grounds of his attack on Cordus. Cordus is described as a "writing fellow" who

> . . . doth taxe the present state,
> Censures the men, the actions, leaves no tricke,
> No practice unexamin'd, paralels
> The times, the governments, a profest champion,
> For the old libertie.
>
> (4:385)

Now in 1616, when Jonson remarked to Drummond of Hawthornden that "Tacitus wrott the secrets of the Councill and Senate," he also confided an English political secret, that the prefatory epistle to Savile's translation of Tacitus, signed A. P, was really written by the earl of Essex (1:142). This is one of the best indications that we have that the original *Sejanus* was in some way connected to the Essex conspiracy. As F. J. Levy has shown, the activists and malcontents who surrounded Essex at the turn of the century were known to be reading Tacitus;[17] and Jonson, if we are to judge from his cautious apology for Essex in *Cynthia's Revels,* was one of them. Such facts make it difficult to accept the notion that four years later Jonson was so impressed by the heinousness of Essex's crime, so convinced of the country's hegemonic needs, that he transformed the earl from Actaeon into Sejanus, and had him cruelly dismembered after all. Yet we can tell that he changed his mind about Tacitus. Sometime before 1616 he had written a sardonic little poem called *The New Crie,* attacking the amateur politicians of London. "The councells, projects, practices they know, / And what each prince doth for intelligence owe," he sneered, parodying for the second time his definition of the Tacitean historian, who "can speake of the intents, / The councells, actions, orders, and events / Of state, and censure them." The men of the new cry have, moreover, the same authority for their disruptive behavior as had Essex, as had Jonson himself. They "carry in their pockets Tacitus,"

> And talke reserv'd, lock'd up, and full of feare,
> Nay, aske you, how the day goes, in your eare.
> Keep a starre-chamber sentence close, twelve days:
> And whisper what a Proclamation sayes.
> . . . .
> They all get Porta, for the sundrie wayes
> To write in cypher, and the severall keyes.
>
> (8:59)

And, most significantly "all forbidden bookes they get." In this poem, perhaps because Jonson had been deeply shocked by the implications of the Gunpowder Plot in 1605, in which he himself was marginally implicated, obliquity has reassumed its dishonest meaning. Fear is now the obsession not of the censor but of the censurer; Tacitus has become a model of subversion; the noble defense of freedom of speech has vanished in the dislike of "forbidden bookes"; "what a Proclamation sayes" has acquired the form of a taboo. Whatever Jonson had originally meant by *Sejanus* in 1603, what it meant to him in 1605 could not, it seems, have remained untouched and unchanged by the writing of this poem. Yet it is typical of his own brand of honesty that it appears *along with Sejanus* and the praise of Savile's Tacitus in the 1616 folio, as part of the record, a record of ambiguity and interpretive difficulty, in which texts and historical events are equally resistant to simple, settled meanings.

The facts that texts can change their meanings in the light of events is, finally, brought dramatically home to us by the later reception history of *Sejanus.* The typology of the tyrannical favorite became firmly attached to the figure of George Villiers, duke of Buckingham, who was, of course, not even in the picture when Jonson wrote *Sejanus.* In the impeachment proceedings against Buckingham in 1626, Sir

John Eliot offered the resemblance in a speech to the House of Commons;[18] and Charles was reported to have said, when the speech was reported to him, "If the Duke is Sejanus, I must be Tiberius." When called to account, however, Eliot disclaimed any intention "to parallel Times, or any other person, but the Duke." He thereby asserted a principle of selective analogy that was as inarguable as it was unconvincing. When, shortly afterward, Buckingham was assassinated, Jonson was momentarily arrested on suspicion of having incited the assassin; almost as if it were believed that, having patented the topicality of the Sejanus story, Jonson was somehow responsible, if only as a prophet, for Buckingham's fate. This strange sequence of events serves to remind us of the indeterminate and shifting nature of historical analogy. Not only cannot we, must not we, be sure what Jonson intended; but the analogic potential of his text changes according to the reader's historical circumstances, beyond authorial control. In 1605 Jonson had emphasized in his address "To the Readers" that the text was "not the same with that which was acted on the publicke stage," a remark itself open to more than one interpretation; but even when the text was fixed in print, the impact of the context left it, if anything, more subject to contingency.

We can add, then, to the principles of interpretation understood by Chamberlain four more exhibited by Jonson:

5. Disclaimers of topical intention are not to be trusted, and are more likely to be entry codes to precisely that kind of reading they protest against.

6. Censorship encouraged the use of historical or other uninvented texts, such as translations from the classics, which both allowed an author to limit his authorial responsibility for the text ("Tacitus wrote this, not I") and, paradoxically, provided an interpretive mechanism. That is, the reader was invited to consider not only the timeliness of the retelling of another man's story, but the implications of the model, and the methods of selection, transmission, and adaptation.

7. It cannot be assumed that the hermeneutics of censorship depend on any crude opposition between a government and its critics, or on what has been called a Whig view of history. In Jonson we reapproach a figure normally thought of as a court poet, and whose career as such had been formally initiated in January 1605, *before* the publication of *Sejanus,* by the Twelfth Night production of his *Masque of Blackness.* Later there was a dramatic reversal of roles, during the revolution, when first the Long Parliament and then Crom-

well became the censors, and royalist writers their cautious censurers; but we will also encounter other court poets, even the king's great preacher and Anglican spokesman, John Donne, developing oblique strategies of communication and referring, as they did so, to censorship as their motive and constraint.

8. Jonson, it seems, changed his mind, and he certainly changed his social status. We cannot afford to ignore the psychological dimension of this problem, the confusing knowledge that writers did change their opinions, even their deepest convictions, shift their allegiance, and then, perhaps, retain an uneasy coexistence with their former selves. Jonson himself, as an arriviste, frequently expressed discomfort with himself — by loud expressions of personal integrity, and occasional admissions of shame.[19] Others found their loyalties divided by events, or merely found them occasionally strained. Oversimplifying, I name this complex phenomenon ambivalence, to distinguish it from the ambiguity that announces it. Ambivalence unites intellectuals whom overt political allegiance might seem to have sundered; and functional, conscious, textual ambiguity is their common resource. I do not, of course, exclude the possibility of unconscious tension or suppressions; but when political censorship is *acknowledged* by a writer as his context, the tensions between self and society are likely to have been brought within reflective reach, the presence of a deliberated subtext largely ousting the dramas of the involuntary.

"Betweene our sentence and our powre": *King Lear* and the double text

The question of how censorship affected the public theater must at some point impinge on Shakespeare; and the play on which this question should be focused is *King Lear,* rather than *Richard II,* that oftencited example of Elizabeth's sensitivity to topical implications. Although we have no comparable record for *King Lear* of a royal act of interpretation, we do have evidence of a court performance. The 1608 quarto offers to the reader the text "As it was played before the Kings Maiestie at Whitehall upon S. Stephans night in Christmas Hollidayes," an occasion which the Stationers' Register for November 26, 1607 identifies as "Christmas Last." We know, in other words, that *King Lear* was performed before James himself on 26 December, 1606; and we begin, therefore, with a direct inference that here was a play of direct interest to the king, not because, as with *Richard II,* it had acquired topical significance subsequent to its composition, but rather because its approach to the nature and problems of kingship were from the first perceived to be in some way germane to the new reign. But in what way? Did James see it, as has been argued, as complimentary to himself and his darling project, the union of England and Scotland under a new title of Great Britain?[20] Or did he see it, as Elizabeth saw *Richard II,* as a potentially subversive response to his policies of which he needed to take cognizance? There has in recent years developed a whole range of more or less explicitly Marxist criticism of *King Lear,* readings that try to deal with the fact that this play alone of the major tragedies is clearly and profoundly engaged not only with questions of authority in the state but with socioeconomic issues, feudal rights and obligations, and something that verges upon class analysis.[21]

Indeed, this play may well be the crux by which the methodology and integrity of my argument as a whole can be tested, and not only because the criticism is split so widely down the middle, not only because, as Frank Kermode cogently puts it, the play "has many 'subtexts,' is patient of many interpretations."[22] It is also because what we know "about" *King Lear,* its "sources," its circumstances of production, its most plausible sociopolitical and cultural contexts, not only fails to resolve its internal ambiguities but actually seems to create new contradictions, to highlight new ambivalences in the text. So, for example, Glynne Wickham's theory that the play was designed as "active propagation"[23] of James's plans for the Union — a reading predicated on a theory of representation by inversion, with Lear, the divider of the kingdom, functioning as an antitype to James, the unifier, — is based on the fact that James's policy was widely disseminated in the published text of his speech at the opening of his first Parliament on 19 March 1604, as well as on other unmistakable propaganda for the Union, such as Anthony Munday's pageant for the Lord Mayor of London, October 29, 1605. Such an interpretation lends importance to Shakespeare's references in *King Lear* to the "British powers" and, in the quarto only, to the "Brittish partie." On the other hand, the case for reading Lear as not an antitype but a type of James is based on such well-documented characteristics of the new king as his absolutist rhetoric, his abandonment of the cares of government for the pleasures of hunting,[24] on the prominence of his court fool Archie Armstrong, and on the fact that from the beginning of the reign there was dissatisfaction with his use of the prerogative, his lavish creations of knighthoods for his Scottish followers, for example, and his grants of monopolies. Such a reading gives special meaning to a speech of the Fool that appears only in the quarto text: "No faith, Lords and great men will not let me, if I had a monopolie out, they would have part an't";[25] but it will have to wrestle, somewhat uneasily, with the fact that the characters in the play most dissatisfied with Lear's one hundred knights are the implacable Goneril and Regan.

The play functions, in other words, as an exceptionally exacting test case of the historical method of interpretation in general, and in particular of my claim that such multivalency in a text whose sociopolitical ambience cannot be doubted is a sign that the writer is working under constraint. It is my contention that here, as in Jonson's *Sejanus,* we have a play that was indeed designed to be ambiguous, but that unlike *Sejanus, King Lear* was also intended to be experienced differently by different audiences, or even to mediate between them, by showing that the questions under dispute were not capable of easy resolution. Something is present in the text of what both James and his opponents wanted to hear; but beyond such slight gratifications is a larger analysis, comparable to that of *Richard II* but more finely reticulated, of the conflict between the loyalty due to the sovereign and the perception that a particular sovereign's inadequacies are dangerous to the nation. And this functional ambiguity cannot, I would further contend, be fully grasped without an extensive exploration of the play's political contexts — a considerably more extensive one than has hitherto been conducted by either side of the argument for subversion or legitimation.

The second major challenge in any discussion of *King Lear* and censorship is to determine the scope of the question: that is to say, it has usually been posed in the past solely as an editorial problem, as a possible explanation for certain disparities between the first quarto and the folio texts. Reopening this question has a certain institutional significance. For in posing it previously as a problem of textual difference — and hence of a difference of detail — editors and bibliographers have been moved not by an interest in censorship itself and its cultural consequences for the drama, but rather by their concern for a stable and sacramentalized text as the basis for exegesis. It is ironic to discover that these premises have been carried over into what is perhaps the most destabilizing event in textual studies during this century, the division of the text of *King Lear* into two separate texts of equal authority, and the sanction given by Oxford University Press to the radical theories of Michael Warren, Gary Taylor and others, who argue that the differences between the quarto and the folio are authorial in origin.

In *The Division of the Kingdoms*,[26] the volume in which this revisionary movement has itself become institutionalized, the question of censorship as a possible explanation for passages excluded from the folio is reopened in an essay by Gary Taylor;[27] and it is a further irony that Taylor's arguments *against* such an explanation are throughout framed by a premise typical of New Criticism, that the greater the artist, the less likely he was to have chosen to deal with the topical and hence to have given the censor any concern. Taylor begins his argument with the statement that "censorship imposes the political restraints of a particular time and place upon a potentially timeless work of art," (p. 75); and his concern throughout is to substitute for the hypothesis of such external restraints the internal ones of artistic second thoughts. Thus the folio's elimination of references to France and a foreign invasion in the last two acts, previously suggested by W. W. Greg and Madeleine Doran as a consequence of censorship,[28] is to be defended instead "on purely artistic grounds" and in the knowledge that "Jacobean censorship of references to foreign powers always involves negative portrayal of contemporary figures" (p. 80). Likewise, the omission of Edgar's cynical talk to his brother of a "prediction" of "unnaturalnesse betweene the child and the parent, death, dearth, dissolutions of ancient amities, divisions in state, menaces and maledictions against King and nobles, needles diffidences, banishment of friends, dissipation of Cohorts, nuptial breaches" (Act 1, Scene 2, C2v) cannot be a consequence of censorship, for three reasons. First, the "predictions" are too general to be applied with any certainty to Jacobean events; second, what the folio removes from Edmund in dark forecasts it gives back to Gloucester, meditating on the "late eclipses"; and third, there are "two obvious dramatic motives for the folio's omission: to play down the mocking tone . . . , and to remove a frankly topical exchange, once its dramatic currency had been devalued by the passage of time" (p. 85). One might see a certain self-contradiction here, since the predictions are either too general to be topical, or too general to be worth removing; and since their rewriting and replacement in Gloucester's speech connects them directly to the remarkable eclipses of September and October 1605 and rescues them from Edmund's cynicism, one could even argue that the revision embedded the predictions more firmly in Jacobean history. What is most of interest here, however, is the critic's certainty that the historically determined text must be "devalued" as history moves on.

The same certainty is manifest in Taylor's discussion of why the folio should have omitted the Fool's rhyme about sweet and bitter folly in Act 1, scene 4, along with its reference to the sale of monopolies, to the king's having given away all his titles (other than that of fool), and perhaps to the "incredible competitive gluttony" for which James's court banquets were already notorious. In this instance, Taylor concedes that the passage could have been ordered deleted by Sir George Buc, Master of the Revels, as a precondition of performance, because he would not have been able to miss, in this one area of the text, a whole series of allusions that were unmistakably to James himself, and unmistakably critical of him. But, Taylor significantly adds, if that were the cause of the folio's excision, the playwright might even have welcomed it as his own revision: "Shakespeare's own impulses to comment upon contemporary abuses may have led him to write at greater length than the play required. The censor, by curbing that impulse, may actually, in applying the restraints of a particular time and place, have done the timeless work of art a service" (p. 109).

Finally, there is a remarkable passage in which Taylor argues why it is that we need not consider censorship as the cause for the folio's most striking omission, the mock-trial that Lear in his madness conducts, arraigning his wicked daughters for their crimes against him and humanity. Predictably, Taylor concludes that the reason for the scene's removal from the folio was the dramatist's later insight, gained from stage experience, that it was dramatically redundant; but he bolsters this conclusion by remarking that the scene could not have attracted the attention of the censor because it was so "uncontroversial," so politically neutralized, because it had already been subjected to the dramatist's self-censorship, because Shakespeare as he wrote must have had "half a mind's eye on the censor." It is for this reason, Taylor argues, that the scene was not, in the quarto, what it might have been without such "anticipation of censorship," that it was not a major critique of Jacobean justice, that it did not demonstrate dramatically "that the economically and politically powerless, deprived of any resort to real justice, must content themselves with fantasies of legal retribution" (p. 90). And he correctly points out the limitations in previous editorial approaches to stage censorship, that they have focused on "known or probable cases of the censor's direct interference with an author's manuscript, post partum," whereas "the anticipation of censorship must have influenced, far more persuasively, what dramatists attempted."

What this essay evinces, in other words, is a conflict between an inherited concept of great art as ahistorical, and an emergent or reemergent sense of the intellectual space that the artist in this period had to clear for himself between external pressures of different kinds. What Taylor appears to intuit here (though it runs counter to his main hypothesis) is the very argument of my Introduction, that "literature" in the early modern period was conceived in part as the way around censorship. In Taylor's hypothetical reconstruction of what the mock-trial might have been like had not Shakespeare written with "half a mind's eye" on the Master of Revels, not to mention James himself as a spectator, there is, half-articulated, one of the cardinal principles of the hermeneutics of censorship: that the institutionally unspeakable makes itself heard inferentially, in the space between what is written or acted and what the audience, *knowing what they know,* might expect to read or see. Yet the logical extension of this insight is, surely, to ask how the inevitable presence of such contraints would have affected more than these details of the text's evolution, how, for example, the expectation of censorship would have affected Shakespeare's choice of the Lear story as a suitable subject for tragedy in the first place.

But before going on to ask that central question, there are two other points that Taylor makes in this essay that are germane to understanding censorship as a code, as a tacit contract between writers and the authorities. The first, already mentioned, is the theory that the erasure of the Fool's rhyme about sweet and bitter folly, along with its gibes at monopolies, knightings, and royal banquets, was probably caused by the accumulation of visibly topical references in one area of the text, references which might have passed unnoticed had they not been seen in *conjunction.* This observation could be reversed, forming another principle of the hermeneutics of censorship: in a work of oblique sociopolitical import any markedly topical allusions will tend to be widely scattered through the text, so that they appear to be random shots at local irritations, rather than a sustained and coherent attack on a government or a court. Needless to say, this scattershot approach would also have the practical effect of greatly complicating the censor's task, requiring close reading of the sort for which few civil servants would have the necessary concentration.

Taylor also implies that the susceptibility of any play to censorship would have been increased in proportion to the amount of provocation that the theater was giving at that time. *King Lear,* if one assumes a date of composition somewhere between the end of 1605 and the court performance of December 1606, would have been presented for licensing just after "a series of increasingly serious theatrical scandals" (p. 105). These included the trouble over Jonson's *Sejanus* in 1603, over Samuel Daniel's *Tragedy of Philotas* in 1604, and four plays in which James himself had been the perceived object of satire, *The Dutch Courtesan,* Marston's *The Fawn,* and the collaborative *Eastward Ho* and *Isle of Gulls.* As Taylor points out, Buc ought to have been made particularly nervous, throughout 1606, by his earlier imperceptiveness (an observation which might well bear on *all* the folio's major omissions, not merely the Fool's criticisms, one would think). But the general logic of Taylor's argument is here less important than what these facts of theater history tell us about the interactions of censorship and culture. They remind us both that activity is generated *reciprocally* by writers and censors; and that flurries of prohibitions, penalties, or of "scandals" in the theater were likely to be symptomatic of tensions generated outside the theater. In the case of *King Lear,* its place in this sequence of plays requires us to ask what in the first three years of James's reign was exciting the theater to such provocative behaviour, and what attitude Shakespeare himself was likely to have towards both the "scandals" and their causes.

We know that Shakespeare was on the cast list for the 1603 performance of *Sejanus.* That in itself suggests that he quickly learned from experience what kinds of discretion were expected from dramatists under the new regime. It has also been proposed that phrases from *Eastward Ho,* whose anti-Scottish humour landed Jonson and Chapman in prison, became embedded in the text of *King Lear.*[29] Yet if Sonnet 107 refers to the accession of James as a "most balmy time," when "peace proclaims olives of endless age" and the moon (Elizabeth) has fortunately proved mortal,[30] we have an equally strong inference that in 1603 Shakespeare was prepared to share in the general optimism of that year.

We also know that that optimism did not last long. By the time that James met with his first Parliament, there had already developed a substantial critique of what he himself called his "Christmas," the irresponsible disposition of titles and other privileges to his Scottish followers; and that it was this behaviour that had already, before he announced it as policy, prejudiced the House of Commons against his plan for the Union. What happened was an almost immediate split in the culture, insofar as we can use that term to refer to what was being said and published. On the one hand, the reading public was being bombarded with documents supporting the king's program. These included *A Treatise of Union of The Two Realmes of England and Scotland* by Sir John Hayward (London, 1604), an obvious attempt by a man imprisoned for indiscretion in the previous reign to establish his credentials with James; William Herbert's *Prophecie of Cadwallader,* (London, 1604), which presented James in its conclusion as the "second Brute" who would unite the kingdoms which the first Brutus had divided between his three sons; the anonymous *Miraculous and Happie Union of England and Scotland,* attributed to William Cornwallis; John Gordon's *Sermon of the Union of Great Brittanie,* delivered on 28 October, 1604; George Thomson's Latin poem, "De reductione regnorum Britanniae ad unum principem"; Robert Pont's Latin dialogue, *De unione britanniae,* published in Edinburgh in 1604, which concludes with the dreadful pun: "Sith God hath made al under one, / Let Albione now al-be-one"; the anonymous *Rapta Tatio . . . tending to the Union,* published in London in 1604 and addressed to the cities of London and Edinburgh; David Hume's Latin treatise, *De unione insulae britannicae,* published in London in 1605 but written from a Scots perspective; the already-mentioned pageant by Anthony Munday, entitled *The Triumphes of Re-United Britania* and, like Herbert's *Prophecie,* featuring a praise of James as the second Brutus foretold by Merlin; and two tracts by John Thornborough, Bishop of Bristol, to which we shall return.

Most important of all, however, was the publication of James's own speech at the opening of Parliament in March 1604, in which he expatiated on the many and great blessings which he, in his own person, brought with him to bestow on England, and spoke scathingly of the "frivolous objection of any that would be hinderers" of his plan for the greatest blessing of all, the achievement of the union of the kingdoms.[31] The effect of this speech was, to use a Foucauldian term, to establish the Jacobean discourse, to make available to the reading public in a highly dramatic form a representation of the king's character: his tone of voice, his peculiar blend of idealism and egotism, the odd mixture of familiarity and formality that marked his public pronouncements. It was typical of James that he concluded by remarking that some of his hearers in Parliament might have felt that his speech lacked eloquence, that it smacked of the impromptu, but that this should be read as a virtue:

> it becommeth a King, in my opinion, to use no other Eloquence then plainnesse and sinceritie. By plainnesse I meane, that his Speeches should be so cleare and voyd of all ambiguitie, that they may not be throwne, nor rent asunder in contrary sences like the old Oracles of the Pagan Gods. And by sinceritie, I understand that uprightnesse and honestie which ought to be in a Kings whole Speeches and actions: That as farre as a King is in Honour erected above any of his Subjects, so farre should he strive in sinceritie to be above them all, and that his tongue should be ever the trew Messenger of his heart: and this sort of Eloquence may you ever assuredly looke for at my hands. (p. 280; see Fig. 1)

The 1604 speech was discussed all over the country, according to the author of *Rapta Tatio,* who declared himself to have been brought out of seclusion by the great interest of the common people in these matters:

> But so full are all thinges every where of his Maiestie . . . by Subjectes who [normally] neither take much joy in any thing, but in Harvestes, Mariages, and Holydayes . . . Above all it may be . . . they seeme full of a speech his Highnesse made in the beginning of the Parliament.[32]

On the opposite side from the propagandists were the reform-minded members of the House of Commons, who were from the start deeply suspicious of what the Union would mean in economic terms, and who saw the beginning of the new reign as an opportunity to press for the redress of grievances. On 23 March 1604 Sir Robert Wroth raised the question of monopolies in the House;[33] and in the debates on the Union there was anxiety expressed that the king's English subjects would suffer in the inevitable competition for place and privilege. What increased their suspicion was that their debates, down to the very words and speakers, were obviously being reported to the king. The Commons quickly realized that what was at stake was their freedom of speech. On June 20, 1604, there was read in the House *The Form of Apology and Satisfaction,* a document addressed to James and designed to lay to rest any "misinformations" he had re-

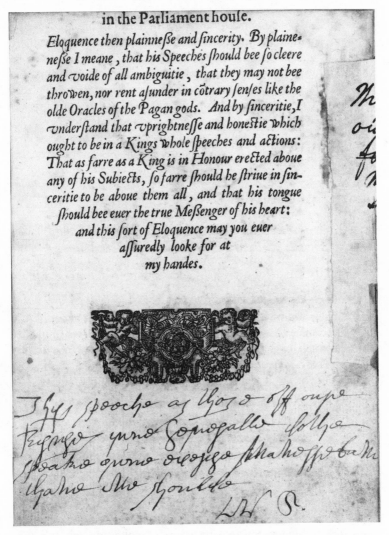

in the Parliament houſe.

Eloquence then plainneſſe and ſincerity. By plaine-
neſſe I meane, that his Speeches ſhould bee ſo cleere
and voide of all ambiguitie, that they may not bee
throwen, nor rent aſunder in cōtrary ſenſes like the
olde Oracles of the Pagan gods. And by ſinceritie, I
vnderſtand that vprightneſſe and honeſtie which
ought to be in a Kings whole ſpeeches and actions:
That as farre as a King is in Honour erected aboue
any of his Subiects, ſo farre ſhould he ſtriue in ſinceritie to be aboue them all, and that his tongue
ſhould bee euer the true Meſſenger of his heart:
and this ſort of Eloquence may you euer
aſſuredly looke for at
my handes.

*Figure 1. James I, Speech at the opening of Parliament, March 1604. By per-
mission of the Folger Shakespeare Library (STC 14390).*

ceived about their deliberations; but for all its humble style, the *Apology* contained a firm reminder to the new monarch that there were traditions of parliamentary discourse in England of which he seemed unaware. "Let no suspicion," wrote the apologists, cross the minds of the king's advisors in the Commons, "that their privileges . . . should by sinister informations or counsel be violated or impaired. or that those which with dutiful respects to your Majesty speak freely for the right and good of their country should be oppressed or disgraced."[34] In particular, they singled out the first of Thornborough's pamphlets, *A Discourse plainly proving the evident Utility and urgent Necessity of the desired happy Union of England and Scotland,* and complained that the publication was "injurious and grievous,"

> being written expressly with contempt of the Parliament and of both Houses in the highest degree; undertaking to deface the reasons proposed in the Commons . . . containing moreover sundry slanderous passages and tending to murmurs, distraction, and sedition. (p. 225)

With the bishop of Bristol's opinions thus themselves added to the list of grievances, it would have been surprising if his next publication, the much longer and more carefully argued *Joiefull and Blessed Reuniting the two mighty & famous kingdomes,* had not also attracted a good deal of publicity. Significantly, Thornborough conceived of the two kingdoms as siblings competing for the favors of their father, James the patriarch, and he developed this metaphor in language that is irresistibly suggestive of the opening scene of Shakespeare's play:

> But we ought to consider, that both English and Scottish . . . without difference may challendge like interest in his Maiesties favor . . . to be divided equally, and graciously among al, by Geometrical proportion as his Maiestie shal bee pleased to deeme meete. Which thing may move al to mutual kindnes, & reciprocate love towards the other . . . not grudgingly, nor contentiously, striving for prerogative of blessing; and birthright, in his Maiesties favour; as if it might be saide to his highnesse, *hast thou but one blessing my father?* . . . Let our strife rather be like that of Ephestion and Craterus, who contended whither should love their king Alexander most; in so much that Alexander was enforced to decide the controversie, adjudging that Ephestion loved the king best, and Craterus Alexander best. So it pleased the king in his sentence equally to divide his love, and

so did they both equally strive to love: . . . And so I doubte not
but our contention is of the like love, & dutie towards our Sover-
aigne. (pp. 59–63)

Thornborough had, in effect, expanded James's own theory of kingship as patriarchy into an imaginary scene in a drama of sibling
rivalry — or rather of two contrasting scenes of different rivalries, the
one, modelled on the Old Testament rivalry of Jacob and Esau, an
unacceptable contest based on greed, the other, illustrated by classical anecdote, a desirable competition in love, or the ability to express
it; and the implication of Thornborough's argument is clearly that
those who resist the Union are following the first model, by allowing
their jealousy of Scotland to interfere with their filial love and duty.
It is the Parliamentarians, in other words, who are the dividers of
the kingdom that the king would reunite.

How can we conceive a relationship between this tract and Shakespeare's play? First, if we assume a date of late 1605 to late 1606 for
the composition of *King Lear,* we can also assume that it followed
all of the other contributions to the Union controversy. Not one of
them alludes to the Lear story, even when, as in Munday's pageant,
or Herbert's *Prophecie,* or Thornborough's *Joiefull and Blessed
Reuniting,* substantial attention is paid to the chronicle history of
Britain. It is hard to believe that Thornborough, in particular, could
have developed the metaphor of sibling rivalry and the competition
to see who "should love their king . . . most" without some references
to *King Lear* if the play were already current in the London theater.
Second, there are two minor instances in which it looks as though
Shakespeare's knowledge of Thornborough's tract was comparable to
that which has been posited for quite different kinds of "sources"[35]
— two small but not perhaps insignificant "echoes." The first of these
is between Thornborough's statement that "both English and Scottish
. . . without difference may challendge like interest in his Maiesties
favor," and the language of Lear's opening challenge to his daughters:

> Which of you shall we say doth love us most?
> That we our largest bountie may extend,
> Where merit doth most challenge it.

> (B1v)

The second is between Thornborough's earlier comparison between
"a people disjointed one from the other" to "Sampsons *Foxes* running divers and contrary waies, with *fire-brands* of dissention among

them" (p. 32), and the language of Lear's reunion with Cordelia in Act 5, Scene 3:

> He that parts us shall bring a *brand* from heaven,
> And *fire* us hence like *Foxes*.
>
> (K4r)[36]

But in a larger sense, what Thornborough's pamphlet provided was a powerful political metaphor, one that apparently penetrated the language of the Union controversy and was assimilated by James himself. On 18 November, 1606, the king opened the third session of Parliament with a long speech in which he urged a final resolution of the issue, and stated that "he did so equally esteem these Two Kingdoms, betwixt which he was so equally divided, as Two Brothers, and as if they had equal Parts of his Affections . . . and after him there could never be any so equally and so amply affected to them both."[37] It was, of course, in the Christmas break that followed this short session, with a vote on the issue still pending, that *King Lear* was performed before the king at Whitehall; and what it offered unmistakably to its royal spectator was a very different view of the relationship between fathers and children than that which his speech took for granted, a vision not of fatherly blessings but of patriarchal injustice and folly, in which echoes of his own propaganda could be heard, but strangely maladjusted. In particular, although the fictional transference from two sons to three daughters made impossible any reductive allegorization of *King Lear,* the original binary structure of the metaphor (and some of James's own vocabulary) was retained in the opening lines of the play, where Kent remarks to Gloucester, "I thought the King had more *affected* the Duke of Albany then Cornwall," and Gloucester replies, "It did allwaies seeme so to us, but now in the division of the kingdomes, it appeares not which of the Dukes he values most," (B1r; italics added).[38]

I do not forget, of course, that the choice of the Lear story by Shakespeare was in part the consequence of the revival of the old chronicle play of *King Leir.* But the question asked by John Chamberlain of Sir John Hayward's *Life of Henry IV,* "why such a storie shold come out at this time," should equally be asked about the old play, which was entered in the Stationers' Register on 8 May 1605, "as it was latelie acted," and duly appeared in a quarto edition. It is highly probable that its appearance at that time was motivated by the publication of John Thornborough's *Joiefull and Blessed Re-*

uniting, itself most likely motivated by Parliament's attack on and suppression of his imprudent and impolitic *Discourse;* and in the context of Thornborough's metaphors of sibling rivalry, a person or persons sympathetic to the Parliamentary opposition to the Union might well have remembered the story of King Lear, and recognized its pertinence to the current political vocabulary. Between the summer of 1605 and the winter of 1606, then, Shakespeare (who had already considered, in *Hamlet,* how a play might catch the conscience of the king) would have had ample opportunity to read the old play, to research other versions of the story in Holinshed, Spenser, *The Myrroure for Magistrates,* to reconceive the story as a tragedy, in defiance of all of his sources, and to add all of those unmistakable resemblances between Lear and James himself. The result was a play so deeply ambiguated, so clearly referential in some way to the Union debate, but so utterly resistant to assimilation by either side in the controversy, that it could safely take its place in a theater unusually vulnerable at that moment to state interference, that it could even, with impunity, be presented before the king.

If, then, we assume that Shakespeare's play was indeed a response to the Union controversy, but one deliberately shaped by its author's understanding of the hermeneutics of censorship, we can recognize its first scene as a paradigm of those hermeneutics, a preliminary statement of the controlling discursive conventions, dramatizing the restraints that the play, by being a play, acknowledges and to which it makes formal submission. In Lear's authoritarian rhetoric (including those striking shifts from the royal "we" to the familial "me"), in his determination that nothing come "betweene our sentence and our powre", there is an implicit critique of James's public pronouncements; and in the contrast between the unscrupulous and self-serving flattery of Goneril and Regan, Cordelia's self-agonizing taciturnity, and Kent's unacceptably blunt counsel we may recognize an analysis of the very situation facing Shakespeare and manifest in the publications of 1604-5. We do not need to allegorize Kent into a figure for the reformist party in the Commons to recognize that his introduction into this scene (one of Shakespeare's main departures from his sources) is as a figure of responsible public service and counsel; but it adds a certain energy to that perception to recognize also a connection between his stand ("Thinkst thou that dutie / Shall have dread to speake when power to flatterie bows?") and the *Apology's* protest lest "those which with dutiful respects to your Majesty speak freely for the right and good of their country should be oppressed or disgraced." In a more complicated way, Cordelia's sincerity, "I am sure my loves more richer then my tongue . . . I cannot heave my heart into my mouth," is a reproach to James's claim, in the speech of 1604, that his "tongue should be ever the trew Messenger of his heart," reminding him that the sincerity of others may very well appear in forms that are unsympathetic to ourselves.

Yet there is equally no doubt that after this first scene, when the balance of sympathy is decisively shifted back to Lear, Shakespeare also renders equivocal the source of state-criticism or reproach. Although we are never encouraged to lose confidence in Kent's honesty, his effectiveness is steadily decreased (especially in the folio version); it is, of course, the Fool who is given responsibility for pointing out to the king his folly; and for all his status as privileged speaker, the Fool, as we all know, quietly disappears in Act 3, Scene 6, as his most explicit political gibes disappear in revision. Most puzzling of all these allusions to the problem of political communication, however, is the fact that it is Goneril who objects to her father's retinue of knights, and that she couches that objection in the language, however "deliberately tortuous,"[39] of parliamentary reformism. Twice she mentions "redresses," and specifies their motivation in the "tender of a wholesome weale," (D1v), concealing in the language of "discreet proceeding" a black threat of compulsion. Whatever Shakespeare's own motivation in writing, or rewriting, "such a storie . . . at this time," it clearly was not to support without question the parliamentary opposition against the king.[40]

In another essay in *The Division of the Kingdoms,* Gary Taylor argues that the most likely date for Shakespeare's revision of *King Lear,* the revision that led to the folio version, was 1609–10.[41] In connection with this theory, it is worth noting that in early 1610 James had become even *more* like Lear, expanding in his own pronouncements on the implications of the patriarchal metaphor, reminding his subjects that the stories of fathers and children are governed by the same rules as the histories of kingdoms. In his notorious speech to the Commons at Whitehall on 21 March, James described his theory of the origins of kingship thus:

> A Father may dispose of his inheritance to his children, at his pleasure: yea, even disinherite the eldest upon just occasion, and preferre the youngest, according to his liking: make them beggers, or rich at his pleasure: restraine, or banish out of his

presence, as he finds them give cause of offence, or restore them in favour againe . . . : So may the King deale with his subjects.[42]

Although this definition was preliminary to a more moderate account of how the balance of powers might actually work, the speech was indicative of James's growing frustration with Parliament and of the dissolution to which he finally resorted in January 1611. In the meantime, another speech of 21 May had deeply aroused the anger of the Commons and again alerted them to the fact that their freedom of speech was endangered. According to John Chamberlain, the speech "bred generally much discomfort to see our monarchicall powre and royall prerogative strained so high and made so transcendent every way."[43] These circumstances might well have figured among Shakespeare's motives for reworking and perhaps restaging his tragedy, as much or more as a desire to improve it artistically.

And if we posit that both the earlier and the later versions of *King Lear* were conceived by Shakespeare in response to constitutional and cultural excitement, to a political discourse in which familial relationships had acquired an intense metaphorical freight, while the question of how the king was to receive uninhibited advice was itself a matter of public concern, we may not be any closer to resolving *King Lear*'s internal conflicts of sympathy and polity, but we may be closer to understanding why they exist. And to read the play not only as a fully meditated (and slowly evolving) response to major political events and statements but as a contribution to them, an attempt, through intellectual and emotional complication of the issues, at conciliation of the parties, is not, surely, to reduce its status as art. Rather, it may help us to replace the concept of literary transcendence, which seems to be currently exhausted, with the more rigorous concept of intellectual independence; that quality which Shakespeare manifests more powerfully than any of his contemporaries, but which in him, no less than in them, was partly the consequence of living with censorship.

"What th' Spanish-treaty meant": the drama of Opposition

In her powerfully documented study of Puritan drama under the early Stuarts, Margot Heinemann introduces a qualification of the concept of "Opposition":

> Where dramatists were writing largely for court circles they could hardly help being cautious and equivocal, perhaps half-hearted in their handling of critical themes. "Willing to wound

> and yet afraid to strike" they inevitably were, much of the time, and not only for reasons of censorship. . . . How to modify the behaviour of kings, to redress grievances, to get some kind of consensus between Crown and Parliament *without* . . . calling into action dangerous and subversive "popular" forces — this was the problem of the Puritan lords and gentry as well as of Presbyterian grandees and big businessmen throughout the period.

There are fertile notions here, but almost all of them need qualification or expansion. There is, first, an assumption that the different strategies employed by writers critical of royal policy or behavior can be explained by differences of class or social status. Thus Thomas Middleton, firmly based in the London middle class, could deliver a blatant attack on James's pro-Spanish policies, if not on James himself, in *A Game at Chess;* but Massinger, the son of a gentleman and dependent on aristocratic patronage, "often appears to pull his punches."[44]

But such alignments, as in the case of Jonson, are insufficiently mobile, allowing neither for the vagaries of temperament nor for the demonstrable fact that the same writer will at different times try different strategies. On the scale of protest, from the utmost outspokenness to the finest of innuendos, Jonson appeared in several positions. In the case of Massinger, the argument that he was inhibited by the patronage of Philip Herbert, earl of Montgomery and fourth earl of Pembroke, is peculiar, given the role of the Pembroke family as loyal opposition. As Heinemann herself observes, William Herbert, third earl of Pembroke and lord chamberlain, was recognized as the leader of the anti-Spanish group in the Privy Council. Not only does he seem to have intervened on behalf of the actors eventually imprisoned for staging *A Game at Chess,* but he also protected and encouraged the virulently anti-Spanish pamphleteer Thomas Scott.[45] It seems reasonable to suppose that his brother shared his views, and would have offered comparable protection to Massinger.

Another questionable assumption by Heinemann is that certain writerly cautions were not the product of censorship. Yet if we are to broaden the concept of "Opposition" to include the voice of the moderate, loyal, but occasionally dismayed, then we ought also to broaden the meaning of censorship. In the seventeenth century, censorship included not only licensing laws and penalties, banned plays and burned books, but also the interruption of public debate in Parliament; constraint of the clergy, individually or as a group, from preaching as they chose; as well as the personal inhibitions of fear, tact, and ambition. Censorship also presumed a range of response by the authorities to criticism, from extreme and savage reprisal to turning a blind eye. Here, too, personal temperament in the first two Stuarts made for unpredictability. A writer who could touch James's vanity might survive his authoritarianism. And most complex of all were the conventions of political discourse, the unwritten rules and contracts evolved, broken, and relearned throughout the century, the formulae of protected speech and privileged genres, of equivocations shared by authors and authorities.

There is no more striking exhibit of these conditions than the Spanish Marriage crisis in the early 1620s, a crisis that engaged Jonson as well as Middleton and Massinger. In fact it was a double crisis, for James's unpopular plan to marry his heir to the Spanish infanta was inextricably involved with the loss of the Palatinate. James's refusal to intervene on behalf of his daughter Elizabeth and her husband, Frederick, the Elector Palatine, was predicated on a chance of negotiating with Spain for a peaceful settlement. Elizabeth, queen of Bohemia, thereby became for England a symbol of Protestantism left in the lurch. And James himself produced a striking political statement, not of creative diplomacy, but of ambivalence. Refusing any form of official military intervention in his own name, he allowed Sir Horace Vere to take a volunteer force to Europe to assist Frederick, while at the same time permitting Lord Vaux to collect volunteers to fight on the side of Spain.

The result was confusion and suspicion on all sides. Alarmed but stubborn, the king issued a series of proclamations to restrain the press and any other forum in which criticism of his policies might be heard. On 4 August 1621, John Chamberlain, alert as ever to the literary and political texture of daily life, reported that "there is come out a new proclamation against lavish and licentious talking in matters of state, either at home or abrode, which the common people know not how to understand, nor how far matter of state may stretch or extend; for they continue to take no notice of yt."[46] On 24 November, Chamberlain added that the House of Commons had taken exception to this proclamation, "very wisely (forsooth) as yf they might reach to what was spoken there."[47] In other words, the king's desire to muzzle opposition had suddenly taken on a new legal or constitutional seriousness, as censorship threatened, or appeared to threaten, parliamentary freedom of speech.

Chamberlain's news acquires a special pungency or intentionality when we recall that the man to whom he wrote, Sir Dudley Carleton, English ambassador at the Hague, was also the host of the exiled king and queen of Bohemia in 1621. But Chamberlain's obvious partisanship ("very wisely forsooth") did not impede his interpretive ability. And there followed, indeed, a remarkable constitutional exchange between the king and Parliament. The texts involved were not of the sort we usually associate with problems in hermeneutics — official letters, petitions, journal entries — yet it is perfectly clear from reading them that the context, an ambiguous statement of repressive intent, had sharpened the interpretive faculties and honed the language of all concerned. On 4 December 1621, James wrote to the Commons to "acquaint that House . . . that none therein shall presume to meddle with any thing concerning our Government or Mysteries of State, namely, not to speak of our dearest Son's Match with the Daughter of Spain, nor to touch the Honour of that King, or any other Our Friends or Confederates."[48] The Commons responded with a petition requesting, among other things, clarification of the king's intentions, in the hermeneutical sense:

> Whereas your Majesty, by the general Words of your Letter, seemeth to restrain us from intermeddling with Matters of Government . . . the Generality of which Words . . . (*as we hope beyond your Majesty's Intentions*) might involve those Things which are the proper subjects of Parliamentary Actions and Discourse; and whereas your Majesty's Letter doth seem to abridge us of *the ancient Liberty of Parliament for Freedom of Speech* . . . we are therefore now again inforced humbly to beseech your Majesty to renew and allow the same. (pp. 292–93; italics added)

James perceived the point, and the implied counterthreat. His response was a statement of careful positivism. He complained that the Commons had made "so bad and unjust a Commentary upon some Words" of his letter that "a Scholar would be ashamed so to misplace and misjudge any Sentences in another Man's Book" (p. 326). He defined state meddling as referring solely to "Matters of War or Peace, or our dearest Son's Match with Spain, by which particular Denominations *We interpret and restrain* our former Words" (italics added); and he assured the Commons that their "Privileges" should remain as inviolate as his "Prerogative," a careful balance of language and power. The Commons, however, insisted on explicitness. On 18

December, they wrote into their journal their insistence that their privileges were not dependent on any such compromise, but "the ancient and undoubted Birthright and Inheritance of the Subjects of England" (p. 360). James lost his patience. In January 1622, he dissolved the House, and with his own hands tore the offending text from the parliamentary journal. Too much transparency had made the discourse nonviable.

The channels of public debate were thereby closed, but the Spanish Match and the Palatinate remained open and burning issues. Into the fray went Thomas Scott, Puritan divine, with a series of pamphlets, whose titles expressed the openness of his challenge. Between 1620 and 1624, Scott proclaimed in *Vox Populi, Vox Coeli, Vox Regis,* and *Tom Tell Truth* the nature of the new "voice" that was now required—truthful, audible, and backed up by absolute authority.[49] In *Vox Coeli,* the Spanish ambassador, Gondomar, is blamed for a state of repression in England such that "no cinsere advise, honest Letter, Religious Sermon, or true picture can point at the King of Spaine, but they are called in; and their Authours imprisoned" (pp. 60–61). In a popular variant of Jonson's adage in *Sejanus,* Scott warned James that censorship only encourages defiance: "For . . . if one penne, or tongue be commanded to silence, they will occasion and set tenne at libertie to write and speake; as Grasse or Cammomell, which the more it is depressed, the thicker it will spread and grow" (p. 61). The successful publication and dissemination of his own grassroots protest proved the point.

Most significant, in *Vox Regis,* in the course of a defense of his own style, Scott suggested alternative media for discussion of the crisis. "Might I not borrow a Spanish name or two," he asked, "to grace this Comedie with stately Actors? Or must they onely be reserved for Kingly Tragedies? Why not Gondomar as well as Hieronymo or Duke D'Alva?" (p. 10); a suggestion that suddenly gives "Spanish" drama a new significance. This was the context of his cogent remark, cited earlier, that "sometimes Kings are content in Playes and Maskes to be admonished of divers things."

In the early 1620s there was, in fact, a sudden interest in plays with Spanish themes or titles. In 1624, *The Spanish Viceroy,* sometimes attributed to Massinger, was performed without license. It has since disappeared without trace.[50] So too has *The Spanish Contract,* advertised 26 April 1624.[51] On the other hand, James let Middleton's *Game at Chess* play for twelve days before acceding to Gondomar's

request that he suppress it.[52] Some plays were more oblique. We do
not know the date of *The Noble Spanish Soldier*, published in 1634,
but both Dekker and Rowley were collaborating with Middleton and
Massinger during the Spanish Marriage crisis, and the play in its final
form contains a debate on literary censorship. A poet, called on by
the Spanish king's discarded fiancée to write a satire on the subject,
replies:

> I doe not love to plucke the quils
> With which I make pens, out of a Lions claw:
> The King! sho'd I be bitter 'gainst the King,
> I shall have scurvy ballads made of me,
> Sung to the Hanging Tune. I dare not, Madam;

whereupon the woman attacks him for moral and political cowardice. The "true Poet," she asserts, will always speak out against infamy
in high places: "his lines / Are free as his Invention; no base feare /
Can shake his penne to Temporize even with Kings."[53] Yet *The Noble
Spanish Soldier*, in its ambiguous attitude to Spain, appears to temporize, thereby permitting its own survival.

Another survivor was *The Spanish Gypsy*, product of a collaboration between Middleton and William Rowley, which had the distinction of being acted by the Lady Elizabeth's Company at Whitehall
on 5 November 1623, "the prince only being there."[54] This tiny record itself deserves interpretation. The Lady Elizabeth's Company, also
known in 1623/24 as the Queen of Bohemia's Company, was undoubtedly associated in the public imagination with the cause of the Palatinate. A private showing to the "prince alone" at Whitehall suggests
that the play had a special message for Charles; and the date of the
performance, only a few days after the prince's return from Spain
without his Spanish bride, seems more than coincidental. The context of interpretation, then, was the public knowledge that the Spanish
Match had proved a fiasco, and widespread suspicion that neither side
had been negotiating in good faith. We do not, of course, know how
that private performance might have been adapted to speak to the
occasion, and the play's published text seems innocent enough. But
there is contemporary evidence that it was regarded as topical commentary. In a collection of satires, *An Age for Apes*, published in
1658 but clearly retrospective, Richard Brathwaite wrote:

> I hold it to be oyle and labor spent
> Here to discourse what th' Spanish-treaty meant,

But nere had businesse so strange a carriage:
To make more shows and lesse intend a marriage,
But this was so well shadow'd, give it due,
By th' Spanish Jipsy and her wandring crue.[55]

In Brathwaite's hermeneutic, a "well-shadow'd" play not only succeeds better than open discourse in making its message *acceptable* to those whose actions it would influence. It is also the most appropriate medium for a world of political negotiation in which ambiguity prevails, in which the authors of high policy decline to make their intentions plain, and in which an attempt to discover "what th' Spanish-treaty meant" is doomed to failure.

Philip Massinger: some repressions of our own

Massinger deserves more detailed attention here, in part because the history of his work's reception is so enlightening. In Thomas Davies's edition of 1761, Massinger is presented as an outspoken political critic, who "boldly attacked the Faults of Ministers and of Kings themselves . . . pointed his Arrows against Carr and Buckingham, against James and Charles the First." He was admired by Coleridge as a "Democrat," and linked by Byron with Shakespeare and Otway, an odd but revealing triangle of preference.[56] And in 1876 the great historian S. R. Gardiner paid him the compliment of his undivided attention. His article on Massinger's relation to contemporary issues endorsed a position like that of Davies, arguing that certain plays, *The Maid of Honour, The Bondman, Believe As You List,* were constructed as oblique political commentary, encouraged by and instrumental to the Pembroke family.[57]

Being taken seriously by a historian has its dangers for a literary figure. The year after Gardiner's essay appeared, Leslie Stephen published one of his own, depreciating Massinger as an artist in proportion to his didacticism. Repeated by Arthur Symons and canonized by T. S. Eliot in *The Sacred Wood* (1920), a recognizably modernist view of Massinger had emerged. To a generation that was taught to admire Webster, Massinger's deliberative plays were lexically drab; while for critics who promoted esthetic distance the idea of a political function for drama was obnoxious.

It is not improbable that Massinger will do well in the next cycle. In the interim, some confusions need to be cleared away, with respect to both his intentions and his methods. I focus on *The Maid of Honour,* as his first independent production, and one that epitomizes many of his values. Before *The Maid,* Massinger had collaborated in 1619 with John Fletcher in a demonstrably political play. *Sir John Van Olden Barnavelt* was originally prohibited by the bishop of London, but eventually released, and played to packed audiences. In the winter of 1621/22, while James was locked in a contest of wills with Parliament over their right, if any, to discuss his foreign policy, Massinger's new play appeared. It opened with a fictional problem in international relations that was patently a metaphor for the Palatinate crisis. The peace-loving king of Sicily, Roberto, receives an ambassador from Ferdinand of Urbino appealing for military assistance against threatened invasion. Roberto refuses, on the grounds of an idealized pacifism:

> . . . wee that would be knowne
> The father of our people in our study,
> And vigilance for their safety, must not change
> Their plough-shares into swords, or force them from
> The secure shade of their owne vines to be
> Scorch'd with the flames of warre.

> (I.1.164–69)

The passage contains two biblical allusions, Isaiah 2:4 and I Kings 4:24, 25 ("And Solomon had . . . peace on all sides round him. And Judah and Israel dwelt safely, every man under his vine and his fig-tree"). But it also connects at least the second of those allusions to a recent political text, which serves as both intermediary and true object. In March 1621, James had addressed the opening session of Parliament in a somewhat defensive way, conscious of the pressures that required him to summon it at all, and hoping to appease it by invoking the ideals of his reign, the Solomonic typology he had elected:

> And now I confess that when I looked before upon the face of government, I thought (as every man would have done) that the people were never so happy as in my time . . . and for peace, both at home and abroade, I may truely say more setled, and longer lasting, then every any before, together with as great plenty as ever: so as it was to be thought, that every man might sit in safety under his own vine and his own figge-tree.[58]

Behind the doubts ("I thought . . . it was to be thought") lie the facts of the German wars, the grievances about sales of monopolies and patents, the drastically bad harvest of the previous summer. The speech, a statement of conciliatory purpose, was promptly published. James's own impulse to propaganda gave Massinger the cipher he needed. Roberto was James, quoting himself, and refusing to intervene in the Palatinate.

S. R. Gardiner's famous essay on Massinger made the same point over a century ago, but without reference to James's speech. He was confused by the play's date of publication, 1632, and was obliged to read it as a Caroline text, designed to refer only retroactively to James, and to use that reference as an ironic frame for Charles's actions. So, when Roberto agrees on a cynical compromise:

> . . . since these Gallants weary
> Of the happinessse of peace, desire to taste
> The bitter sweets of warre, wee doe consent
> That as Adventurers, and Voluntiers
> (No way compell'd by us) they may make tryall
> Of their boasted valours,
>
> (I.i.252–57)

Gardiner recognized Charles's permission to the marquis of Hamilton to assist the king of Sweden with a volunteer force, in the autumn of 1631. The allusion to Vere's volunteers in 1620 could function, Gardiner believed, only as a sign that history repeats itself, that Charles was reliving his father's failures.

Despite the sophistication of this argument (which could certainly help to explain the play's *publication* in 1632), Gardiner's failure to date *The Maid of Honour* correctly has been used to cast doubts on his whole hypothesis. Exceptions have also been taken to the "vagueness of the parallels" he suggested; and the fact that Massinger seems to handle the issues he poses with impartiality has been used to "make the idea that he was conducting political propaganda an absurdity."[59] By not meeting his editors' standards for propaganda—crudeness and consistency—Massinger has been rescued, despite himself, from the reproach of topicality. This view contrasts intriguingly with Heinemann's, who equally felt, though from a perspective sympathetic to politicized drama, that Massinger "often appears to pull his punches." Yet a principle of inexact analogy, with specific entry codes (the Solomon/James allusions), would resolve some difficulties; and the others (impartiality, pulling punches) could be profitably renamed ambivalence. *The Maid of Honour* has no blacks and whites like Middleton's chess pieces, no consistent allegory of international relations.

What it offers instead is a thoughtful but not detached analysis of
a national problem, the location and definition of honor in the modern world. Figuratively embedded in the play's title, honor is actually presented as in short supply. Instead of taking sides, as Middleton could in *A Game at Chess,* Massinger dramatizes ambivalence
and inconsistency, values insecurely held and positions insufficiently
thought through. In Act I, the spokesman for honor is Bertoldo, the
man of action, arguing against his sovereign's pacificism in favor of
military intervention:

> . . . May you live long, Sir,
> The King of peace, so you deny not us
> The glory of the warre . . .
> . . . Rowze us, Sir, from the sleepe
> Of idlenesse, and redeeme our morgag'd honours.
>
> (I.1.235–36)

But at the end of Act V, Bertoldo has been defeated, imprisoned,
has thrown childish tantrums at his helplessness, has been ransomed
by Camiola, the Maid of Honour herself, and has then broken his
marriage contract with her for political expediency. The effect of
this perfidy is to make Camiola give up on a world in which the virtue she represents is so neglected, and to depart for a monastery,
leaving behind injunctions that recall, ironically, Bertoldo's emptied
words:

> I conjure you
> To reassume your order; and in fighting
> Bravely against the enemies of our faith
> Redeeme your morgag'd honor.
>
> (V.ii. 286–89)

The echoes of Shakespearean dialectic, of Prince Hal, Falstaff, and
Hotspur, were probably intended.

The play promotes, then, a critique of values, in order to show both
how they inevitably conflict (pacificism versus activism), but also how
they may, in proportion as they are grandly stated, be held trivially
or inconsistently. The only solution to this ethical instability is to tran-
scend it, as Camiola does, by retreat into the life of the contemplative. But the problem, as broad and unrelenting as anything in Webster or Tourneur, was made relevant and specific to its original audi-

ence by its topical introduction, by being keyed in, so to speak, to the Palatinate.

A similarly timely reexamination of the venerable term "honor" appears in several of Ben Jonson's poems of this period. *An Epistle to a Friend, to persuade him to the Warres* opens in Bertoldo's language:

> Wake, friend, from forth thy Lethargie: the Drum
> Beates brave, and loude in Europe and bids come
> All that dare rowse: or are not loth to quit
> Their vitious ease, and be o'rewhelm'd with it.
> It is a call to keep the spirits alive
> That gaspe for action, and would yet revive
> *Mans buried honour . . .*
>
> (8:162; italics added)

And it ends, after several iterations of "honour," with Camiola's call for a continued crusade:

> . . . now goe seeke thy peace in Warre,
> Who falls for love of God, shall rise a Starre.

Yet Jonson, who had fought in the Low Countries in 1591/92, might have excused himself at the age of thirty-eight from any active combat. With all of the ambivalence of his laureate's position, he confronts that fact in *An Epistle answering to one that asked to be Sealed of the Tribe of Ben*. On the one hand is the intellectual's professed indifference or superiority to politics:

> Let these men have their wayes, and take their times
> To vent their Libels . . .

"What is't to me," Jonson declared, what is happening in Europe today, "I wish all well." But a moment later, another, younger self emerges:

> But if, *for honour,* we must draw the Sword,
> And force back that, which will not be restor'd,
> I have a body, yet, that spirit drawes
> To live, or fall a Carkasse in the cause.
>
> (8:218–19; italics added)

There is a conduit in this poem between Jonson's own vacillation and his sense of obscurity and cynicism on a national and international scale. As Richard Brathwaite declared it "oyle and labor spent / Here to discourse what th' Spanish-treaty *meant,*" Jonson asked himself in 1623 "What is't to me . . . / Whether the Dispensation yet be sent, / Or that the Match from Spaine was ever *meant*?" In this central poem of self-definition, the distortion of public meaning and value divides the poetic ego against itself; Jonson's envy of Inigo Jones, who planned the wedding masque for Charles and the infanta, is mixed with a profound distrust of the "late Mysterie of reception" from which he had been excluded. All he meant, literally, by that phrase was the wedding masque, but we may find it strangely, hermeneutically, chosen.

These poems of Jonson's, from *Under-wood,* were published posthumously in 1640. So while they provide a gloss on Massinger's intentions in *The Maid of Honour,* and share both its historical context and its lexicon, their ambivalence is more self-analytical and less strategic. The *Under-wood* poems, and the source of their ambivalence, will be discussed in more detail. In the meantime, we must return to the crucial and as yet undetermined question of Massinger's intended audience.

Without some grasp of the intended audience, or whether there might be more than one, any theory of function or intention remains inadequate. But because we have no record of the original production of *The Maid of Honour,* we have to direct the question to later plays for which the documentary evidence survives. *The Bondman* was licensed for production in December 1623. It, too, was interpreted by Gardiner as a commentary on the German wars and Anglo-Spanish relations. In rejecting this hypothesis, Massinger's editors remarked that "if one tries to follow the political allegory out, there are many contradictions, and one may feel dubious about Massinger's urging his monarch on to action in a tragicomedy at the Cockpit."[60] Yet these same editors record two crucial items of the stage history of *The Bondman,* both of which relate to the question of audience and intention, though they seem, perhaps, to lead in opposite directions.

The first is that it was written for the Queen of Bohemia's or Lady Elizabeth's Company, newly formed in 1621/22, short-lived but intensely active. Sir Henry Herbert licensed thirteen new plays for them between May 1622 and February 1625, when the company seems to have disappeared,[61] leaving something of a mystery in the minds of stage historians. As I have suggested above, the new company must have been associated in the public mind with the fortunes or misfortunes of its absent patroness, and the plays would therefore have attracted an audience already sympathetic to her cause. On the other hand, there is a record of a *private* performance, on 27 December 1623, at Whitehall, "the prince only being there." This fact completely undermines the belief that a play written for the public theater could have no message intended for the king (or the king's son). In all, the Queen of Bohemia's company gave five such private performances for Charles at Whitehall during this period, including Middleton and Rowley's *The Changeling* (4 January 1624).

In the case of *The Bondman,* the timing of the event is also significant. In October, Charles had returned from Spain without the infanta; and, as both he and his father made clear, the marriage negotiations would proceed no further without some commitment from Spain to restore the Palatinate. On 28 December, the day *after* the private performance of *The Bondman,* James signed the warrant for a new parliament, putting paid to the Match and his peace policy simultaneously. It is hard not to believe that *The Bondman,* with its opening scenes of preparation for a great war, its heroic language, its injunctions to the citizens to support the war financially, was a comment on the new anti-Spanish militancy of Charles and Buckingham; but since in the play the chief consequence of that foreign campaign was rebellion of the slaves at home, and included a lecture by their leader on its cause — the descent from a benevolent patriarchy to governmental tyranny — it would seem that Massinger was, again, delivering a mixed message. There is both a parliamentary and a prophetic ring to the rhetoric of Pisander, the leader of the slave rebellion:

> this hath forc'd us,
> To shake our heavy yokes off; and if redresse
> Of these just grievances be not granted us,
> Wee'le right our selves.

> (IV.ii.84–87)

The play's tragicomic structure averts the fulfillment of that "if," as later Stuart history could not. It offers a workable compromise, as *The Maid of Honour* did not; and it seems to have offered, therefore, a peculiarly direct response to the dilemma of the moderates, as posed by Heinemann: "how to modify the behaviour of kings, to redress grievances, to get some kind of consensus between Crown and Parliament *without* . . . calling into action dangerous and subversive 'popular' forces." We do not need to argue a tight fit between events and characters in history and fiction; the ethos of the play's negotiated compromise would, given the actual situation, have ensured its own applicability.

There is, also, indisputable evidence that Massinger's plays were seen in his own day as bearing on contemporary politics, evidence that also supports the case for a contractual or conventional hermeneutics. In January 1631, Sir Henry Herbert noted in his office book:

> This day being the 11 of Janu. 1630, I did refuse to allow of a play of Messinger's, because itt did contain dangerous matter, as the deposing of Sebastian king of Portugal, by Philip the [Second,] and ther being a peace sworen twixte the kings of England and Spayne.[62]

On 6 May, Herbert licensed *Believe As You List* for performance. In those four months, Massinger had rewritten his play to the extent of giving it a Carthaginian setting; yet the surviving autograph manuscript still shows signs of the original version, which must have been based on the history of King Sebastian of Portugal. Either the deposed Sebastian or his pretended survivor had in the 1580s been an exile and supplicant for aid in Europe. The play focuses on his betrayal by the king from whom he has sought assistance, but who has responded instead to the diplomatic pressures of another great European power. Removing England and Spain from the cast of characters, and relocating the action in the distance, both temporally and geographically, had the effect of transforming the play into an allusion *to* the Sebastian story, rather than a dramatization *of* it; and it did nothing to remove the further allusion to the situation of Frederick, king of Bohemia, whose story, Massinger implied, was equally a tragedy of betrayal.

It has been pointed out that "the application of the tragedy is far from unambiguous."[63] Of course. That crucial ambiguity was the key to its final allowance, as the minimal alterations Massinger made to his text were the signs of his submission to the conventions of political drama, his willingness to encode, up to a point. Yet the play's prologue, like Hayward's dedication to Essex or the prefatory material to *Sejanus,* challenged the audience to see what they could "find":

> yf you finde what's Roman here,
> Grecian or Asiaticque, drawe to nere
> a late, & sad example, tis confest
> hee's but an English scholler at his best,
> a stranger to Cosmographie, and may erre

> in the cuntries names, the shape, & character
> of the person he
> presents, yet he is bolde in me to
> promise, be it new, or olde, the tale
> is worth the hearing . . .
> . . . .
> then whether hee hath hit the white
> or mist, as the title speakes, beleeve you
> as you list.

The title, in other words, defines the hermeneutical status of the text. It reminds us of Shakespeare's *As You Like It;* but where that title was an invitation to wish fulfillment, to the desire for happiness, *Believe As You List* provokes and resists cognition, opens a credibility gap and dares us to close it.

No discussion of the dramatics of censorship in Massinger would be complete without some approach to *The Roman Actor,* published in 1629, and, as its title page informed the reader, "divers times . . . with good allowance Acted, at the private Play-house in the Black-Friers, by the Kings Majesties Servants." It was licensed for performance in October 1626. As with *Sejanus,* then, we face a Roman drama, this time set in the reign of Domitian, whose original state as it was acted at Blackfriars is entirely conjectural; and as with *Sejanus,* the text as eventually published unmistakably dramatizes certain aspects of the hermeneutics of censorship, in this case those that directly involve the theater. Finally, as with *Sejanus,* the text of 1629 offers us an extraordinarily difficult problem of interpretation, and illustrates the same pattern of instability, the same subjection to shifting contexts and exegetical climates. In June 1822, for example, the play was "compressed" so as to offer to the public only those sections of the first act that dealt directly with stage censorship, the trial of Paris and his fellow actors on the grounds that they

> . . . search into the secrets of the time,
> And under feign'd names, on the stage, present
> Actions not to be touch'd at; and traduce
> Persons of rank, and quality of both sexes,
> And with satirical and bitter jests
> Make even the senators ridiculous
> To the Plebeans.[64]

There seems little doubt that this publication, and the production in which Kean acted the role of Paris, constituted a gesture of defiance of the repressive Tory administration of Castlereagh, which had, in 1819, in response to the Peterloo Massacre, passed the Six Acts restricting public meetings, imposing stamp duty on periodicals containing news, and increasing the penalty for seditious libel. In August 1822 Castlereagh died, making way for the liberal reforms of Robert Peel. In 1929, by contrast, William Lee Sandidge's edition of the play presented it, from a modernist perspective, as a defense of the theater against the restrictive intentions of the *Puritans,* comparable to Heywood's *Apology for Actors* in 1612 but transcending it by being a defense "not for a specific time, but for all time."[65] And in 1983 Jonathan Goldberg read *The Roman Actor* from a postmodernist perspective, with an emphasis on its plays within a play, on the representational anxieties it produced, on the mirror relationship of the theater of politics and the politics of theater.[66]

My own preference is for a reading of *The Roman Actor* that focuses more precisely on the interpretive *system* invoked and provoked by the text as published in 1629, as well as on the significance of its timing. From Goldberg's reading, in a book entitled *James I and the Politics of Literature,* one might infer that one was looking at a Jacobean play;[67] whereas in fact *The Roman Actor* was first performed in the second year of Charles's reign, and published in a year when that reign was in crisis, the king engaged in a battle with the House of Commons for the supremacy in government, a battle which inevitably involved the question of parliamentary freedom of debate. In that political theater, as we have already seen, Jonson's *Sejanus* had become part of the terms of reference, when Sir John Eliot adapted its Roman typology to the Buckingham impeachment proceedings. It can scarcely be a coincidence that Eliot's notorious analogy, and his imprisonment for it, took place in May 1626, to be followed by the licensing of *The Roman Actor* in October; and that the same pattern was repeated in 1629, when Sir John Eliot was again among those arrested in March for parliamentary insubordination to the king, an event that, given the old-style dating, must have been *followed* by the 1629 publication of the play in quarto. In so clearly imitating the trial scene in *Sejanus,* and in having Paris, like Cordus, give a defense of his art and its objectivity, Massinger invoked Jonson as well as Suetonius and Dio Cassius as his "sources." And he also, in the opening speeches of his play, explicitly raised a question that Jonson had asked at least of himself, concerning the relationship of culture to royal patronage, and the status of a theater that must balance that dependency against its time-honored role of sociopolitical criticism. Paris, who, as one of his fellow actors points out, holds his "grace and power with Caesar," is convinced that the consul's threats to "silence" his company ("For being galld in our last Comedie") will be ineffective against Domitian's pleasure in their work. But although in the trial scene he does succeed in clearing himself of the initial charge of seditious representation, it is that same Caesar who finally stabs him to the heart.

Perhaps also in imitation of Jonson, Massinger's published text appeared with a similar barrage of commendatory poems, several of which would seem to be provoking the reader to read between the lines. Thomas May's contribution was to assert that "Paris . . . / Acts yet, and speakes upon our Roman Stage." John Ford called attention to "Domitians pride," and Robert Harvey to the fact that this section of Domitian's history leads directly to his "Evening fate." Joseph Taylor introduces the shadow of the "sowre Censurer," who may be either critic or censor; and "Tho. G." (probably Thomas Goffe) suggested in another pun that Massinger's book (*liber*) should be free (*liber*) from the teeth of envy, that it should scorn the frequent fires of the blind devourers of paper (Crebra papyrivori spernas incendia paeti), lines that certainly seem to evoke the threat of censorship in one of its more extreme manifestations. Again, Latin serves the same purpose as the incomplete signature of the author. But T. I., whom Sandidge identified as Thomas Jeay, was rather more daring, invoking in his poem both the drama's responsibility to inform the monarch of his faults, and the penalty the dramatist risks thereby:

> Each line thou hast taught CEASAR is, as high
> As Hee could speake, when groveling Flatterie,
> And His owne pride (forgetting Heavens rod)
> By His Edicts stil'd himselfe great Lord and God.
> By thee againe the Lawrell crownes His Head;
> And thus reviv'd, who can affirme him dead?
> . . . .
> And if it come to tryall boldly looke
> To carrie it cleere, Thy witnesse being thy Booke.[68]

Alerted by this remarkably lucid and daring (and collaborative) account of how the theater can "revive" the past to meet the needs of the present and to circumvent the censors, the reader of *The Roman Actor* was thus instructed how to read the trial of Paris, and in particular how to understand his long speech of defense. On the surface merely a long version of the conventional argument that the comic and satirical theater does not attack particular persons, but only delivers general moral lessons in which the spectator may coincidentally find that the cap fits, in reality Paris's speech is a cunningly constructed account of the hermeneutics of censorship, in which the word "censure" reappears constantly with growing thematic force.

He begins by responding to the charge that the actors have represented "Actions not to be toucht at" and "traduced" members of the government; he asserts that such readings are solely a product of the reader's misinterpretation:

> If I free not my selfe
> (And in my selfe the rest of my profession)
> From these false imputations, and prove
> That they make that a libell, which the Poet
> Writ for a Comedie, so acted too,
> It is but Justice that we undergoe
> The heaviest *censure*.

> (I.iii.44–49)

And he proceeds through the argument that the theater has always been responsible for regulating morals by example, to the case-by-case proof of how it is *not* responsible for the personal application of its lessons:

> . . . if a Matron
> However great in fortune, birth, or titles,
> Guiltie of such a foule unnaturall sinne,
> Crie out tis writ by me, *we cannot helpe it:*
> · · · · · · · · · · · · · · ·
> . . . if a Patrician,
> (Though honourd with a Consulship) finde himselfe
> Touch'd to the quicke in this, *we cannot helpe it.*
> · · · · · · · · · · · · · · ·
> Nay e'ne your selfe my Lord, that are the image
> Of absent Caesar feele something in your bosome
> That puts you in remembrance of things past,
> Or *things intended tis not in us to helpe it.*
> I have said, my Lord, and now as you finde cause
> Or *censure* us, or free us with applause.

> (I.iii.118–142; italics added)

And before sentence is given, Domitian's return is announced, suggesting to the consul Aretinus, the addressee, my Lord himself, that it would be strategic to "reserve" to Caesar "the *Censure* of this cause."

It should be obvious by now that Massinger's refrain, "we cannot helpe it," is part of an ingenious deployment of one of the central disclaimers in the discursive code of self-protection, a transfer to the reader, or to the bosom of "my Lord," of unacceptable intentions, "things intended." But at the same time the speech makes it very clear that if the drama were to speak of dark dealings in high places, its "libels" would not have wanted substance:

> . . . And for traducing such
> As are above us, publishing to the world
> Their secret crimes we are as innocent
> As such as are born dumbe.

(I.iii. 106–9)

That there are secret crimes that could be published is left, given the conditions of publication in this society, for an apparently innocent syntax to depose.

There is one final inference of *The Roman Actor,* which it would be left for Prynne's *Histriomastix,* four years later, to remove from the territory of the inferential and place squarely before the Caroline reading public; that the court of Charles I had a growing reputation for an obsession with stagecraft, that the histrionical tendencies of both king and queen were becoming a matter of common gossip, if not of common reprobation. In Prynne's equally obsessive anti-theatricality, the disastrous effects of playacting in the careers of various Roman emperors, especially Nero, acquired a topical and tendentious character that his judges felt unable to ignore; and we can guess that it was partly because he chose to make this point in the form of a prose treatise—because he did not elect to make use of the structural protection of the play, the illusion that history was *only* literature—that he became a tragic actor in the live theater of politics. But before moving to that phase of the argument, I want to broaden its base, generically and perhaps ideologically. Another figure whose career, like Massinger's, bridges the reigns of Charles I and James I is John Donne, whose interest in interpretation is usually considered only in terms of theology and religious exegesis. Yet Donne's political experience was comparable to that of Jonson and Massinger; and he was more explicit than either of them about the hermeneutical climate in which he was bound to operate.

Take heed what you hear: Donne's ambiguous prose

Like Jonson, Donne's early poetry is scarred in places — and in significant places — by the signs of a repressive culture. Raised as a Roman Catholic, Donne was undoubtedly extrasensitive to the potential dangers involved in holding or disseminating the views of a religious minority; yet it was secular ambition and a corresponding anxiety about sociopolitical inhibitions and tensions that had more obviously seeped into the vocabulary and even the structure of many of his Elizabethan and early Jacobean poems, along with a number of specific references to censorship. In the second satire, for example, Donne concludes an extended attack on the misuses of words, language, in his society — an attack which is focused on the legal profession — with a piece of self-reassurance: "but my words none drawes/Within the vast reach of th'huge statute lawes."[69] The implication is that satire is a safe mode of self-expression so long as it remains private and unpublished, a perception shortly to be substantiated by the Bishops' Order of 1599 which forbade the publication of satire. In the fourth satire, Donne doubly complicates this relatively simple position, by creating a strategy of self-representation and self-expression that both gave him a certain protection and emphasized the dangers he thought he faced. He imagines himself trapped on his way to court by a court gossip, who not only suggests insidiously that in Elizabeth's last years "'Tis sweet to talke of Kings," that is, to anticipate her demise and a male successor, but makes him a captive audience to a long satirical diatribe against the administration at home and abroad:

> More than ten Hollensheads, or Halls, or Stowes,
> Of triviall houshold trash he knowes; He knowes
> When the Queene frown'd, or smil'd, and he knowes what
> A subtle States-man may gather of that;
> He knowes who loves; whom; and who by poyson
> Hasts to an Offices reversion;
> . . . .
> He thrusts on more; And as if he'd undertooke
> To say Gallo-Belgicus without booke
> Speakes of all States, and deeds that have been since
> The Spaniards came, to the losse of Amyens.
> . . . .
> He like a privileg'd spie, whom nothing can
> Discredit, Libells now 'gainst each great man.

He names a price for every office paid;
He saith, our warres thrive ill, because delai'd;

(1:162–63)

The allusion to state spy-systems connects this poem to Jonson's *Se-janus;* and Donne's strategy of having another figure, of whom he purports to disapprove, do his libelling for him, is analogous to Jonson's use of Tacitus as a screen. But unlike Jonson, Donne here articulates, with fine insight, the psychological consequences of a repressive culture. As he listens to this list of venalities and atrocities, Donne's satirical persona experiences not only fear but a subtle form of guilt by association, a metamorphosis of complicity:

I more amas'd then Circes prisoners, when
They felt themselves turne beasts, felt my selfe then
Becomming Traytor, and mee thought I saw
One of our Giant Statutes ope his jaw
To sucke me in;

(1:163)

For Donne, the human product of state censorship is not the heroic individual whose outspokenness deserves written memorial, but the deeply divided and half-felonious self.

This strategy is repeated in *Elegy* 14, subtitled "A Tale of a Citizen and his Wife," which opens with a disclaimer against satirical intent, an assertion of the speaker's harmlessness:

I sing no harme good sooth to any wight,
To Lord or foole, Cuckold, begger or knight,
To peace-teaching Lawyer, Proctor, or brave
Reformed or reduced Captaine, Knave,
Officer, Jugler, or Justice of Peace,
Juror or Judge; I touch no fat sowes grease,
I am no Libeller, nor will be any,
But, (like a true man) say there are too many.

(1:105–6)

In fact, the arrangement of persons and professions here makes its own social comment, the pairing of lord and fool, knight and beggar, officer and juggler suggesting identification rather than differentiation. But the main satirical intent of the poem is reserved for a conversation between the speaker and a London citizen, whom the

speaker coaxes out of his natural taciturnity in order the better to
flirt with his wife behind his back. Behind his back in another sense,
then, the poem delivers an attack on the times, which, because of
the focusing of the citizen's nostalgia, are recognizable as the early
years of James's reign:

> . . . for he gave no praise,
> To any but my Lord of Essex dayes;
> Call'd those the age of action; . . .
> . . . .
> Our onely City trades of hope now are
> Bawd, Tavern-keeper, Whore and Scrivener;
> The much of Privileg'd kingsmen, and the store
> Of fresh protections make the rest all poore;
>
> (1:107)

This allusion to the sale of monopolies connects the voice of the London citizen to that of Shakespeare's Fool in *King Lear;* and as in *King
Lear* the voice of social criticism is presented as the voice of irrationality. "Thus ranne he on," says Donne's cynical speaker, "In a continued rage: so void of reason/Seem'd his harsh talke." And the effect
on the listener is to make him "sweat for feare of treason." Yet behind these generic fences we can perceive, intact, the subversive in-
stinct, limited and marginalized though it may be; and because of
its obvious presence here, we might well reconsider the cause and function of many of the metaphors in Donne's love poems, his constant
references to kings and their favorites, to the state as the frame of
reference for the definition of amorous privacy. When, in *The Sunne
Rising,* the male lover delivers to the sun the injunction to "Goe tell
Court-huntsmen, that the King will ride," he certainly permitted his
readers the same kind of reflection on James's unpopular obsession
that could have been occasioned by Shakespeare's representation of
Lear as huntsman. And when in *The Anniversarie* the lover contrasts
his own situation to that of "All Kings, and all their favorites," not
only with respect to their permanence, but in their freedom from fear
of treason, he reminded his audience of that other world outside the
bedroom that is represented by the satires and the satirical elegies,
a world in which men "sweat for feare of treason" because of conversation held in the street. But it is not only in "paroles indiscrètes,"
as Montesquieu called them, that Donne's society manifested its dis-
contents, and Donne took notice of them. In *Elegy 11* he included

in a curse against an enemy the dreadful fate of being in possession
of "libels, or some interdicted thing,/Which negligently kept," will
bring the possessor to ruin. And in *Pseudo-Martyr,* that remarkable
act of submission to the system that Donne published in 1610, supporting the Oath of Allegiance, he sought in his "Advertisement to
the Reader" to defend himself against Roman Catholic controversial-
ists by identifying them with the very spies and state-censors whose
operations discolored his earlier satirical writing:

> I hope either mine Innocence, or their own fellowes guilti-
> nesse, shall defend me, from the curious malice of those men,
> who in this sickly decay, and declining of their cause, can spy
> out falsifyings in every citation; as in a jealous, and obnoxious
> State, a Decipherer can pick out Plots, and Treason, in any fa-
> miliar letter which is intercepted.[70]

Donne had good reason to identify the familiar letter as a dangerous genre, dangerous because written, a transitional genre between
private speech and public communication, and often, indeed, intercepted. Donne's own familiar letters were, most of them, published
after his death by John Donne, Jr., in a volume entitled *Letters to
Severall Persons of Honour* (1651), and they are invaluable documents
for anyone trying to establish his father's political opinions. One has
to be somewhat wary here, not only because the chronology of most
of the letters can be only hypothetically reconstructed, but also because familiar letters have generic conventions, matters to be discussed
in Chapter 5, but which include the *expectation* of confidentiality,
even of secretiveness. Nevertheless, even if we allow for such expectations, Donne's letters produce, as a group of texts, an effect of strain,
even of danger, in excess of generic shaping; and more important for
this argument, they show that his response to a climate of censorship
and other related forms of inhibition was a constant interest in, even
an obsession with, problems of interpretation and misinterpretation.
In 1609, for example, the year in which he completed *Pseudo-Martyr,*
Donne wrote to his friend Sir Henry Goodyere a critique of another,
unidentified book written to the same purpose. Although on the main
issue, whether Roman Catholics should be forced to take the oath,
there was, he felt, "perplexity . . . and both sides may be in justice,
and innocence," nevertheless that particular controversialist had
broken the conventions of that kind of discourse by "miscitings, or
misinterpretings" of other men's words. "I looked for more prudence,

and humane wisdom in him," Donne explained, "because at this time the watch is set, and every bodies hammer is upon that anvill."[71] The very indeterminacy of the issue required a hermeneutical delicacy or integrity, an attention to authorial intention that prohibited the wresting of texts to one's own purpose. Another letter, roughly contemporaneous and also to Goodyere, addresses the question of doctrinal certainty in similar terms:

> And when we are sure we are in the right way . . . it concerns us as much what our companions be, but very much what our friends. In which, *I know I speak not dangerously nor misappliably to you,* as though I averted you from any of those friends, who are of other impressions than you or I in some great circumstances of Religion. (pp. 28–29; italics added)

These special conditions, of trust and intimacy, of cognitive shortcuts and particular understandings, are involved again in May 1612, in a letter to George Garrard. The occasion of the letter was the recent death of the lord treasurer, Robert Cecil, earl of Salisbury, an event followed by a spate of satires. Donne took the occasion to meditate on "libel," not only on the nature, function, and sanctions of satire as a genre, but also on its peculiar status as prohibited and usually anonymous discourse. His first whimsical suggestion is that the recent libels have been so "tastelesse and flat" that they must have been written by Salisbury's friends:

> It is not the first time that our age hath seen that art practised, That when there are witty and sharp libels made which not onely for the liberty of speaking, but for the elegancie, and composition, would take deep root, . . . no other way hath been thought so fit to suppresse them, as to divulge some coarse and railing one. (pp. 89–90)

Poor satire, in other words, drives out or censors good or effective sociopolitical criticism.

Donne then pursued the question of whether all satires ought to be prohibited. "I dare say to you," he continued, "where I am not easily misinterpreted, that there may be cases, where one may do his Countrey goode service, by libelling against a live man." The distinction he wished to draw was between satire that intends to reform its subject, and hence must be published in his lifetime, and that which, appearing only after his death, is malign to no purpose. Posthumous

satire of a powerful statesman is also, of course, cowardly, since it
has avoided his wrath by delay. The point is well taken; yet Donne's
language is more informative than, perhaps, he knew. "I dare say,"
which momentarily invokes the satirist's own audacity, is quickly coun-
teracted by the now-characteristic note of caution, "*where I am not
easily misinterpreted.*" With his own satires of the 1590s behind him,
Donne was not quite ready, yet, to abandon the genre; but his language already showed the effects of a repressive culture.

In the last part of the letter, Donne recalled that some of the Church
Fathers had written "libellous books against the Emperours of their
times" (p. 79), but *not* during their lives. "I am glad," Donne commented drily, ". . . for that must have occasioned tumult, and contempt, against so high and Soveraign persons." Remembering also
that those libels were atypical, because not anonymous, he added:
"which excuse [atypicality] would not have served in the Star-chamber,
where sealed Letters have been judged Libels." This sudden, and certain, and threatening topicality closes the gap between the letter writer
and his subject, as letters themselves become potentially libelous, or
prohibited discourse. Genre, then, is to be determined not by intention (satire is a critique of the powerful, intended to improve them),
but by reception (satire is literally the *product* of censorship, that which
the powerful interpret as offensive to themselves).

The death of Cecil might have been seen as an opportunity for
James's government to relax, to abandon the spy systems of the king's
first decade for a more genuinely pacific cultural climate. But more
tensions were brewing, in the affairs of the Palatinate. Donne, who
had expressed high hopes for the marriage of Princess Elizabeth to
the Elector,[72] was appointed by James to accompany Viscount Don-
caster on his 1619 mission "to compose the discords of that discom-
posed State," as Izaak Walton put it.[73] Donne's continued devotion
to the queen of Bohemia and her cause is well documented, and needs
to be remembered when reading, in a letter to Sir Henry Goodyere,
that "the Palatinate is absolutely lost" (p. 230). But the military details that follow are no more shocking than his account of the political climate at home:

> Mr. Gage is returning to Rome, but of his Negotiation I dare
> say nothing by a Letter of adventure. The direction which his
> Ma^{ty} gave for Preachers, had scandalized many; therefore he
> descended to pursue them with certain reasons of his proceed-

> ings therein; and I had commandment to publish them in a Sermon at the Crosse . . . where they received comfortable assurance of his Ma[ties] constancy in Religion, and of his desire that all men should be bred in the knowledge of such things, as might preserve them from the superstition of Rome. (pp. 231–32)

The sermon to which this letter refers was preached on 15 September 1622. James's *Directions to Preachers* had just been issued, via the archbishop of Canterbury; and their ostensibly theological thrust had, as Donne's excerpt makes clear, political correlatives. Preachers were forbidden

> to soare in poynts too deepe, To muster up their own Reading, to display their own Wit, or ignorance in medling with Civill matters or (as his Majestie addes) in rude and undecent reviling of persons.[74]

Donne's task in the sermon was to defend both James's foreign policy and the repression of criticism it necessitated. He cited precedents for restraint of the pulpit under previous monarchs, including Elizabeth. He argued that the king's own learning required the best possible construction of his intentions in the *Directions;* only a "Libeller" could believe them meant to encourage "Ignorance, or Superstition," among the people. And he suggested that James's apparent inactivity on behalf of his daughter might conceal an effective strategy:

> As God sits in Heaven, and yet goes into the field, so they of whom God hath said, Yee are Gods, the Kings of the Earth, may stay at home, and yet goe too. They goe in their assistance to the Warre; They goe in their Mediation for Peace; They goe in their Example, when from their sweetnesse, and moderation in their Government at home, there flowes out an instruction, a perswasion to Princes abroad. Kings goe many times, and are not thanked, because their wayes are not seene. (p. 187)

James was pleased with the sermon, which was promptly published on his order in three separate issues. Yet there is contemporary evidence that others heard the sermon in a sense less helpful to James. John Chamberlain wrote to Dudley Carleton that Donne preached "to certifie the Kings good intention . . . but he gave no great satisfaction, or as some say spoke as if himself were not so well satisfied."[75] And Donne's own letter to Goodyere suggests a tension between the authorized message of the sermon and its author's actual feelings. On the one hand are impersonal, passive, conditional constructs: "*they* received comfortable assurance"; "*his* desire that all men *should* be bred in the knowledge of such things, as *might* preserve them." On the other, we hear of personal constraint—"I dare say nothing"; "I had commandment to publish"—as if he were speaking and not speaking equally under duress.

Just as it is impossible to tell if the text we have of *Sejanus* and other published plays is identical with that actually delivered from the stage, so, too, Donne's tone of voice from the pulpit might have given the audience of his sermon the other meaning that Chamberlain reported. Yet even in the text we have there are signs of ambivalence. Why, for example, dwell on the unpopular forced loan, so inaptly named a "benevolence," that he himself had paid earlier in 1622? Why qualify so carefully his praise of James's pacificism: "our Peacemaker, who hath *sometimes* effected it *in some places,* and always seriously and chargeably and honourably endeavored it in all places" (pp. 192–93; italics added)? And why, in the passage cited above, call attention to the domestic political ideal of "moderation," if not to suggest, both to his royal and to his popular audience, that the *Directions* could be interpreted very differently as an immoderate and authoritarian speech act.

Required to explain from the pulpit the pulpit's repression, Donne could not, in 1622, have been unaware of a painful contradiction. He solved it, in part, generically, by defining his role as the best, the most generous, interpreter of the king's intentions. The worst interpretation is here, in passing, defined as satire, or libel. The terms of this solution had been evolved, and more fully articulated, in a sermon of late 1620, when the news of Frederick's defeat had first reached England, and Donne had had to respond—or had felt he had to—to those who were "scandalized." The 1620 sermon equate "scandals" with misinterpretations; and its language, as a contribution to the hermeneutics of censorship, deserves quotation at some length: "It concerns us," Donne wrote,

> to devest that natural, but corrupt easinesse of misconstruing that which other men doe, especially those whom God hath placed in his own place, for government over us; that we doe not come to think that there is nothing done, if all bee not done; that no abuses are corrected, if all be not removed. (3:182)

The defense of the king's inactivity was here, too, presented as a problem in cognition; but in this earlier sermon Donne was considerably harsher on those who chose the "worst" reading of events:

> To be unsensible of any declination, or any diminution of the glory of God, or his true worship and religion, is an irreligious stupidity; But to bee so ombragious, so startling, so apprehensive, so suspicious, as to think everything that is done, is done to that end; this is a seditious jealousie, a Satyr in the heart, and an unwritten Libell; and God hath a Star-Chamber, to punish unwritten Libels before they are published; Libels against that Law, Curse not, and speak not ill of the King, no not in thy thought. (3:182)

This recalls Jonson's *The New Crie,* in its desire to fix the responsibility for overdetermination on outsiders, and to sanction censorship. The implied contrast between the territories of light (a divine Star-Chamber) and of darkness (those "ombragious" minds who deal in shadows and innuendo) matches the required contrast between sermon and satire, preacher and libeller, good and bad readers of history. For our purpose, its special interest lies in Donne's desire (and capacity) to integrate historical and formalist concerns, to generate genre theory out of the political demands that were made of him. It is not without irony that his editors in 1959 introduced the sermons of 1621/22 as "of an age and not for all time . . . *sermons upon emergent occasions* . . . called forth by a particular set of circumstances, and when those circumstances passed, the sermons lost their value" (4:23–24; italics added). It is to be hoped that we will not need such apologies much longer.

There is, finally, direct evidence that Donne himself suffered from the effects of censorship, or rather that he became a near victim, apparently for engaging in oblique criticism of Charles and Henrietta Maria in a sermon supposed to support their interests. On 1 April 1627 Donne preached on Mark 4:24 — "Take heed what you hear" — and developed his text into an appeal for loyalty to the crown, an attack on seditious "whispering." His language, as before, overtly disenfranchised the king's critics, making them the villains in a Senecan tragedy of state:

> This whisperer wounds thee, and with a stilleta of gold, he strangles thee with scarfes of silk, he smothers thee with the down

of Phoenixes, he destroyes thee by praising thee, and undoes
thee by trusting thee. (7:406)

But Seneca, although explicitly cited, is not the only classical model
for this passage. The whisperer destroys, Donne continues, "by trusting thee with those secrets that bring thee into a desperate perplexity,
Aut alium accusare in subsidium tui (as the Patriarch, and Oracle
of States-men, Tacitus, says).[11] The sudden entry of Tacitus as an authority, a patriarchal source of wisdom rather than an underminer,
is startling. If that historian's name involved for Donne the same complex of responses as, I have argued, it did for Jonson, its invocation
here can be neither casual nor innocent. Tacitus was not normally
one of Donne's oracles, to say the least, and his bitter account of a
political climate that encouraged men to turn informers against their
friends was a peculiar locus classicus to muster in support of the
crown.

That Donne *was* suspected of equivocation is known — recorded,
in fact, by himself, in another of those revealing personal letters. To
his friend and patron, Sir Robert Carr (Somerset's cousin), Donne
sent a frantic appeal for assistance, explaining that Laud had demanded a text of his sermon for close reading. The context, as he
further explained, was the dispute between Charles and Laud on the
one hand, and Archbishop Abbot on the other, a dispute that had
begun in 1625 over Richard Montague's *Appello Caesarem*[76] but had
recently been refocused by Abbot, using the pulpit as a medium of
political criticism. To Carr, Donne explained that, since *his* sermon
had been written two months previously, it should not be read as sup-
portive of Abbot, whose provocative sermon he had not read; and
that therefore, "exceptions being taken, and displeasure kindled at
this, I am afraid, it was rather brought thither, then met there" (p.
306). The disclaimer, the complaint about overdetermination, the familiar phrase "exceptions being taken," all place this letter squarely
in the hermeneutics of censorship; but what is truly remarkable is
the *private* admission to Carr that changes the nature of the disclaimer
completely: "Freely to you I say, I would I were a little more guilty" (p. 305).

Donne's editors, reading the sermon in the light of this letter, concluded that its genuinely loyalist intentions had been misunderstood
because of two tactless allusions to royal wives "that might have been
interpreted as . . . somewhat lacking in respect to Henrietta Maria"

(7:41). In both instances, the issue was the role of the wife in assisting or subverting the national religion. One was particularly striking in view of the scandal, in June of the previous year, over the queen's "pilgrimage" to Tyburn, site of the execution of Roman Catholics, martyrs or traitors, depending on one's point of view. The result, on 31 July, had been the dismissal of all of her French household, who were ignominiously sent back to their own country as a bad influence. Donne wrote:

> Very religious Kings may have had wives, that may have retained some tincture, some impressions of errour, which they may have sucked in their infancy, from another Church, and yet would be loth, those wives should be publicly traduced to be Heretickes, or passionately proclaimed to be Idolators for all that. (7:409)

It is hard to conceive that this was *unintentional* tactlessness, or even that it was tactlessness at all. It seems far more likely that Donne, whose responsibility it was to define the via media in religion, was cautiously, and with the utmost precision, mediating a compromise between Charles and his Puritan critics, one that he meant to be intelligible to both sides. The queen was not to be "publicly traduced"; but she ought to be (and had been) privately disciplined.

But there are other signs of evenhandedness in the sermon, moments hard to miss, one would think, where Donne moves from intimation to affirmation, if not to provocation. One of the most peculiar is a passage in the sermon's center, a moment marked by Donne himself as unique in his career:

> I enter with such a protestation, as perchance may not become me: That this is the first time in all my life . . . this is the first time, that in the exercise of my Ministry, I wished the King away; That ever I had any kinde of loathnesse that the King should hear all that I sayd. (7:403)

This is no mere gesture of self-depreciation. It introduces the cause of his anxiety, his determination to strike a balance perhaps ungrateful to the king's ears, "to speake of the Duties of subjects before the King, *or of the duties of Kings*" (italics added). The note of controlled and muscular fear is both nicely calculated and (to me) upsetting. That it was calculated is made clear by a passage only at first sight less subjective where, at the beginning of the sermon, Donne opened up his text — "Take heed what you hear" — and applied it to the preacher's mission. Preachers were thereby enjoined neither to delete from nor to add to the Word they received from Christ:

> Be not over-timorous so to prevaricate and forbear to preach that, which you have truely heard from me; But be not over-venturous neither, to pretend a Commission when you have none, and to preach that for my word, which is your own passion, *or their purpose that set you up.* (7:294; italics added)

Be bold, be bold, but not too bold. On the indeterminate edge between cowardice and courage the preacher's stance is uneasy, like Britomart in Busyrane's castle, or Milton's Christ on the pinnacle; yet in this context, "their purpose that set you up" is an overtly political phrase. The church must not become a tool of the state. The state, in turn, must allow its preachers to say what they ought. "It is better to hear the Rebuke of the wise, then to heare the songs of fools, says the wise king" (7:411). So wrote Donne, reminding Charles of his father in more ways than one.

It is interesting to hear this sermon of 1627, written when he was fifty-five, taking him in some ways back to the imperatives of Satire 3 and his twenties; fascinating to find that once again the problematics of political discourse remind him of satire, and its mixed motives:

> We make Satyrs; and we looke that the world should call that wit; when God knowes, that that is a great part self-guiltinesse, and we doe but reprehend those things, which we our selves have done, we cry out upon the illnesse of the times, and we make the times ill. (7:408)

For Donne, the connection between satire and political outspokenness was a psychological knot that he was still, in his fifties, trying to disentangle.

Having "faithfully exscribed" his sermon, Donne provided Laud with a copy, and then wrote another extraordinary letter to Carr:

> Sir,
>
> I was this morning at your door, somewhat early; and I am put into such a distaste of my last Sermon, as that I dare not practise any part of it, and therefore though I said then, that we are bound to speake aloud, though we awaken men, . . .

> yet after two or three modest knocks at the door, I went away.
> (pp. 307–8)

He proceeds to argue that Charles must have approached the offending sermon with some preconceived bias, so carefully had it been prepared to serve his interests, as Donne understood them:

> I have cribrated, and re-cribrated, and post-cribrated the Ser-
> mon, and must necessarily say, the King who hath let fall his
> eye upon some of my Poems, never saw, of mine, a hand, or an
> eye, or an affection, set down with so much study, and diligence,
> and labour of syllables as in this Sermon I expressed those two
> points, which I take so much to conduce to his service, the im-
> printing of persuasibility and obedience in the subject, And the
> breaking of the bed of whisperers. (pp. 308–9)

Apart from the intriguing suggestion that Charles had been reading
some of Donne's love poetry, the emphasis on artfulness in the sermon is suspicious; and equally disingenuous, I suspect, is the interpretation to which the latter directs Carr, who was presumably to pass
it on:

> So, the best of my hope is, that some over bold allusions, or
> expressions in the way, might divert his Majesty, from vouch-
> safing to observe the frame, and purpose of the Sermon. When
> he sees the generall scope, I hope his goodnesse will pardon col-
> laterall escapes. (p. 309)

This defense is typical of the hermeneutics of censorship, in its emphasis on the importance of authorial intention in controlling meaning, its disavowal of allusion, its appeal against selective reading. Yet
this, like Cordus's defense in *Sejanus,* can be no simple and trustwor-
thy disclaimer. The letter began, after all, by quoting the sermon on
the preacher's duty to "speake aloud," while admitting that he went
away "after two or three modest knocks at the door." This is a witty
metaphor for the style of courtiership, not only at the anxious moment but over the long career. With Donne, wit and "self-guiltinesse"
reciprocally excited each other; and these late documents invite a
trusted reader (not ourselves) to ask how often he had chosen, as the
style appropriate to a repressive culture, the modest knock that would
not awaken his audience. Donne's letter to Carr suggests a line of
defense; but it simultaneously reminds him of the sermon's central

issue—the problem of combining obedience with outspokenness, of offering the king palatable advice while avoiding "the bed of whisperers." I see no evidence from these documents of his old age that he felt he had found a solution.

The case of William Prynne

Possibly in 1627, Donne wrote to an unidentified friend about the increasing austerity of his intellectual life: "I make account that to spend all my little stock of knowledge upon matter of delight, were the same error, as to spend a fortune upon Masks and Banqueting houses" (p. 228). This dour comment makes it clear how widespread was the criticism of Caroline culture as it had developed under the influence of Henrietta Maria, and that it was not only Puritans who were outraged by the focus on court theatricals. This criticism came to a head, as is well known, in the publication of William Prynne's massive diatribe against the stage, *including* private theatrical performances at court. My purpose in rehearsing this well-known event is to highlight the workings of censorship in this case, and to show the quite extraordinary focus on interpretation that survives in the actual records of the trial.

Histriomastix appeared in the booksellers shortly after the court performance of Walter Montague's *The Shepherd's Paradise* in January 1633, and there seems little doubt that here again Chamberlain's question of "why such a [book] shold come out at this time" was extremely germane to its reception. When Prynne was brought to trial for sedition and libel before the Star Chamber, one of the charges against him was that he had insulted the queen, who had herself performed in Montague's play, by including in his index a reference to "women actors, notorious whores." That was only the most immediately offensive of his numerous attacks on court theatricals, which became, in the second part of his massive text, as much his topic as the immorality of the public stage. Like Donne, Prynne argued before his judges that the timing was pure coincidence: that he had begun his work as early as 1624, when he first arrived in London and was shocked by the tone of the theaters; that he had obtained a license for its publication in 1630, and seen it through the press in 1632; in other words, that it should have been read as an orthodox Puritan treatise of moral and religious intent. Yet into the second part Prynne had incorporated a long section proving that "it hath beene always reputed dishonorable, shamefull, infamous, for Emperors, Kings, or

Princes too come upon a Theatre to dance, to masque, or act a part in any publike or private Enterludes."[77] Consciously or not, his book suggested an analogy between the Caroline court, with its histrionical tendencies, and that of the Roman emperor Nero. After one long passage of denunciation taken directly from Tacitus, the consequences of such an analogy were implied:

> Such was the Playerlike citharedicall life of this lewd vitious Emperour: which made him so execrable to some noble Romanes, who affected him at first, before he fell to these infamous practices; that to vindicate the honour of the Romane Empire, which was thus basely prostituted, they conspired his destruction. (p. 852)

Histriomastix was, in other words, a peculiarly infelicitous combination: one thousand tedious pages long, it combined what *might* have been political warning with a crushing insensitivity to the media which *might* have made it palatable. That drama could have any didactic or analytical function was endlessly denied; yet Prynne himself made copious use of the dramatists' sources of indirection: old stories, other men's words. Like Jonson in *Sejanus,* for example, Prynne quoted extensively from Tacitus; and in his defense he drew attention to those methods:

> Yf Mr. Pryn had conceyved that there had been in it any thinge of that construction, which hee doth confesse that the same may be wrested to, hee would never have soe publicquelye avowched [his book]; and all that in the particulers hath been scited against him is not possitive from himselfe, but as consequence of thinges written by other authours.

Prynne's judges, however, also chose to ignore the conventions. They argued a specific and dangerous application of his words:

> In . . . which . . . thoughe not in expresse tearmes, yet by examples and other implicite meanes, hee laboures to infuse an opinyon into the people, that for acteinge or beinge spectatours of playes or maskes it is just and lawfull to laye violent hands upon kinges and princes. Yf hee had possitively named his Ma[tie] in theis places his meanynge would have been to playnne, therefore he names other princes, and leaves the applicacion to the reader.

And they refused him the protection built into the censorship laws at the time of the "statute of silence":

> Itt is said, hee had noe ill intencion, noe ill harte, but hee maye bee ill interpreted. That must not bee allowed him in excuse, for he should not have written any thinge that would bear construccion, for hee doth not accompanye his booke, to make his intencion knowne to all that reades it.[78]

In these records of the Star Chamber, the hermeneutics of censorship took a turn for the worse. In order to preserve the illusion of power, there were to be sacrificed the power of allusion, the saving grace of indeterminacy, the principles of authorial intention and of the readers' responsibility. By making Prynne a martyr, Charles took an irrevocable step toward civil war and a polarized culture. From that point, those who needed a symbol of his autocracy were not obliged, as Jonson had been, to turn to Roman history, for Prynne's ears entered the territory of legend and symbol. Sir John Suckling, in a play called *The Sad One,* significantly unfinished and unpublished in his lifetime, shows that even a Cavalier poet recognized the new typology: as his Docodisapio ("teacher of wisdom"?) remarks of the current repression in Sicily:

> Why there's another abuse i' th' State, a man shall have his ears cut off for speaking a truth. A sick Government, Drollio, and a weak one, believe't; it never thrived since Spain and we grew so great. There's a mystery in that too, Drollio.[79]

Thomas Carew: a "previledged Scoffer"?

If Prynne's *Histriomastix* and its punishment represented a massive failure of tact on both sides, a breakdown of the communicative strategies and conventions, there is clear evidence in the events that followed of attempts at reconstruction. One year later, three dramatic statements were made, by or to the court, all of which in different ways obliquely referred to *Histriomastix* and the nature of its challenge to Caroline policy and culture. On 6 January 1634, the court saw a revival of John Fletcher's tragicomedy *The Faithful Shepherdess,* in the same costumes used for the previous Twelfth Night entertainment, that fateful performance of Montague's *Shepherd's Paradise.* The full meaning of this event will be explained in Chapter 4, where I discuss the political significance of pastoral romance as a genre. On

3 February, James Shirley's masque *The Triumph of Peace* was produced by the Inns of Court at Whitehall, and repeated, so great was its success, ten days later. The work was commissioned by Charles, and yet, as Stephen Orgel points out, it seems to have been a case of "Charles' critics retaining Inigo Jones in an attempt to speak to the king in his own language." Criticisms of the abuse of the royal prerogative, recommendations that Charles behave like a constitutional monarch, have infiltrated even the published text of the masque. Also, Orgel discovered an interpretation of the *Triumph* by Bulstrode Whitelocke, member of the planning committee for the masque, where he reported on the reception of the antimasque of "projectors," or would-be monopolists. The antimasque, Whitelocke recorded, "pleased the spectators the more, because by it an *information was covertly given to the King* of the unfitness and ridiculousness of these Projects against the Law" (italics added).[80] Since William Noy, Charles's attorney general, was the man primarily responsible for staging the antimasque, such an interpretation is, as Orgel points out, doubly peculiar. Not only does it indicate that the king's own masque, commissioned in his own defense, had, as it were, turned witness for the prosecution, in a way that even ordinary spectators could grasp; but it also requires us to suppose that the attorney general, the man responsible for evading the antimonopoly legislation of 1624, should offer a critique of his royal master's policies. Yet however skeptical we might feel about such a degree of deviousness, the importance of Whitelocke's account for the hermeneutics of censorship is inarguable. He clearly assumed not only the possibility of "covert" signification, but also that its intended audience was the king himself, that its object was criticism in the peculiarly protected form of a work by royal commission.

Five days after the repeat performance of *The Triumph of Peace* there occurred a still more ambiguous dramatic event; Thomas Carew's masque *Coelum Britannicum* was produced at court. When published later in 1634, its title page strongly suggested that it too was the product of a royal command; for it carried a motto from Ausonius: "Non habeo ingenium; Caesar sed iussit: habebo. Cur me posse negem, posse quod ille putat?" ("I have no wit; but Caesar has commanded: I will [therefore] have it. Why should I deny an ability that he thinks I have?") The invocation of Caesarian injunction sounds oddly threatening in the context of current disputes over the royal prerogative; and equally suggestive was Carew's choice of a model, Giordano

Bruno's *Spaccio de la bestia trionfante,* dedicated in 1584 to Sir Philip Sidney. The model carried with it, presumably, the reputations of both Bruno and Sidney as questioners of royal authority.

Carew's strategy in the masque was overtly ambivalent or bifocal. He offered two different representations of England's "heaven" or superior powers: one the model court desired by Charles and Henrietta Maria; the second, the court of Jupiter which is to be reformed according to that model. As a manuscript account of the masque put it:

> Mercury descends to their Ma:[ties] declaring the resolution of the Gods to purge the Heavens of those Constellations w:[ch] antiquity had fixed there, as eternall Registers of their Luxuryes w:[ch] they renounce and intend a reformation in Conformity to their Ma:[ties] exemplar Court, made such by the sedulous imitačon of the unparalled Coniugall love and other heroicall vertues of soe Royall Presidents.[81]

And as Dunlap shows, many of the reforms actually described in the masque reflect, in topical detail, recent Caroline legislation—control of the taverns, or restraint of the country gentry from residing in London. The masque is structured, in other words, on a compliment that declares itself a critique, the notion of a government reforming itself according to an ideal of itself. Charles is both the old, decadent Jupiter and the new deity who will replace him.

Underlining this bifocality, of course, are the chief speakers or interpreters of the heavenly transition—Mercury, god of eloquence, and Momus, "a previledged Scoffer," as the manuscript calls him, the representative of satire and scandal.[82] It is Mercury who gives the uplifting account of the "exemplar Court" and its cosmic influence; even he has been reformed and comes

> Not, as of old, to whisper amorous tales
> Of wanton love, into the glowing eare
> Of some choyce beauty

(p. 154)

but to express the newly fashionable Neoplatonic codes of conduct. It is Momus whose irrepressible prose account of the same events lets in all the ironies and skepticism that formal compliment holds at bay. Momus suggests that Charles's recent legislation is unrealistic, "too strict to be observed long"; that control of the taverns is the effect of some "heavenly Beverage" on the royal mind, an intoxication "which hath rendred the Ideas confus'd in the Divine intellects." He alludes to recent parliamentary history, the "riotous assembly" of 1628, and to the debate over the royal prerogative: "Though I am but a Woollsacke god, and have no vote in the sanction of new lawes, I have yet a Praerogative of wresting the old to any whatsoever interpretation, whether it be to the behoofe, or prejudice, of Iupiter his Crowne and Dignity" (p. 157). And he reflects sardonically on the gap between public iconography and political reality:

> There were some innocent, and some generous constellations, that might have been reserved for Noble uses: as the Skales and Sword (Libra) to adorne the statue of Justice, since she resides here on earth onely in Picture and Effigie. The Eagle had beene a fit present for the Germans, in regard their Bird hath mew'd most of her feathers lately . . . and then had you but clapt Perseus on his Pegasus . . . there had beene a Divine St. George for this Nation. (p. 164)

In all of these comments there is a focus on interpretation, or misinterpretation, as part of the political process. The Caroline reforms are based on "confused" ideas, or on the confusion between Platonic idealism and workable legislation; the debate over the sovereign power and its basis in law has involved the legal profession in "wresting the old [texts] to any whatsoever interpretation"; and the desire for a public symbolism, the Caroline focus on iconography, merely draws attention to the icon's emptiness.

In Momus we have, then, a highly developed spokesman for an advanced hermeneutics; and that it is specifically the hermeneutics of censorship seems equally clear. Like Jonson's Cordus, Momus employs the disclaimer, denying, and therefore implying, that his speech will contain "state-formality, politique inferences, or suspected Rhetoricall elegancies" (p. 160); but the objective historian has been replaced by another safety device, the jester, the wise fool, the "previledged Scoffer." Like *Sejanus,* also, *Coelum Britannicum* alludes to contemporary censorship, playing on the name of the Star Chamber, and connecting it to the royal program of moral reform:

> It is therefore . . . enacted . . . to remove all imputation of impiety from the Coelestiall Spirits, and all lustfull influences upon terrestrial bodies . . . that there be an Inquisition erected to ex-

punge in the Ancient, and suppresse in the moderne and succeeding Poems and Pamphlets, all past, present, and future mention of those abjur'd heresies, and to take particular notice of all ensuing incontinences, and punish them in their high Commission Court. (pp. 158–59)

This announcement must exist in parodic relation to Prynne's attack on lascivious fictions, and it surely anticipates some of Milton's ironies in *Areopagitica;* yet terms like "Inquisition," "suppresse," and "punish" do not easily consist with the ideal of an unimpeachable and benevolent government. The government that had, the previous year, brutally suppressed and punished one of its citizens, merely on suspicion of "politique inferences," has a long way to go, Carew suggests, before true stellification can occur. The privileged speaker, however, introduces a timely, as well as a topical message into a privileged genre and may thereby help to avoid another such confrontation.

Areopagitica: "those fabulous Dragon's teeth"

The test of this chapter must inevitably be Milton's *Areopagitica.* It is, after all, the only seventeenth-century response to censorship that has acquired the status of high art. Unfortunately, in the canonical process, it has become isolated from the discourse that preceded and generated it, a striking instance of Fredric Jameson's contention that "by definition the cultural monuments and masterworks that have survived tend necessarily to perpetuate only a single voice in this [class] dialogue." The earlier parts of this chapter happen, by coincidence, to fulfill the obligation that Jameson requires of all sociopolitical criticism, to reconstruct other voices in the ideological antiphony. There is one crucial distinction between Jameson's program and my own, however: I do not regard the notion of class as a significant determinant in the thinking of writers like Jonson, Massinger, or Donne. Jameson's theory of political response is that it is always broadly (and hence narrowly) dichotomous, based on a simple opposition between ruling class and opposition. Normally, he proposes, "A ruling class ideology will explore various strategies of the legitimation of its own power position, while an oppositional culture of ideology will, often in covert or disguised strategies, seek to contest and undermine the dominant value system." Yet we have already seen Jacobean and Caroline writers experiencing both social and ideological mobility, or watched them combine legitimating tactics required or needed by the authorities with covert or oblique criticism of their regimes. Jameson's position is germane to Milton's *Areopagitica* because it specifically adduces the case of the Puritan revolution. A period of such explosive sectarianism was a challenge to any theory based simply on class dualism, Jameson perceived; and his solution was to declare the 1640s in England a historical moment when "two opposing discourses fight it out within the general unity of a shared code . . . the shared master code of religion."[83] It was the need to attack the "hegemonic theology" from within, in other words, that led temporarily to dispersal and pluralism.

But the *Areopagitica* requires a still more complicated theory. Milton himself was, as we all know, ideologically mobile. He was instinctively an elitist at a time when the identity of the political elite was, to say the least, indeterminate; and in 1644 he was already disillusioned by the Long Parliament, with whose Presbyterian leaders he had thought to make party, until his campaign for legal divorce made him a political liability. To put it more generously, the *Areopagitica* was motivated by his discovery that oppositional culture (to use Jameson's term) was *not* clearly identifiable, that to judge from their institutions, "New Presbyter [was] but Old Priest writ large."[84] Significantly, the institution in question was censorship. The Parliamentary licensing act of 14 June 1643 had carried the shadow of the Star Chamber into the new age of enlightenment, threatening not only its continuation but Milton's ability to believe in its arrival.

The *Areopagitica* did not, moreover, try to clarify matters by sorting everybody into two sharply polarized camps. Its response to the discovery that the ideological divide had been crossed was a rousing defense of pluralism, and, more important for our purpose here, a powerful manifesto for indeterminacy. This is what makes the *Areopagitica* a text in the hermeneutics of censorship, at a particularly dynamic convergence with biblical hermeneutics. The only dualism envisaged by Milton is an emblem of double meaning, an ancient ambiguity, perceived in the Roman temple of Janus:

> And now the time in speciall is, by priviledge to write and speak what may help to the furder discussing of matters in agitation. The Temple of Janus with his two controversal faces might now not unsignificantly be set open.[85]

But the two "controversal" faces of Janus are themselves part of a broader polysemy, a myth of dispersal in which, after the original revelation by Christ, a "wicked race of deceivers . . . took the virgin Truth, hewed her lovely form into a thousand peeces and scattered them to the four winds" (3:549). Good and wise men are to work together at the task of reconstruction, seeking individually "those dissever'd peeces which are yet wanting to the body of Truth" (3:551) and which will not be fully reunited until the Second Coming. Even then, Milton suggests, though Truth must not be conceived of as shiftily protean, "yet is it not impossible that she may have more shapes than one" (3:563).

Or, to shift to an architechtonic metaphor, the sectarian impulses that the Presbyterians would inhibit by censorship should really be perceived as functional, in the most basic sense, to the rebuilding of the national religion:

> There must be many schisms and many dissections made in the quarry and in the timber, ere the house of God can be built. And when every stone is laid artfully together, it cannot be united into a continuity, it can but be contiguous in this world; . . . nay rather the perfection consists in this; that out of many moderat varieties and brotherly dissimilitudes that are not vastly disproportionall arises the goodly and the gracefull symmetry that commends the whole pile and structure. (3:555)

It was a brilliant stroke, of course, to convert the most frustrating conditions of the intellectual life — disagreements and misunderstandings — into a cause for celebration. And, as with John Chamberlain's canny relativism ("every thinge is as yt is taken"), this metaphor has uncanny relevance to modern and postmodern disputes about form and meaning. If the edifice in question were not the church but the academy, such controlled and "brotherly" pluralism might have its attractions; all the more so because, at this stage of his career, Milton's respect for indeterminacy is really a healthy positivism, certainty deferred but not indefinitely. Opinion was to be rescued from the disesteem of a Platonic epistemology; but it was also redefined as "knowledge in the making."

Milton's other stroke of brilliance was to raise to the level of philosophical principle the choice of overt rather than covert discourse. Jonson, in *Timber,* had defined the transparent culture theoretically possible under a wise monarch. Milton transferred this principle to a parliamentary system, arguing that open criticism of one's government was actually proof of loyalty: "For he who freely magnifies what hath been nobly done, and fears not to declare as freely what, might be done better, gives ye the best covenant of his fidelity" (3:488). He also proposed that publication was itself a form of legitimation:

> What can be more fair, than when a man . . . shall not privily from house to house, which is more dangerous, but openly by writing publish to the world what his opinion is, what his reasons, and wherefore that which is now thought cannot be sound. Christ urged it as wherewith to justifie himself that he preacht in publick; yet writing is more publick then preaching. (3:548)

And where Jonson had advised pragmatically that "the mercifull Prince . . . needs no Emissaries, Spies, Intelligencers, to intrap true Subjects," Milton wrote, transcendently, that Truth herself "needs no policies, nor stratagems, nor licensings to make her victorious" (3:563). The echo of *Timber might* have been a coincidence; but I doubt it.

There is, in fact, much to suggest that Milton knew the stratagems of those who preceded him in debates about censorship. He too adopts, or rather adapts, the stance of the privileged speaker — "And now the time in speciall is *by priviledge,* to write and speak what may help" (italics added) — in a serious pun on the "cum privilegio" that signified a licensed text. But instead of the limited freedoms taken by court appointees, or the divine or democratic authority assumed by Thomas Scott, the privilege Milton claims is that of the intellectual, self-appointed; "studious labours" and "naturall endowments" (3:490) had convinced him of his natural, "peculiar" election[86] to advise his country's elected representatives.

He was also familiar with some of his subject's most venerable topoi. In his brief history of censorship from early Christian times, Milton pointed to Augustus as a model of imperial tolerance, citing the same passage in Tacitus that Jonson's Cordus had used in his own defense:

> And for matters of State, the story of Titus Livius, though it extoll'd that part which Pompey held, was not therefore suppresst by Octavius Caesar of the other Faction. (3:499)

Later, in arguing that censorship will not restrain sectarianism, but rather invest heterodox opinions with the importance of anything prohibited, Tacitus reappears via Sir Francis Bacon:

"The punishing of wits enhaunces their autority," saith the Vi-
count St. Albans, "and a forbidd'n writing is thought to be a
certain spark of truth that flies up in the faces of them that seek
to tread it out." (3:542) [87]

Again, the origin was Tacitus (*Annals* IV, 35), describing the aftermath of Cordus's trial in the Roman Senate:

> The Fathers ordered his books to be burned by the aediles; but
> copies remained, hidden and afterwards published: a fact which
> moves us the more to deride the folly of those who believe that
> by an act of despotism in the present there can be extinguished
> also the memory of a succeeding age. On the contrary, genius
> chastized grows in authority [punitis ingeniis gliscit auctoritas].[88]

Finally, there is Milton's highly interesting use of his title page as
entry code to his subject, a code that in this instance combines the
plainest intentionality with the finest allusiveness. On the one hand,
the *Areopagitica* proclaims its topic (a "Speech . . . For the Liberty
of Unlicens'd Printing"), its author ("Mr. John Milton"), and its audience ("the Parlament of England"). On the other, it recommends
itself with a motto from Euripides' *The Suppliants*:

> This is true Liberty when free born men
> Having to advise the public may speak free,
> Which he who can, and will, deserv's high praise,
> Who neither can nor will, may hold his peace;
> What can be juster in a State then this?
>
> (ll. 438–41)

Milton was here quoting Theseus quoting the formula with which,
after the democratic reforms of 436 B.C., the herald opened the proceedings of the democratic assembly in Athens, the Ekklesia.[89] The
ambiguity implicit in this contrast of institutions connects to another
ambiguity in the pamphlet's very title, since the *Areopagiticus* of
Isocrates (355 B.C.) was actually a reactionary document, urging the
Areopagus to *institute* censorship.[90]

But Milton's allusiveness did not, I think, rest here. In *The Suppliants,* Theseus is spokesman for Athenian justice against Theban
tyranny, represented by Creon's refusal to release the corpses of the
Seven against Thebes; and at the source of that whole tragic legend
stood the myth of Cadmus and the sowing of the dragon's teeth, an

appropriate myth of origin for a self-destructive society, twice invoked
by Euripides in *The Suppliants* as the cause of present trouble. It was
also, as Milton certainly knew, twice invoked in Plato's *Laws,* the
primary classical authority for state censorship, and a text he specifically needed to refute. In the first book of the *Laws* (641c), Plato's
Athenian remarks that education has never been Cadmean, that is,
fratricidal; but in the second book (663–64), he cites the myth of Cadmus and the dragon brood as "a great example of how it is possible
to persuade the souls of the young of just about everything." Hence
it proves the efficacy of a state-controlled culture in which "only those
convictions which would do the greatest good for the city" shall be
permitted expression. The lawgiver should encourage only such literature as "will tend to make the whole community speak about these
things with one and the same voice."[91]

To Milton, intent on a defense of multivocality, the Cadmean legend reads differently. Rather than being proof of public docility and
gullibility, it becomes in *his Areopagitica* a metaphor for intellectual
energy. Books, he admits, are "as lively, and as vigorously produc-
tive, as those fabulous Dragons teeth; and being sown up and down,
may chance to spring up armed men" (3:492). But rather than accepting a theory of the survival of the fittest, Milton argues that the state
might "as good almost kill a man as kill a good book," and may do
more damage by the latter:

> Who kills a Man kills a reasonable creature, God's Image, but
> hee who destroyes a good Booke, kills reason it selfe, kills the
> Image of God, as it were in the eye. . . . We should be wary there-
> fore what persecution we raise against the living labours of pub-
> lick men, how we spill that season'd life of man preserv'd and
> stor'd up in Books; since we see a kinde of homicide may be
> thus committed, sometimes a martyrdome, and if it extend to
> the whole impression, a kind of massacre. (3:492–93)

The choice offered allusively to the Long Parliament is, therefore, not
only between different versions and phases of Athenian democracy;
it is also between Athens, the city of light, and Thebes, the city of
doom.

This is, of course, only one of dozens of allusions, some classical,
some Christian, some literary, in the body of the text; but it has not
been given the attention Milton himself invokes on his title page,
whose chief message is that the classical tradition was itself not uni-

vocal on the subject of freedom of speech. And in case we should miss the point, Milton later inserts into his mockery of censorship a reminder that facades need careful inspection: "The Windows also, and the Balcone's must be thought on, there are shrewd books, *with dangerous Frontispices* set to sale" (3:524; italics added).

What *has* been frequently observed is that Milton's position was not objective (he was frustrated by the hostile reaction to his divorce pamphlets), or consistent (he excluded Roman Catholic propaganda even from the right to a first hearing). Even his distinction between prelicensing and later suppression, when a book had been tested and found obnoxious by a wide audience, was called into question by his later conduct, when, as part of his service to the Council of State in 1651, he acted as official licenser of newsbooks.[92] But no evidence of his own ambivalence is more tantalizing than the ghost of a line preserved in the Trinity manuscript version of his sonnet *On the New Forcers of Conscience under the Long Parliament.* When Milton turned in 1644 from support of the Presbyterians to attack, he made explicit in the sonnet what the *Areopagitica* only implies, that Parliament ought to reject its Presbyterian leadership, and "clip [them] as close as marginal P[rynne]'s ears." The early vindictiveness that threatened his current opponents with the fate of a victim of the Star Chamber is in striking contrast to Sir John Suckling's uneasy Cavalier conscience: "a man shall have his ears cut off for speaking a truth." Did Milton's own conscience get to him before the edition of 1673, jarred perhaps by the threatened suppression of *Paradise Lost,*[93] to produce the cooler final version, "Clip your Phylacteries, though baulk [i.e., spare] your Ears?" But to hear these two men, Puritan spokesman and Cavalier poet, taking stances on Prynne's ears originally so opposite, so opposite also to what we might have *expected* of them, is a salutary caution. In the hermeneutics of censorship, every thing is indeed only "as yt is taken."

Since the subject of this chapter is interpretation, its objective being to reground that supposedly literary activity in history and politics, I do not deal with texts that merely argue for or against censorship, such as William Walwyn's *The Compassionate Samaritane,* which immediately preceded Milton's *Areopagitica,* or Jeremy Taylor's *The Liberty of Prophesying* (1647), or John Goodwin's *Fresh Discovery of the High Presbyterian Spirit* (1654).[94] Subsequent chapters will show the response of intellectuals to censorship under Cromwell and the later Stuarts in ways that extend the range of ideology and event into genre theory and iconography. But there is one stage in the history of censorship later than the seventeenth century that belongs in the present inquiry. In 1695 precensorship by licensing was abolished, and control of the press passed into the territory of common law, where cases for libel and seditious libel were heard in the courts. Occasionally prosecutions were instigated by Parliament, as in the case of Daniel Defoe's *Shortest Way with Dissenters* in 1702. But after 1695, as before, one of the primary issues in cases of libel remained the question of intention, particularly when irony (Defoe's method), allegory, or innuendo was used or suspected. As Swift remarked in the 1735 edition of *Gulliver's Travels*, "People in power were very watchful over the press, and apt not only to interpret, but to punish every thing which looked like an *innuendo*."[95] But we should now have little difficulty in recognizing the familiar protest against overdetermination by a far from ingenuous author, Swift's friend Bolingbroke, who published a series of articles in the *Craftsman* under the pseudonym of Humphrey Oldcastle, in which Jacobean history was retold as a medium of covert attack on Walpole. We recognize here the old strategy of John Hayward, and recognize also the disclaimer in *The Doctrine of Innuendo's Discuss'd* (1731), where Bolingbroke's articles are described as "Matters of Fact extracted from the best Historians, of Things transacted some Ages ago." Therefore, the anonymous author argued, "how invidious is it in any Man to wrest an Author's meaning, and draw Parallels where none were design'd."[96] In 1729 the case of *Rex v. Clarke* set a precedent for restraining interpretation to "such as the generality of readers must take it in, according to the obvious and natural sense of it"; although journalists like Richard Steele continued to argue that if a passage were *capable* of an innocent interpretation, that ought to prevail. As the *British Journal* put it (with an intriguing parenthesis) in 1722:

> When words used in their true and proper sense, and understood in their literal and natural meaning, import nothing that is criminal, then to strain their genuine signification to make them intend sedition (which possibly the author might intend too) is such a stretch of discretionary power, as must subvert all the principles of free government.[97]

The debate over intention continued throughout the eighteenth century, along with doubts as to whether juries were sufficiently competent readers of texts ("a plain Jury of Freeholders may happen not to be so well versed in the Arts of Composition, and Figures of Rhetorick, as to be able to trace out the exact Meaning of these Mysterious Writers, through all their Innuendo's, and double Entendres").[98] But by the end of the century it was the juries who, by refusing to convict for seditious libel, allowed public opinion to intervene between a government and its critics, and so prepared for the end of political censorship in England.

3   Lyric and Society

The poem of the mind in the act of finding
What will suffice. It has not always had
To find: the scene was set; it repeated what
Was in the script.
          Then the theatre was changed
To something else. Its past was a souvenir.
It has to be living, to learn the speech of the place.
It has to face the men of the time and to meet
The women of the time. It has to think about war
And it has to find what will suffice. It has
To construct a new stage. It has to be on that stage
And, like an insatiable actor, slowly and
With meditation, speak words that in the ear,
In the delicatest ear of the mind, repeat,
Exactly, that which it wants to hear, at the sound
Of which, an invisible audience listens,
Not to the play, but to itself . . .
                    — Wallace Stevens, "Of Modern Poetry"

In his 1601 comedy, *The Poetaster,* Ben Jonson dramatized a successful relationship between poetry and the state, with Jonson himself
as the Roman poet Horace, saved from his detractors, and established
in the goodwill and protection of Augustus. Yet that play on its first
appearance caused so much scandal, on account of its thinly veiled
insults to contemporary writers,[1] that Jonson appended an "Apologeticall Dialogue." Here he appeared again, not as Horace, but simply
as "Author," to discuss the problems of a writer's relation to society.
At the end of this striking act of defamiliarization, the author exits,
promising to write in future only for an audience of one, "so he judicious be." "Leave me," he says:

> . . . There's something come into my thought,
> That must, and shall be sung, high, and aloofe,
> Safe from the wolves black jaw, and the dull asses hoofe
>
> (4:324)

These lines project a move from comedy to tragedy, and in fact predicted *Sejanus,* a play that enacts a totally destructive relationship
between the intellectual and the state. The difference is partly to be
explained by a shift in Jonson's public attitude to Elizabeth made
possible by her death, and a desire to warn her successor of the cul-

128

tural disadvantages of a repressive regime. But Jonson's own experience of censorship in the case of *The Poetaster* may have helped to shape *Sejanus;* for the "Apologeticall Dialogue," "only once spoken upon the stage," was itself "suppressed by authority."[2] Conversely, this historical fact helps us to interpret those striking metaphors at the end of the dialogue. The intellectual space, "high, and aloofe," in which the writer seeks voluntary isolation, is delimited for him by two hostile forces: on the one hand, "the dull asses hoofe," philistinism, the uneducated audiences that preferred Shakespeare's plays to his own; on the other hand, the "wolves black jaw," political power as intimidation.

These lines reappear in a new and significantly altered context in a poem in Jonson's *Under-wood. An Ode: To himselfe* is inarguably lyric in form and by virtue of the traditions it invokes:

> Where do'st thou carelesse lie,
>   Buried in ease and sloth?
> Knowledge, that sleepes, doth die;
> And this Securitie,
>   It is the common Moath,
> That eats on wits, and Arts, and (oft) destroyes them both.
>
> Are all th'Aonian Springs
>   Dri'd up? lyes Thespia wast?
> Doth Clarius Harp want strings,
> That not a Nymph now sings?
>   Or droop they as disgrac't,
> To see their Seats and Bowers by chattring Pies defac't?
>
> If hence thy silence be,
>   As 'tis too just a cause;
> Let this thought quicken thee,
> Minds that are great and free,
>   Should not on fortune pause,
> 'Tis crowne enough to vertue still, her owne applause.
>
> What thou the greedie Frie
>   Be taken with false Baytes
> Of worded Balladrie,
> And thinke it Poësie?
>   They die with their conceits,
> And only pitious scorne, upon their folly waites.

Then take in hand thy Lyre,
    Strike in thy proper straine,
With Japhets lyne, aspire
Sols Chariot for new fire,
    To give the world againe:
Who aided him, will thee, the issue of Joves braine.

And since our Daintie age,
    Cannot indure reproofe,
Make not thy selfe a Page,
To that strumpet the Stage,
    But sing high and aloofe,
Safe from the wolves black jaw, and the dull Asses hoofe.
                                                        (8:174–75)

The theme of this poem, like that of the "Apologeticall Dialogue," is the author's isolation from his culture, his "silence" in a society overrun by cheap versifiers, poetasters, fashionable hacks; and, as at the conclusion of *The Poetaster,* continued articulateness will depend on a successful shift into a different genre. "Then take in hand thy Lyre," Jonson encouraged himself, choosing the most lyric of instruments. The genre of elitist communication is to be narrowed from comedy, through tragedy, to lyric. The address to a "judicious audience" of one is now an address to himself. Yet, for all its claims to transcendence, the personal space is still defined by default, in response to an apparently frustrate public life; the self is generated conceptually out of loss of self-esteem. The poem's resolution is still governed by the black teeth of fear and the dull thud of humiliation. Marked and shocked, the self gathers itself together, and declares itself an autonomous state.

The previous chapter has examined the impact of censorship on public or socially extrovert modes of expression: the drama, the sermon, the political pamphlet addressed to Parliament. All are forms that invite societal response and therefore assume certain inhibitions. But if there were one genre for which we might expect immunity in return for privacy, it would be the lyric. Such, at least, would be the assumption of a modernist poet or critic, and of many postmodernists also. This is the legacy of Romanticism, of the Romantic poets' dominance over the lyric, and its completed transformation in their hands into a vehicle of self-expression. When T. S. Eliot delivered his lecture on "The Three Voices of Poetry" in 1953, and declared that in lyric the poet represents "his own thoughts and sentiments . . . to himself or to nobody,"[3] he translated Plato's vocalic distinction between the three major genres into a postromantic premise. As W. R. Johnson has argued, this premise required Eliot to dismiss as fictions the social modes of address in earlier lyric; classical and neoclassical lyricists were "disguising their interior monologues by presenting them as utterances of praise or blame, as attempts at communication with other beings, as shared speech."[4] The result was a theory of lyric freed from the apparent contradictions of earlier practice and the tiresome indeterminacy of terms like "ode" and "elegy," and a radical severing of the genre (if it could still be called one) from its history. The definition of modern poetry by Wallace Stevens offered in the epigraph to this chapter, and published in 1942, was more truthfully a definition of the modernist conception of lyric, whose contraction into "the delicatest ear of the mind" was counterbalanced by its imperialist expansion. Territory previously occupied by dramatic poetry — by real theater — was absorbed metaphorically, the "act of the mind" replacing scene, script, stage, actor, and play, the audience expected to listen only to itself. And it was primarily the act of "finding" that distinguished this program from earlier, pre-scripted conceptions of lyric, invention replacing convention and forgetting its own origins in memory.

A similar elision was performed by Theodor Adorno, lecturing in 1957 on "*Lyrik und Gesellschaft*": "The great poets of the more distant past who might be counted as lyric poets according to literary historical concepts of lyric poetry, Pindar and Alcaeus, for example, . . . are very distant indeed from our primary idea of lyric poetry."[5] Speaking to a radio audience at the height of New Criticism's reign, Adorno took as his premise that lyric and society had been separated in his culture, that there was common assent to the principle of lyric as the purest form of poetry, "free from objective weight, able to conjure up a life unencumbered by the compulsion of prevailing practise, of utilitarianism, of the pressure of stubborn self-preservation." The purpose of his lecture was to counter or at least to complicate this consensus, by proposing that the ideal of purity was inevitably a social product. "It implies the protest against a social condition which every individual experiences as inimical, alien, cold and oppressive."[6] Society itself, then, was the original lyricist, inscribing in the individual the protest necessary to produce the subjective, isolated voice.

Adorno's approach was clearly a response to developments in Marxist esthetics, his friendship with Brecht, and his own work in the Institute for Social Research in Frankfurt. Yet his intuitive response to lyric remained, in this lecture, essentially romantic or post-romantic. Although he argued that "a collective undercurrent" primes all lyric, and praised both Brecht and Garcia Lorca for making that undercurrent audible once more, he also insisted that the truly societal dimension of a text is not to be confused with "the level of social concern of the work, and especially not that of its author."[7] And, most revealing of all:

> The historical relationship of subject to object, of the individual to society, must have found its precipitate in the medium of the subjective, self-reflecting spirit. It will be the more perfect, the less the structure has treated the I-society relationship as a theme, indeed, *the more spontaneously* it crystallizes out of itself in the structure. (italics added)[8]

In that crucial "spontaneously" ("unwillkürlicher"), Adorno's thesis revealed its uneasy compromise between the tenets of Marxism and New Criticism, both of which, of course, depreciate authorial intention.

As Adorno himself admitted, his lecture was open to the charge of betraying its Frankfurt School imperatives: "You can accuse me of being so afraid of crude sociology that I have sublimated the relationship between lyric poetry and society so that nothing actually remains of it."[9] For different reasons, the same charge could be laid against the dominant school of criticism of the 1970s, the Franco-American alliance of poststructuralists and deconstructionists. Its effect on lyric theory is well illustrated by Paul Fry's study of the English ode, which begins by citing with approval, as "something that can and should be said about all important odes", Allan Tate's comment on his own *Ode to the Confederate Dead*. Its generic self-classification was ironic, according to Tate, because "the scene of the poem is not a public celebration, it is a lone man by a gate." For Fry, it was the triumph of modernism to perceive that the gate is always closed, to admit the "cut-off-ness" of all lyric poetry. Given such a premise, the public, ceremonial function of the ode has to be devalued; and the only poems considered are those in which something "personal and dissident" can be discerned, something textually problematic or capable of a deconstructive analysis. It is not without interest for my argument, however, that among the odes so privileged were certain seventeenth-century poems:

> Whether they are covertly antinomian like [Milton's] Nativity
> Ode, colored by sedition like [Drayton's] "Agincourt" and [Jonson's] Desmond ode . . . or simply drawn to an imagery of dwindling and misshapenness like the great odes of Jonson and Dryden, odes also subvert the persuasive power of their formality.
> Their circles are empty and broken; . . . they institute sea
> changes between the present and the absent, all in the service
> of some excluded force that keeps returning, uncannily, from
> within.

For behind this incantation lies evidence for an alternative conclusion: namely, that seventeenth-century poets were attracted to the ode because they wished precisely to interrogate the poet's calling. What they understood of the ode's history suggested an ambiguous form, looking inward and outward simultaneously, and dramatizing, whether in Pindar's voice or Horace's, the demands of both subject and object. Ben./Jonson split himself between two pindaric strophes, in formal imitation not only of severed friendships but of two different concepts of self. Marvell began his *Horatian Ode* by balancing a reclusive poetics against Cromwell's charisma and the chance to participate in the making of history. Abraham Cowley made the formal and historical properties of his *Pindarique Odes* figures for the civil war and his own uneasy stance as observer and prophet during the republic. These strategies cannot be explained by a merely subversive or deconstructive hypothesis.[10]

Yet the concept of subversion should not be completely abandoned, since censorship, in some sense, was certainly one of the "modes of production" of the three examples just named. It ought to be remembered that the *Horatian Ode,* approved by Eliot for its supposed detachment, was thought dangerous enough in 1681 to be canceled from all but a few copies of Marvell's *Miscellaneous Poems,* surviving only by chance. The poem's author was dead, and so were both its objects, Cromwell and Charles I, yet in the context of Shaftesbury's constitutional challenge to Charles II, the text, one must assume, had been reproblematized. This chapter will not reconsider the *Horatian Ode;*[11] but it will consider sociopolitical motives and pressures, censorship among them, in two highly original, yet conventional, lyricists. Jonson's *Under-wood* will stand as the chief example of lyric's evolution in the reigns of James I and Charles I. Cowley's *Pindarique Odes* were recognized as the major lyric experiment of the Protectorate. Between them, we may sketch the outline of a lyric theory that can accommodate the return to classical models, accept the integrity of sociopolitical modes of address, and perceive the essential relationship of both of these to the evolution of a poetic self.

Cries and Whispers:
self-expression in Jonson's *Under-wood*

At first sight, Jonson's *Ode: To himselfe* seems atypical of *Under-wood,* a collection of poems all of which Jonson would himself have loosely classified as lyric,[12] but which today would usually and pejoratively be designated occasional or epideictic. Yet if we look carefully, there is something about the miscellany that prohibits such a separation. *Under-wood* was published posthumously in 1640, but almost certainly arranged by Jonson late in life, presumably with publication as one of his objectives. In it, poems written for past occasions were selected and arranged in roughly chronological order. The effect is a retrospective of Jonson's career, a retelling of his relations with the state, the stage, friends, patrons, politicians; and inserted between the occasional poems are intermittent assertions of autonomy, like the ode to himself, or the *Epistle answering to one that asked to be Sealed of the Tribe of Ben,* poems that assert a personal identity in defiance of societal pressures. The *Epistle answering* concludes with a definition of Ben-hood, the status symbol to which the "one" he is answering presumably aspires:

> Well, with mine own fraile Pitcher, what to doe
> I have decreed, keep it from waves, and presse;
> Lest it be justled, crack'd, made nought, or lesse.
> Live to that point I will, for which I am man,
> And dwell as in my Center, as I can.

(8:219)

Not only does this poem defy Adorno's thesis that the true lyric of social protest will treat the I-society relationship involuntarily, not thematically; but the status even of Jonson's spoken withdrawal is complicated by the poems that surround it, poems that explain how remarkably involved with others his life has been. The effect is doubly disconcerting. On the one hand, statements of aloofness or autonomy are bracketed, set in the frame of what in a Romantic poem we would call surmise; on the other, in the echo of such rejections, poems

of ceremony and compliment darken and lose their interpretive bland-
ness. What the *Under-wood* poems require of their readers is a si-
multaneous recognition of when and for whom they were first written; of how those original occasions serve as *one* of the conditions
of their placement in the new historical structure of the volume, a
structure inevitably affected by the poet's own processes of after-
thought; of what new relationships and interactions are formed between them by this process of collection, which is also recollection;
and of how these new relationships are both the effect of textual jux-
tapositions — key terms which tie them together in ways that could
not have been foreseen when they were first written — and extratextual
reverberations — conditions of meaning that have accrued to them
since they were first written because of what history has subsequently
wrought upon their subjects.

To exhibit these conditions of interpretation, and in the process
gain some purchase on the multivalency of the term "history" itself
in this argument, it is best to begin with the brief and apparently inconspicuous poem *The mind of the Frontispiece to a Booke,* a poem
that Jonson placed immediately following his *Ode: To himselfe.* Its
enigmatic title would not, however, have concealed from a well-
informed reader the fact that Jonson had written this poem in 1614,
to accompany Sir Walter Ralegh's *History of the World* into print.
Ostensibly, in its original form and location, the poem was part of
an emblematic construction, the verbal corollary to and explication
of Raleigh's elaborately engraved frontispiece, which offered the Jacobean audience a view of history as *historia,* the discipline, the written record of real events, conceived of essentially in terms of classical
historiography. (See Fig. 2) Jonson's poem actually translated, in its
last two lines, the most famous ancient definition of history from
Cicero's *De oratore* (2:36):

> Times witnesse, herald of Antiquitie,
> The light of Truth, and life of Memorie.

But in the first part of the poem, he put a rather unusual stress
on the vital role that history, as a written record, plays in setting the
record straight:

> From Death and darke Oblivion (neere the same),
> The Mistresse of Mans life, grave Historie,
> Raising the World to good, or Evill fame,
> Doth vindicate it to AEternitie.

Figure 2. Frontispiece, Sir Walter Raleigh, The History of the World *(1614). By permission of the Folger Shakespeare Library (STC 20637).*

High Providence would so: that nor the good
Might be defrauded, nor the Great secur'd,
But both might know their wayes are understood,
Are the reward, and punishment assur'd.[13]

Now it is impossible to understand this emphasis, which is simultaneously lugubrious and sinister, implying a world in which the "good" and the "Great" are distinct, a world in which justice is not normally done, without recourse to the original context; which here includes not only Ralegh's frontispiece and indeed the whole text of the *History of the World,* but also the circumstances of its conception and publication.

The *History* was conceived by Ralegh while he was a prisoner in the Tower, living under suspended sentence of death for his implication in the Bye plot, and dependent upon Prince Henry for his economic and perhaps personal survival.[14] We know that English historiography had, since the middle of the sixteenth century, always existed in precarious relationship to governmental controls. Baldwin's preface to the *Myrrovre for Magistrates,* the changes ordered by the Privy Council in Holinshed's *Chronicle* of 1587, the Bishops' Order of 1599, which included the specific direction that "noe English historyes be printed excepte they bee allowed by some of her maiesties privie Counsell," the imprisonment of Sir John Hayward for his history of Henry IV in 1599, all tell the same story, one that was unlikely to change under James. At issue, as we have seen, was the principle of historical analogy, a pivotal concept in the hermeneutics of censorship, as well as the belief that the history of the realm, not only in terms of access to state documents but in terms of interpretation, belonged to the monarch. By conceiving of Prince Henry as the primary audience of his history, therefore, Ralegh had both accepted and subverted this hegemonic principle, since the prince was widely recognized as an ideological alternative to his father, especially in his active Protestantism, and his known dislike of his father's conciliation of Spain;[15] and when Henry died, in November 1612, the historian's project, deprived of its initial motivation, faltered and petered out, somewhere between the second and third Punic wars. Given the possibility of identification between the ancient Carthaginian empire and the contemporary Spanish one, Ralegh's decision to dead-end his narrative at that point may have been less arbitrary than it seems.[16]

Ralegh's decision to publish the *History* without a royal protector was patently an affront to the convention of state control over such material. The edition was prudently anonymous, as indeed was Jonson's poem; and at the end of his preface the unidentified author of the *History* offered one of those disclaimers that alerted his readers to the hermeneutics of censorship. Even though he has chosen to write of the "eldest times," rather than the more obviously touchy subject of earlier English monarchies, his text may still be subject to the overdetermination of hostile readers,

> wherein also why may it not be said, that in speaking of the past, I point at the present, and tax the vices of those that are yet lyving, in their persons that are long since dead; and have it laid to my charge. But this I cannot helpe, though innocent.[17]

Sure enough, James perceived the gesture for what it was, and had the edition confiscated. Yet when in 1616 Ralegh was released from prison and sent on a buccaneering adventure for the king's financial gain, his chief literary production was also publicly recognized as his, and calmly appropriated to the system. As Ralegh set off on his ill-fated voyage to the New World in search of gold, James not only allowed for the appearance of a new edition of the *History* under Ralegh's name, but himself marketed the confiscated edition of 1614.[18]

Such ironies were surely available to Jonson, when he chose to reprint his poem in *Under-wood;* and not the least of them would have been the final, fatal turn of Ralegh's personal history, when in default of finding El Dorado he sacked the Spanish towns on the Orinoco, and returned to find himself facing at last the original charge of treason, a sacrifice to James's renewed interest in a Spanish marriage for the remaining heir to the throne, and to the importunities of the Spanish ambassador, Gondomar. After 1618, then, the date of Ralegh's execution, Jonson's poem had inevitably changed its meaning. Its opening emphasis on "Death, and darke Oblivion" carries not only the universal significance of Ralegh's invocation to Death at the *close* of his *History,* a muse recognized only in the project's failure, but also the personal significance given to it only by that unmentionable addressee, the "mind" of "a Booke" in which Jonson himself had had a personal interest.[19] After 1618, Jonson's understanding of *historia,* the written record of events, and of the historian's responsibilities was likely to be even darker, the emotional power of his poem recharged by history as fact, as events in series. When he saved the poem for *Under-wood,* he altered its eighth line, with its hope that in a world governed by *historia* we may all eventually know justice, "the reward, and punishment assur'd," at least in theory, at least in the life of the mind. In its place he wrote this more conventional, yet ultimately far more cynical, proposal: both the "good" and the "Great" might know their ways understood "when Vice alike in time with vertue dur'd." For the reallocations of *historia* he substituted the ethical indifference of history as we actually experience it; and with the author of the *History of the World* "defrauded" of his just fame, Jonson accepted a ghostly version of the historian's role, to vindicate, as it were, in whispers.

In the third line of the Ralegh epitaph (for that is what the poem became), Jonson used the word "raising," a term of special significance for him in the world of Jacobean politics. The word reappears at the end of his complimentary poem on Sir Francis Bacon's sixtieth birthday. Celebrating at the same time Bacon's new title of Viscount St. Albans, Jonson invoked the expansive tone of ceremonial lyric; its ability to publicize, to make accessible to others that which is of value in character or event:

> 'Tis a brave cause of joy, let it be knowne,
> *For 't were a narrow gladnesse, kept thine owne.*
> Give me a deep-crown'd Bowle, that I may sing
> In *raysing* him the wisdome of my King.
>
> (8:225, ll. 16–20; italics added)

Although in its original context the poem's goodwill must have been transparent, its cheerfulness depends on an optimistic reading of the ways and means of success under James I; but if in the spring of 1621 Jonson had felt he might safely "sing / In raysing him the wisdome of my King," what must he have felt when he copied the poem into his personal collection after Bacon's impeachment? By what wisdom, the *Under-wood* setting must inquire, was Bacon sacrificed later in that very same year, 1621, to the struggle between king and Parliament?

Similar conditions control the meaning, the *feeling*, of *An Epigram on Sir Edward Coke, when he was Lord Chiefe Justice of England*, the retrospective enforced by the title and the opening lines:

> He that should search all Glories of the Gowne,
> And steps of all *rais'd* servants of the Crowne,
> He could not find, then thee, of all that store

> Whom Fortune aided lesse, or Vertue more.
> *Such, Coke, were thy beginnings . . .*
>
> (8:217, 11. 1–5; italics added)

Again, that word "rais'd" offers a historical perspective on the Jacobean arrivistes, among whom, of course, Jonson would have to count himself. In retrospect, the connection with the poem on Bacon is more than textual, since Coke had played a major role in Bacon's impeachment; while Jonson's praise of Coke's "manly Eloquence . . . thy Nations fame, her Crownes defence" must have acquired a different resonance after 1628, when Coke's leadership of the rebellious House of Commons had wrested from Charles the Petition of Right. These poems interrogate each other. The story told by and between them is the old story of fortune's slippery wheel, updated to fit the new social mobility of the seventeenth century, but no less dangerous to the individual than it used to be.

This point is made explicitly, and in decisively lyric form, by a striking disturbance of the volume's implied chronology. Immediately after his poem on Ralegh's *History,* Jonson inserted into *Under-wood* the pindaric ode to James Fitzgerald, earl of Desmond, "writ," as its title proclaims, "in Queene Elizabeths Time, since lost, and recovered" (8:176). The poem is far less known than the ode on Cary and Morison, but it is no less interesting for its discovery of a pindaric subject to match the form. Jonson calls on Invention to

> Wake, and put on the wings of Pindar's Muse,
>   To towre with my intention
> High, as his mind, that doth advance
> Her upright head, above the reach of Chance,
>   Or the times envie:
>   Cynthius, I applie
> My bolder numbers to thy golden Lyre:
>   O, then inspire
> Thy Priest in this strange rapture; heat my braine
>   With Delphick fire:
> That I may sing my thoughts, in some unvulgar straine.
>
> (8:176–86)

Fitzgerald was a notable victim of Elizabethan politics. His father had been executed for treason in 1583. He himself had been sent to Ireland and kept a prisoner in Dublin Castle from 1579 to 1584. He was then transferred to the Tower of London until 1600. To Jonson, he was therefore a stoic hero, his integrity created by default, the elevation of his mind produced by the injustice he had suffered for the sins of the fathers:

> Nor thinke your selfe unfortunate,
>   If subject to the jealous errors
> Of politique pretext, that wryes a State,
>   Sinke not beneath these terrors:
>   But whisper, O glad Innocence,
> Where only a mans birth is his offence.

But Jonson had his own "politique pretext" or subtext here. The role of lyric is doubly to enlarge the prisoner, and to make accessible to someone other than Fitzgerald himself those qualities of patience and loyalty that will produce his release from the Tower:

> Then shall my Verses, like strong Charmes
> Breake the knit Circle of her stonie Armes,
>   That holds your spirit
>   And keepes your merit
> Lock't in her cold embraces, from the view
>   Of eyes more true.

Jonson predicts forgiveness by Elizabeth, and concludes by exhorting the earl to deserve his release:

> O then (my best-best lovd) let me importune,
>   That you will stand
> As farre from all revolt, as you are now from Fortune.

To Paul Fry, the peculiar syntax of this ode, especially the confusing use of feminine pronouns, signals constraint. The poet's mind, the Tower, darkness, and the queen ("our faire Phoebe") are difficult to distinguish from each other because Jonson himself was unclear in his objectives. On the one hand, the ode may have been "a seditious coterie poem that resorts to the indirection of Pindar to mystify prying readers"; on the other, its obscurity may signal "a measure of private doubt about the prisoner" and the quality of his allegiance to the crown. Jonson's "ignorance of the facts," Fry concluded, was "as great as his fear of the censor."[20] Fry shows too much ambivalence here, and not enough chronology. If the ode was intended originally as a means to the earl's release, its efficacy would have depended on successful access to a double audience, the queen and her political prisoner. What might be seen as the ode's confusions — its curious overlapping of female figures — might better be understood as poetic strategy designed to present Elizabeth with a tactful critique of her policy. By transferring responsibility for Fitzgerald's condition to the "stonie Armes" of the Tower, and the "gloomie-sceptred hand" of darkness, Jonson permitted the queen herself to discard those cold and repressive attributes. So long as the prospect of royal clemency remained, the poem had no need of subversion.

When Jonson "recovered" it for *Under-wood,* however, its title signaled a new historical context. Placed immediately after the poem on Ralegh, which in turn followed the *Ode: To himselfe,* its darker side, its potential for alienation, was released. The pindaric voice, singing "high and aloofe," aligned itself in hindsight with other victims of "the wolves black jaw"; Fitzgerald, like Ralegh, was dead at the age of thirty-one, his health having been undermined, unquestionably, by his twenty-one years in prison. The warnings initially addressed to him now speak, in the half-light of *Under-wood,* only to the poet himself.

> Nor thinke your selfe unfortunate,
> If subject to the jealous errors
> Of politique pretext, that wryes a State,
> Sinke not beneath these terrors:
> But *whisper* . . .

The crucial word "whisper" is a sure sign of the hermeneutics of censorship. In Sidney's *Arcadia,* the shepherd Dorus had compared his predicament as an unhappy love lyricist to the absolute failure of civic self-expression in *Arcadia:*

> Better yet do I live, that though by my thoughts
>   I be plunged
> Into my life's bondage, yet may disburden a passion
> (Oppressed with ruinous conceits) by the help of an
>   outcry:
> Not limited to a whisp'ring note, the lament of a
>   courtier.[21]

This poem was one of Sidney's many signals that the *Arcadia* was a fictionalized account of and stratagem against the restriction on discourse imposed on an Elizabethan courtier. Fifty years later, not much had changed. In a poem that marks the boundary between the Jacobean and Caroline poems in *Under-wood,* Jonson defined the court of Charles I as a place where "scarce you heare a publike voyce alive, / But whisper'd Counsells, and those only thrive" (8:234).

This inconspicuous poem can, if we allow its influence to spread, alter the character of Jonson's Caroline lyrics. Rather than an uninteresting collection of court flatteries, relieved only by the powerful ode on Cary and Morison, they take their place in the ironic economy of *Under-wood,* where nothing is quite as it seems at first sight. The poem of whispers was addressed to an unidentified bishop. He was almost certainly John Williams, bishop of Lincoln, a figure of much political and moral authority in Charles's reign. Williams had been selected by James to take on the Lord-Keepership after Bacon's fall in 1621. In October 1625, shortly after his accession, Charles removed him from office, ostensibly to separate the functions of church and state, more probably to rid himself of an advisor with strong parliamentarian principles.[22] Jonson's poem turns Williams's defeat into a moral victory:

> That you have seene the pride, behold the sport,
> And all the games of Fortune, plaid at Court;
> View'd there the mercat, read the wretched rate
> At which there are, would sell the Prince, and State:
> That scarce you heare a publike voyce alive,
> But whisper'd Counsells, and those only thrive;
> Yet are got off thence, with cleare mind, and hands
> To lift to heaven: who is't not understands
> Your happinesse, and doth not speake you blest,
> To see you set apart, thus, from the rest.
> T' obtaine of God, what all the Land should aske?
>
> (8:234)

Williams thus becomes, like Fitzgerald and Ralegh, an enforced recluse, "set apart" by his integrity, and hence a lyric object (and subject) in Jonson's developing sense of the genre. Yet the very next poem records Jonson's own failure to achieve a similar independence. *An Epigram To K. Charles for a 100 pounds he sent me in my sicknesse* congratulates Charles for his curative powers over both the King's Evil, scrofula, and the "Poet's Evill, Povertie." In collecting this poem for posterity Jonson added in the margin a crucial date, 1629. It is the first poem in the miscellany to be so dated. In this instance, the date serves as a vital interpretive gloss; for in placing the poem in the opening year of Charles's personal rule, or the Eleven Years' Tyranny, as some would later call it, Jonson explained its closing conceit:

> What can the Poet wish his King may doe,
> But, that he cure the Peoples Evill too?

>   (8:235)

Charles's decision to rule without Parliament was, of course, the result of a constitutional stalemate between king and Commons. It is unlikely that Jonson would not also have known what role Bishop Williams had played in the Lords, during the stormy passage of the Petition of Right. Trying to improve the scope of the petition by inclusion of a clause against arbitrary imprisonment, Williams had been frustrated by Richard, Lord Weston, the new treasurer, whose rival amendment, reasserting the king's absolute sovereignty, was only a part of his strategy to emasculate the petition. Such facts should undoubtedly affect our reading of Jonson's poems to Weston which dominate the last sections of *Under-wood;* especially because the first of these is an *Epistle Mendicant,* emphasizing Jonson's extreme dependency. Inhibited by disease and poverty, Jonson compared himself to "Poore Wretched states, prest by extremities," that are forced to seek help from "Princes aides." The frankness of Jonson's self-abasement is startling, especially in its proximity to his critique (8: 242) of the new vogue of flattery in Caroline culture. It is not that Jonson deconstructs his own poems of compliment. Rather he presents them in candid retrospect as the necessary consequences of the poet's calling when poets and statesmen had substantial need of each other.

We should not be surprised, therefore, to find in Jonson's poems to Weston that key word "rais'd," connecting this relationship to those with Ralegh, Bacon, and Coke, as well as to Jonson's own ambiguous social status. Celebrating Weston's elevation to earl of Portland in 1632, Jonson was even at the time of writing concerned with the negative aspects of promotion, the envy it breeds in others overlooked, the need for poetic interpretation to set such moments in a good light: the envious are urged to "reade the King / In his great Actions: view whom his large hand / Hath rais'd to be the Port unto his Land!" (8:250). The same case was made more expansively for Weston's son's marriage in 1632, in an elaborate *Epithalamion* modeled on Spenser's. "All is a story," wrote Jonson, "of the King and Queene." Their presence at the wedding symbolized their joint role as the fount of honor, honor which devolves on Weston in the form of "greater Name" or additional titles. He, in turn, a "Mine of Wisdome, and of Counsells deep," had talents equal to his hegemonic function, "to worke downe / Mens loves unto the Lawes, and Lawes to love the Crowne" (8:255). But all is not unqualified enthusiasm. Reusing a classical tag on the subject of court advancement, one that he had translated for *Timber,* Jonson reminded his audience both of Weston's unpopularity and of a convention of high-minded rationalization:

> . . . for when a noble Nature's rais'd,
>   It brings Friends Joy, Foes griefe, Posteritie Fame;
> In him the times, no lesse then Prince, are prais'd,
>   And by his Rise, in active men, his Name
>   Doth Emulation stirre;
>   To th'dull, a Spur
>   It is: to th'envious meant
> A meere upbraiding Griefe, and tort'ring punishment
>   (8:256)[23]

The source of this stanza in a letter by Sidonius was discovered by Richard Peterson,[24] whose work on Jonson's poetry of praise has vastly improved our understanding of his classicism, that network of allusions to which we must have access if our interpretations are to be secured. But for all its penetration, Peterson's study clearly exhibits the barrier between the history of ideas and a fully historicized approach to writers and their ideology. In an entire chapter devoted to the significance of Jonson's "rais'd" here and elsewhere, Peterson deals only with its moral and esthetic possibilities. While Jonson obviously believed what he wrote before 1616 to the countess of Rutland, that "it is the Muse, alone, can raise to heaven" (8:114), he had also learned a great deal about terrestial promotion since the publication of *The Forrest.* And he clearly admitted, in *Under-wood,* that though a political rise might sometimes demand endorsement in the language of classical idealism, it was also capable of different kinds of analysis.

In *Timber,* in fact, the classical source of the compliment to Weston occurs in a context of very different timbre. It is part of a series of notes on monarchy and the selection and control of a king's ministers. The term "rais'd" occurs notably three times in a comparison of the bases of sovereignty (8:598–99), in which Jonson remarks on the advantages of a ruler who comes to power "by the suffrage of the people"; and immediately after the Sidonius translation is a note of warning to dishonest ministers, "the great theeves of a state":

> Let them but remember Lewis the eleventh, who to a Clarke of the Exchequer, that came to be Lord Treasurer, and had (for his device) represented himself sitting upon fortunes wheele: told him, hee might doe well to fasten it with a good strong nayle, lest, turning about, it might bring him, where hee was, againe. As indeed it did. (8:604)

It would be surprising if this warning did not silently accompany the Sidonian compliment to Treasurer Weston into the *Under-wood;* particularly since, in the penultimate stanza of the *Epithalamion,* Jonson had made another potentially gloomy classical allusion. Punning on the idea of the family tree that will grow from this marriage, Jonson described Weston himself as

> . . . the maine tree, still found
> Upright and sound,
> By this Sun's Noone-sted's made
> So great; his Body now alone projects the shade.
>
> (8:258)

The allusion is to Lucan's *Pharsalia* (I, 135–43), where the aged and decadent Pompey is described as an oak tree whose roots have rotted, that now "stands by its weight alone, throwing its bare branches to the sky, and making a shade not with leaves but with its trunk" ("Trunco non frondibus efficit umbram"). Obviously, Jonson had converted the allusion into the form of praise; but one has to wonder why the question of decay was raised at all.[25] If Marvell read this poem (as well as Thomas May's translation of Lucan) before the *Horatian Ode,* where Cromwell replaces Lucan's Caesar as the lightning that strikes the ancient tree, he surely noticed the ambiguity of that "still found / Upright." In certain positions, "still" has the ability to suggest temporal and ethical marginality; and Marvell's Cromwell, "still in the Republick's hand" in 1650, was equally subject to the ode's tactical and syntactical dexterity.

One would not need to posit such elusiveness, however interesting it might be to do so, without firm evidence that Jonson was canny by necessity. The crucial text here, in addition to what we have already seen in *Under-wood* (and *Sejanus*), is again *Timber,* where just after his discussion of state ministers Jonson launched briefly into autobiography, a complaint already cited in the previous chapter:

> I have been accus'd to the Lords, to the King; and by great ones. . . . They objected, making of verses to me, when I could object to most of them, their not being able to reade them, but as worthy of scorne. Nay, they would offer to urge mine owne Writings against me; but by pieces, (which was an excellent way of malice) as if any mans Context, might not seeme dangerous, and offensive, if that which was knit, to what went before, were defrauded of his beginning; or that things, by themselves utter'd, might not seeme subject to Calumnie, which read entire, would appeare most free. (8:604–5).

The conditions of political reception are tellingly, if scornfully, delineated, along with one of the characteristic disclaimers in the hermeneutics of censorship—that the only fair reading is contextual. These were the conditions that moved Jonson to the frontiers of lyric theory, that made his lyricism an act of the mind in ways that Wallace Stevens could not have appreciated. At first he was the voice of his "public" lyrics, speaking in a venerable tradition, the voice of social consciousness strained through a fine mesh of caution. Then (but not always later) he discovered the cry of self, "high and aloofe," declaring itself autonomous. Finally, in *Under-wood,* he constructed a third voice, one for which there was no obvious precedent in classical lyric, one that allowed history to tell its own story in the silent connections between poems; a voice that whispered of careerism, of the limits of idealism, of necessity, of the impossibility of independence. The construction of *Under-wood* was, in effect, a lyric act, a prolonged meditation on the I-society relationship; but it was also a direct interrogation of that relationship, not, as in Adorno's hypothesis, a poetry that expresses societal demands and constraints by eliding them. In *Under-wood,* Jonson admitted something that would remain true long after poets achieved some measure of financial independence, that the self is always necessarily a product of its relations.

Accepting this makes it possible to give the poems the kind of reading Jonson asked of his first audience—a reading in the context he constructed for them. And putting the most famous poem of *Under-wood* in its place will have some consequences. The pindaric ode *To the immortall memorie, and friendship of that noble paire, Sir Lucius*

Cary, and Sir H. Morison was written in 1629, in the aftermath of
constitutional crisis and Jonson's own paralytic stroke. It was also
placed in *Under-wood* between the *Epistle Mendicant* to Weston and
the epigram addressed to one of the sons of Ben which explores the
contemporary failure of representation in the Caroline court, the endemic flattery that for Jonson undermines the accurate exchange of
values on which true friendship is based, flattery which can best be
understood in terms of the vogue for an idealized portraiture:

> So doth the flatt'rer with faire cunning strike
> At a Friends freedome, proves all circling meanes
> To keepe him off: and how-so-e're he gleanes
> Some of his formes, he lets him not come neere
> Where he would fixe, for the distinctions feare.
> . . . .
> Though now of flattery, as of picture are
> More subtle workes, and finer pieces farre,
> Then knew the former ages: yet to life,
> All is but web, and painting; be the strife
> Never so great to get them: and the ends,
> Rather to boast rich hangings, then rare friends.
>
> (8:242)

As this poem inevitably summons up the court portraits of Van Dyck,
whose wistful elegance of representation became the hallmark of the
1630s, the halcyon days, so it introduces the major themes of the ode
—friendship, and the relationship of art to life—along with one of
the ode's major metaphors, the circle, which has become the focus
of so much modern criticism. And it is no doubt significant that in
this introductory sketch for the greater poem (for so the placement
makes it appear), the circle appears as a metaphor for the artist's
strategy of avoidance, a means of distancing: "all circling meanes /
To keepe . . . off" the spectator from the kind of scrutiny of his images that would reveal their distance from realism.

Criticism of the ode has been largely dominated by the very idealizing principles that Jonson here throws into question; that is to say,
most readers have preferred to focus on those parts of the poem that
best conform to the expectations of a poem in praise of friendship
and exemplary conduct, especially the idea of perfection exemplified
in Morison, and all the more perfectly exemplified because of his early
death:[26]

All Offices were done
By him, so ample, full, and round,
In weight, in measure, number, sound,
As though his age imperfect might appeare,
His life was of Humanitie the Spheare.

Alternatively, it is possible to focus, as Paul Fry did in his deconstructive reading of the ode, on the obstructions that Jonson has set in the way of such consolation; on the ominous prodigy of the "Infant of Saguntum" who refused to be born into a state of seige, on the small circle of absolute despair that he makes by his hasty return to his mother's womb, and on the other "monstrous issues" of metrics and syntax that reveal the poet to be, finally, "the chronicler of absence and witness of emptiness."[27] It is *also* possible, however, to strike some kind of a compromise between these apparently polarized responses to the ode, and to admit that the text, even when it was first written, gave almost even time to optimistic and pessimistic meditations on Morison's death. Of its twelve stanzas, the first two are given to the aborted birth, the dark view of the unnaturally shortened life of which Morison is the positive example; yet the idealistic premise that "in short measures, life may perfect bee" is also developed in only two stanzas (5 and 7). The third and fourth stanzas are devoted to the other possibility, also expressed in its most exaggerated and cynical form, of the long life without significant ethical shape—the story of the corrupt octogenarian, who began well, but stooped to "sordid flatteries, acts of strife," and of whom the most that could be said, in terms of achievement, was that he "busied the whole State." It is significant that Jonson does not introduce a counterpraise of Cary as the man who will live long and effectively, and indeed almost presents him, by stressing the symmetry between the friends, as not long for this world. The last lines of the poem do not distinguish between "two so early men," who have *already* "sow'd these fruits, and got the harvest in."

This does not mean, however, that Jonson's whole system of values must be thrown in question, or that the quality of the friendship is impugned. Rather, we should notice that the subject of the other two predominantly negative stanzas in the poem (6 and 9) is Jonson himself, the shape of *his* career, and the relationship of that shape to the problem of representation he here faced. In the ninth stanza, Jonson clearly identified himself with his negative typology of the long life:

> Goe now, and tell out dayes summ'd up with feares,
> And make them yeares;
> Produce thy masse of miseries on the Stage,
> To swell thine age;
> Repeat of things a throng,
> To shew thou hast beene long,
> Not liv'd.

The language of this stanza is both an echo of the man "who out-liv'd his Peeres, / And told forth fourscore yeares," and a reversed echo of his address to himself in the *Ode: To himselfe:* "Make not thy selfe a Page, / To that strumpet the Stage, / But sing high and aloofe." And yet as Jonson aligned himself with those old men whose idealism the age had spoiled, he continued to accept responsibility for the ethical stance, the "stand," of which his pindaric takes formal cognizance.

   In the ninth stanza (also a Stand), or more precisely between the eighth and the ninth stanzas, Jonson performed that formal feat of self-denomination that makes this poem especially and uniquely his. The meaning of the famous enjambement (and even of the period which appears in the folio between Ben./Jonson) has been much discussed; but it too surely depends on its context, which is a long, confusing, incomplete sentence about the problem of representation, given an idealistic premise and the threat of approaching silence. As compared with the poet, who is condemned to "tell out dayes summ'd up with feares," Morison has been permitted to leap "the present age" to some kind of atemporal, ahistorical state,

> Of which we Priests, and Poets say
> Such truths, as we expect for happy men,
> And there he lives with memorie; and Ben
> Jonson, who sung this of him, e're he went
> Himselfe to rest,
> Or taste a part of that full joy he meant
> To have exprest,
> In this bright Asterisme:
> Where it were friendships schisme,
> (Were not his Lucius long with us to tarry)
> To separate these twi-
> Lights, the Dioscuri;
> And keepe the one halfe from his Harry.

The poet is not only suspended between two stanzas, but left without a main verb of his own to explain his presence here, in a realm of incompleted intentions, the idealism "he meant / To have exprest" endlessly competing with the realities of experience. In part, his failure is endemic to the epideictic mode, or, more broadly, to language, not because language constitutes reality, but the very opposite; the only truthful representation of life is by life itself:

> Friendship, in deed, was written, not in words:
> And with the heart, not pen . . .

In part, his failure is caused by the failure of his own life to live up to his own expectations; a conclusion which must have been present in the poem when it was first composed in 1629, but which, in the historicizing, confessional economy of *Under-wood* becomes far more painfully manifest.

To return, then, to the question of Jonson's intentions for *Under-wood* as a whole: the most obvious sign of an intention to publish is the prefatory note "To the Reader" in the 1640 folio, indicating to his modern editors that he had "at least begun to arrange" the poems for a new volume (11:47–48). Yet the content of the note was such as to distract modern readers from any notion that the volume was significantly ordered:

> With the same leave, the Ancients call'd that kind of body *Sylva*, or "Υλη, in which there were works of divers nature, and matter congested, as the multitude call Timber-trees, promiscuously growing, a Wood, or Forrest. So am I bold to entitle these lesser Poems, of later growth, by this of Under-wood, out of the Analogie they hold to the Forrest, in my former booke, and no Otherwise. (8:126)

To believe that *Under-wood* was "matter congested" was particularly convenient if one wished to discard most of its poems, selecting only a very few for canonization; and Jonson's apparent depreciation of this volume by comparison with *The Forrest* was a further disincentive to close study. We now have reason to ask, however, whether the note to the reader might not have been intended as a disclaimer, to be read in terms of the hermeneutics of censorship, and to be compared, for example, to Sidney's prefatory "letter" discounting the seriousness of the *Arcadia*. Even within the conventions of modesty topoi, it would have seemed odd for him to designate his poems to Charles and Weston as "lesser" than the verse epistles to the Sidney family; and if this part of his self-presentation is suspect, the focus on miscellaneity may also be deliberately misleading, distracting the attention of the uninformed reader ("the multitude") from the volume's real structure and meaning. In view of the habits of subreading that we have seen were available — indeed, of the interpretive energy of the very word "under" — we may now be "bold" enough to ask why Jonson wished to remark on the boldness of his title, and why he insisted that "Under-wood" be interpreted "no Otherwise." Would not a proper reader immediately ask, "What else could be meant?"

"All the radiant Monsters": Abraham Cowley's *Pindarique Odes*

Implicit in this account of Jonson's lyricism is the premise that the classical lyric tradition offered a more complex genre theory than modern criticism has usually allowed; that it actually prompted analysis of the self's relation to society, and even offered, in Horace's famous elusiveness and Pindar's notorious obscurity, models of tactical reserve. Horace's Roman odes acquired a special relevance to the Caroline era, both in its height and in its collapse. Marvell's *Horatian Ode* was only one instance. In 1648 Sir Richard Fanshawe had reissued his translation of *Il pastor fido* in a new format, accompanied by a collection of his own Caroline lyrics, under this title:

> Il Pastor Fido. The faithfull shepheard. With An Addition of divers other Poems Concluding with a short Discourse Of The Long Civill Warres of Rome. To His Highnesse The Prince of Wales . . . Horat. *Patiarque vel inconsultus haberi.*

The motto from Horace's *Epistles* (I.v.15: "If I suffer and am held unadvised [in so speaking], so be it") became in this context a statement of royalist bravado, a braving of the Presbyterian censors. At the end of the anthology, Horace appeared again, in two contrasting poems cited by Fanshawe as part of his *Discourse* on civil war. The first (*Odes* III, 24) calls out for direct patriotic intervention in the conflict:

> Oh! he that would asswage
>   Our blood shed and intestine rage
> If he would written have

> His Countries Father on his Grave:
> Let him not feare t'oppose
> Unbridled License . . .

The second, Epode XVI, advises his countrymen to give up the struggle and flee to some blessed island where the Golden Age may still exist:

> Now Iron raignes, I like a statue stand,
> To point Good Men to a Good Land.

The choice offered by the Horatian model was that faced by Fanshawe's royalist audience in 1648, the year of the Vote of No Addresses to Charles I. The prince had already left the country for his own safety; for Fanshawe, the function of the Horatian texts was to explain the relationship between loyalty and poetic survival:

> This same despairing Horace did live to see, and particularly to enjoy, other very different times, when the Commonwealth, after the defeat of Mark Anthony at the Battell of Actium, being now quite tired out with civill Warres, submitted her selfe to the just and peacefull Scepter of the most Noble Augustus.

Fanshawe's own convictions kept him tirelessly working for the return of "Augustus" — too soon, as is it turned out — and led to his own capture at the battle of Worcester in 1650; but for others perhaps less brave than himself, Horace, the survivor, showed the ways and means of accommodation.[28]

The example of Pindar was less directly applicable to seventeenth-century poets. Yet the difficulty, the disjunctiveness, of Pindar's style may well have been strategic, given his dependence on powerful patrons in a period of political turmoil. When the Persian invasion began in 480, the Greek city-states divided against themselves, and so, consequently, did Pindar's patrons; yet he managed to survive the war with his reputation unblemished and thereafter divided his services between the Sicilian tyrants Hieron of Syracuse and Theron of Agrigentum.[29] It is probably no coincidence that Abraham Cowley, in introducing the *concept* of the pindaric ode to his countrymen in 1656, opened his experiment with a translation of the Second Olympic, Pindar's celebration of Theron's chariot race victory in 476, a year in which Theron and Hieron were virtually at war; nor that he drew at-

tention, in his annotations, to some of its peculiarities. A preliminary note warned the reader that the ode "(according to the constant
custom of the Poet) consists more in Digressions, then in the main
subject";[30] twice he observed that the "Connexion" between thoughts
or metaphors was "very obscure"; and once he puts into the reader's
mouth the question as to why so much of the ode is committed not
to the chariot race at all, but to the "tragical accidents and actions"
of Theron's legendary ancestors. "I answer," wrote Cowley, "That they
were so notorious, that it was better to excuse than conceal them"
(p. 8).

This initial problematization of the text was, of course, increased
by translation. Cowley's preface to the *Pindarique Odes* emphasized
the difficulties of transmission, and that "nothing seems more rav-
ing" than a literal translation of Pindar, such as the Latin prose version by Benedictus in 1620 (p. Aaa2). For his first two odes, the only
two that actually were translations, Cowley supplied both the original Greek and that Latin translation, to show what he was up against;
and he also supplied a frame of scholarly commentary, without which,
it was implied, we should all be mad together. The pindaric ode was
thus presented as generically enigmatic, unusually dependent for its
interpretation upon readers with special competence.

The theory of the pindaric is further developed in the second and
third odes. Of the second, a translation of Pindar's First Nemeaean,
we are warned that it too will seem out of control. Comparing the
youth of Chromius to that of Hercules, Pindar, "according to his usual
maner of being transported with any good Hint that meets him in
his way," apparently forgot all about Chromios, and concluded his
poem with a "History" of Hercules (p. 11). The history is in fact a
prophecy delivered by Tiresias who, having seen the serpents stran-
gled by the infant Hercules, from this prodigious "beginning . . . told
with ease the things t'ensue":

> From what Monsters he should free
> The Earth, the Ayr, and Sea,
> *What mighty Tyrants he should slay,*
> *More Monsters far then They.*
> How much at Phlægras field the distrest Gods should ow
> To their great Off-spring here below,

Foretold also was how he would finally join the grateful gods in Olym-
pus, walking through groves of light:

> *And as he walks affright*
> *The Lyon and the Bear,*
> *Bull, Centaur, Scorpion, all the radiant Monsters there.*
>
> (p. 14; italics added)

If one of the keys to this genre is the pindaric "maner of being transported," Cowley had given himself greater freedom still. The itali-
cized passages were not in his original.[31] Their effect, however, is to
bring out the potential of Pindar's text, in which the prodigious, the
heroic, the monstrous, and the tyrannical are all imaginatively connected in a world of radiant terror. "Transport" itself, of course, con-
notes a number of ideas that, in this context, actually belong together:
poetic or prophetic inspiration; madness; flight; metaphor; and translation.[32] In the third ode, an imitation of Horace's praise of Pindar,
the concept of unruly transport becomes not merely an occasional
feature but the very essence of the pindaric:

> Pindars unnavigable Song
> Like a swoln Flood from some steep Mountain pours along,
>   The Ocean meets with such a Voice
> From his enlarged Mouth, as drown the Oceans noise.
>
> So Pindar does new Words and Figures roul
> Down his impetuous Dithyrambique Tide,
>   Which in no Channel deigns t'abide.
>   Which neither Banks nor Dikes controul.
>
> (p. 18)

So Cowley, I shall argue, made the pindaric itself into a new figure,
in which form is indistinguishable from content, in which the origins,
functions, prosodic and stylistic features of the genre blend into a
composite idea; and this idea in turn represented, with necessary obscurity, Cowley's own predicament and that of his countrymen, in
the middle years of Cromwell's Protectorate.

The context for this original program was, inevitably, that of Engagement politics, a context that raised crucial questions about the
role of poetry in the state, and the tactics that writers needed in order
to survive massive political change. The choices available to royalist
writers were rather different after the king's death than they had
seemed to Fanshawe, even in 1648. After 1650, it had gradually became
apparent that Cromwell, for all his resistance to parliamentary con-

trol and his obviously dictatorial tactics, himself desired the stability of the realm. As Protector, he embarked on a campaign of moderate reform combined with limited conciliation of the king's supporters, until the Penruddock rising of 1655 convinced him that such leniency was dangerous.[33] The result was the installation of the major generals, and a return to the massive fines or other penalties, including banishment, that had characterized the rule of the Long Parliament. But for the five years from the king's death to the Penruddock rising, the ideological context was that of accommodation to the Commonwealth, whether genuine, expedient, or only pretended. In 1650, the "Engagement to be taken by all men of the age of eighteen" read, "I do declare and promise, that I will be true and faithful to the Commonwealth of England, as it is now established, without a King or House of Lords."[34] It was typical of Cromwell's conciliatory tendencies that the oath itself was suspended during the early months of the Protectorate.[35]

On the royalist side, as was only to be expected, the politics of accommodation took several forms. David Underdown has shown that from the moment of Charles's execution there was increased tension and rivalry between factions.[36] Abroad, the division was between the Louvre faction, centered on Henrietta Maria, who were for immediate action based on an alliance with the Scots; the Swordsmen, centered on Prince Rupert, who were essentially uncoordinated troubleshooters; and the "Old Royalist" group led by Edward Hyde, Ralph Hopton, and Edward Nicholas. Hyde consistently argued against the policy that led Charles II to the battle of Worcester, believing that if the royalists had the patience to wait, they would eventually win the allegiance of moderates of all parties, whereas a league with the Scottish Covenanters was unlikely to engage support in England. Until the disaster of 1650, Hyde's arguments were ignored. But in the aftermath of Worcester the wisdom of patience was widely expressed, as one Cavalier wrote to another: "As wise as those are, that would have the king in action, I think it fit for him to lye still, and expect further events."[37]

The result of the battle of Worcester was a return to the policies of Hyde, and the formation of a resistance group in England known as the Sealed Knot, a group of six selected by Hyde himself and directly authorized by Charles. The goals of the new organization were markedly different from those of the Western Association, the at-home leaders of the conspiracy who had supported the 1650 invasion. The members of the Knot defined their program in a message to Charles in Paris:

> As they would not engage in any absurd and desperate attempt, but use all their credit and authority to prevent and discountenance the same, so they would take the first rational opportunity, which they expected from the divisions and animosities which daily grew and appeared in the army, to draw their friends and old soldiers who were ready to receive their commands together, and try the utmost that could be done, with[out] the loss or hazard of their lives.[38]

They further requested that Charles grant them, in effect, a monopoly on royalist conspiracy in England, to prevent the cause from being set back by the actions of those who "with great zeal and little animadversion embarked themselves in impossible undertakings." It was the failure of this control that led first to the Gerard plot of 1654 and then to the formation of the Action party, with its sequel in the Penruddock rising.

If the royalist leaders could maintain no unified policy, the responses and predicaments of writers who had been closely associated with the court were not likely to be simple. Waller and Dryden wrote panegyrics to the Protector. Richard Fanshawe, after traveling, to his great personal hardship, as a messenger between the queen in France, Charles in Holland, and Prince Rupert at sea, was taken prisoner at Worcester. William Davenant was intercepted on a mission for the queen in 1650, imprisoned in Cowes Castle, and narrowly escaped execution. Cowley himself became a voluntary exile shortly after Henrietta Maria took refuge in France, and by 1646 was established as the private secretary of Henry, Lord Jermyn, the queen's chamberlain. During the next decade he also served occasionally as a royalist agent, in Scotland and in Jersey, as well as habitually decoding secret documents on behalf of the court party in the Louvre.[39] The habits of mind encouraged by such tasks can be imagined. Cowley lived for ten years with secrecy and disingenuity; and it is perhaps not entirely surprising that, when sent to England in 1654 on some unknown mission, he came under suspicion of being a double agent.

In April 1655 Cowley was arrested in London in connection with a royalist uprising in Salisbury, and it was while he was in prison, under constant examination by Cromwell's officers, that he prepared for the press the *Poems* of 1656, containing the *Pindarique Odes.* The meaning and motives of the entire volume have been, ever since, much debated. Both Cowley and his apologist, Bishop Thomas Sprat, were later to protest that the poet's intentions had been misunderstood by the king's party, and modern critics continue to dispute the interpretation of one ode in particular, the *Brutus.* Yet the concept of functional, intentional ambiguity has never been fully applied to the *Brutus,* or the odes as a group; while there is also a strong possibility that the volume really was ambivalent—that Cowley's poetry was, if not exactly a double agent, necessarily facing two ways at once.

The signal that the 1656 *Poems* were to be read as more than a merely "literary" event was, of course, the notorious preface, for which Charles II never really forgave Cowley. "Tucked away" as Nethercot puts it,[40] in an explanation of why he had suppressed some of his earlier works, was a definition of the role of the intellectual during the Engagement—a crucial passage that it was certainly possible to read as conciliatory to Cromwell and a betrayal of his exiled employers. From prison, Cowley urged royalist writers to do everything in their power to avoid reviving the conflict:

> When the event of battel, and the unaccountable Will of God has determined the controversie, and that we have submitted to the conditions of the Conqueror, we must lay down our Pens as well as Arms, we must march out of our Cause it self, and dismantle that, as well as our Towns and Castles, of all the Works and Fortifications of Wit and Reason by which we defended it.[41]

There was at least one aspect of this argument that we now know to have been disingenuous. Cowley claimed, untruthfully, to have destroyed the manuscript of his own royalist epic *The Civil War,*[42] because it was "almost ridiculous, to make Lawrels for the Conquered."

When Bishop Sprat became Cowley's literary editor after his death, in 1667, he published, with Restoration hindsight, an "Account of the Life and Writings" of his friend; and into this biography he inserted a defense of the notorious preface. Sprat read the preface, on the one hand, as completely disingenuous, a conciliatory strategy designed merely to accomplish Cowley's release from prison "to pursue the ends for which he came hither"; and on the other, as a significant contribution to Engagement strategy, as that had been defined by the moderates surrounding Hyde. Cowley's loyalty, Sprat asserted, was never in question; rather, upon his coming over he found the state of the Royal Party very desperate. He perceived the strength of their Enemies so united, that till it should begin to break within itself, all endeavours against it were like to prove unsuccessful. On the other side he beheld their zeal for his Majesties Cause, to be still so active, that it often hurried them into inevitable ruine. He saw this with much grief. And though he approv'd their constancy as much as any man living, yet he found their unseasonable shewing it, did only disable themselves. . . . He therefore believed that it would be a meritorious service to the King, if any man who was known to have followed his interest, could insinuate into the Usurpers minds, that men of his Principles were now willing to be quiet, and could perswade the poor oppressed Royalists to conceal their affections for better occasions.[43]

Unfortunately for Cowley, Charles and Hyde failed to recognize their own policy, if this indeed was what Cowley had "concealed" and "insinuated" in his preface; while at the same time Cromwell's agent 839 reported in November 1655 that Cowley would "pretend to serve [Cromwell's] interest to secure and free himself."[44]

In 1659 Cowley, now in Paris and himself anticipating the Restoration, wrote to Lord Ormonde with a disclaimer typical of the hermeneutics of censorship:

I am fully satisfied in conscience of the uprightness of my own sense in those [two] or three lines which have been received in one so contrary to it, and though I am sure all my actions and conversation in England have commented upon them according to that sense of mine, and not according to the interpretations of others, yet because it seems they are capable of being understood otherwise than I meant them, I am willing to acknowledge and repent them as an error.[45]

Few statements could record so poignantly the central problem of determining and *maintaining* authorial intention. As William Prynne's Star Chamber judges had noted, the author cannot "accompanye his booke, to make his intencion knowne to all that reades it"; and the only gloss on his text available to Cowley was his own conduct which, as the records show, was itself far from unambiguous.

In 1668 Sprat argued that the preface to the 1656 *Poems* was the only part of Cowley's life "that was lyable to mis-interpretation" (A3v).

But several critics have subsequently felt that at least one ode was similarly liable. In 1721, Dr. H. Prideaux assumed that it was the *Brutus* ode that had occasioned Hyde's famous rebuke to Cowley.[46] His assumption derived from another, that the execution of Charles I by his revolutionary subjects was a natural analogy for the assassination of Julius Caesar. It was an assumption shared by Richard Lovelace, whose *Mock Song,* published in *Posthume Poems* (1659), but probably written shortly after the regicide, ironically wished long life to "the brave Oliver-Brutus."[47] Thomas May in his *History of the Parliament of England* (1647), had also suggested the analogy between the English revolutionaries at the battle of Edgehill (though then under the leadership of the earl of Essex) and Brutus and Cassius, whom May, as a convert to the revolution, was prepared to admire:

> Brutus and Cassius delayed the battle, as loath to waste so much blood, if by any other strategem they might have subdued; because they were, saith Dion, good men, and pitied their countrymen, loving the safety, and striving for the liberty even of those men who fought against them, to overthrow that liberty.[48]

Though Lovelace and May spoke from opposite sides of the battlefield, they shared the same Roman tropology, the same recognition that, as May put it, "concerning human actions and dispositions, there is nothing under the sun which is absolutely new." The problem is how precisely to apply the structures of Roman history; or, as May again articulated it, "Whether the parallel will in some measure fit this occasion or not, I leave it to the reader" (p. 272).

At the heart of the questions raised by the name of Brutus was the classical argument for tyrannicide, recently restated in the *Vindiciae contra Tyrannos,* a powerful polemic written in the context of Huguenot policies in France, but published in an English translation in 1648.[49] And in this argument, the historical role of Brutus was analogous to the legendary role of Hercules as tyrant slayer, a role that, as we have seen, Cowley had *inserted* into his translation of the First Nemeaean. In 1649, Milton, in the *Tenure of Kings and Magistrates,* cited the Hercules of Senecan tragedy, "the grand suppressor of tyrants," in support of his own theoretical defense of the revolution;[50] while in 1652 William Sanford, surveying in *Modern Policies* the results of such thinking, remarked sardonically that to depose a monarch, "or if need be to murther him . . . is commendable if you can dress him up like a Tyrant (as recommended by Buchanan, Cicero and Seneca, in *Hercules Furens.*"[51] What these examples indicate, surely, is that Cowley had deliberately chosen a topic on which he could expect his readership to be deeply divided.

At first sight it might have appeared to that audience that Cowley was indeed taking a position—that the ode was to be a straight-forward defense of Brutus against a negative, and hence a royalist, reading of his conduct. "Excellent Brutus," wrote Cowley as an initial premise, "of all humane race, / The best till Nature was improv'd by Grace." And when to such general admiration is added the specific virtue of republicanism, along with an emphasis on Brutus's refusal of single rule after Caesar's removal, it would have been difficult for a reader in 1656 *not* to assume the topical analogy, not to infer that Cowley referred to Cromwell's refusal of the crown in 1652. Yet like Thomas Sprat, the critics of our own century have been anxious to defend Cowley against any imputation of republicanism. For Jean Loiseau, for example, Cowley was unconscious of "le sens perfide que l'on pourra prêter à sa louange."[52] Others have suggested that Cowley's Brutus stood for the *royalist* cause, perhaps even for Cowley himself.[53] If we are not to dismiss such readings as instances of wishful thinking, we must suspect the ode itself of a certain instability, of a capacity, if not to mislead, at least to lead in more than one direction.[54]

On closer inspection (and in view of the methodological problem that a search for ambiguity is almost always successful), any assumption of clarity in the *Brutus* disappears. In fact, Cowley presents his ode as cognizant of the instability of his subject, its liability to misinterpretation. "Th'Heroick Exaltations of Good," we are reminded at the beginning of the second stanza, "Are so farre from Understood / We count them vice." Those who have condemned Brutus for Caesar's assassination are "Mistaken," but they are "Mistaken Honest men," honestly confused by conflicting ethical imperatives. But we are not to be offered a new account of Brutus, his motives and sanctions, that will resolve such confusions. On the contrary, Cowley seems to go out of his way to leave confusion intact. When he presents the classical case for tyrannicide, he does so in a mystifying syntax:

> What Mercy could the Tyrants life deserve
> From him who kill'd Himself rather then serve?

This syntax permits a momentary doubt as to the referent of "Himself," a doubt that has to be resolved by remembering Brutus was a suicide. If the doubt is resolved, it is likely to be revived by discovering in the third stanza an even more opaque construction, in which the crucial rhyme "deserve/serve," which carries the ethical and constitutional argument, is repeated in reverse:

> There's none but Brutus could deserve
> That all men else should wish to serve,
> And Caesar's usurpt place to him should proffer;
> None can deserve't but he who would refuse the offer.

While an assiduous reader who knew what he ought to find could surely decipher this network of negative constructions and floating pronouns, a reader who was not so sure might easily be influenced by the *metrical* equivalence of "Tyrants . . . deserve" and "Brutus . . . deserve" to receive the ode's insidious message that the two chief protagonists in this ancient drama were difficult to distinguish; a message surely also carried by the discovery in the same stanza that in the vagaries of historical record one adjective applies equally to them both:

> Ingrateful Brutus do they call?
> Ingrateful Caesar who could Rome enthrall!

And what are we to make of the peculiar placing of that word "usurpt," given the royalist habit in the 1650s of referring to Cromwell as the Usurper. Whose place has been usurped by whom? Such ambiguity may well have been intended to be useful to Cowley, as he sat in prison, hoping perhaps that Cromwell would see in the *Brutus* only a Roman model for his own political conduct, while Charles might be induced to look beyond the poem's conclusion to the defeat of Brutus at Philippi. But beyond fulfilling the requirements of self-interest, if such they were, the poem is manifestly a statement of undecidability, a statement in which metrics, syntax, and the obscure connections of the text with its two historical contexts, past and present, all collaborate.

Indeed, if we approach the *Pindarique Odes* from the perspective of the *Brutus,* what emerges is a repeated strategy of provoking political questions while refusing to supply unequivocal answers. There is a certain pattern of references to tyranny; yet we cannot determine clearly who, in Cowley's political theory, deserved such a title in his own time. We must notice the topical application of *Destinie,* with its opening metaphor of a chess game in which the pieces seem to move independently:

Here a proud Pawn I'admire
That stil advancing higher
At top of all became
Another Thing and Name.
Here I'm amaz'ed at th'actions of a Knight,
That does bold wonders in the fight
Here I the losing party blame
For those false Moves that break the Game.
That to their Grave the Bag, the conquered Pieces bring,
And above all, th'ill Conduct of the Mated King.

(p. 29)

But we must also observe how carefully Cowley balanced his evalua-
tive responses, the "proud Pawn" and the "ill Conduct of the Mated
King" deserving comparison with Marvell's evenhandedness in the
Horatian Ode. But where Marvell aspired to a historian's objectivity,
the distance invoked by Cowley in his pindarics seems visionary and
transcendental. "Lo from my'enlightened Eyes the Mists and shadows fell," he wrote in *Destinie:*

And, lo, I saw two Angels plaid the Mate
With Man, alas, no otherwise it proves.
    An unseen Hand makes all their Moves.

.   .   .   .

Some Wisemen, and some Fools we call,
Figures, alas, of Speech, for Destiny plays us all.

(p. 30)

The stress on figures and their potential for misunderstanding is
virtually the subject of the penultimate ode, *The 34 chapter of the
Prophet Isaiah,* a biblical metaphrase which, like the translations from
Pindar, was heavily annotated. It is obvious that Cowley here extended
his concept of the pindaric transport to include Hebraic prophecy.
Just as in *The Extasie* he had imagined himself mounting like the
prophet Elijah straight to heaven, an Old Testament counterpart to
Hercules, so here Isaiah's style is directly compared to Pindar's:

The manner of the Prophets Writing, especially of Isaiah, seems
to me very like that of Pindar; they pass from one thing to another with almost Invisible connexions, and are full of words
and expressions of the highest and boldest flights of Poetry . . .
and the connexion is so difficult, that I am forced to adde a little,
and leave out a great deal to make it seem Sense to us. (p. 50)

But it is also clear that in making "Sense" to his audience in 1656 Cowley had created a text of hermeneutical density, a vortex of possible or alternative meanings. Both the ode and its commentary exploit the original ambiguity: did Isaiah's predictions refer to the history of Judea in his own times or to the apocalypse, the end of all time? It would therefore have appealed both to millenarians and to those, like Milton, who dealt in analogies between English and Jewish history. But the problem of temporal ambiguity would be apparent to any reader trying to decide whether Isaiah's predictions had already been *twice* enacted, or whether they were still to come. "A dreadful Host of Judgements is gone out," wrote Cowley in his opening stanza, " . . . To scourge the Rebel World." Did the ghastly images of military slaughter that followed primarily suggest the recent civil war or some further judgment to fall upon a rebellious nation? Despite the fact that Cowley's translation omitted verses 7 through 10, his commentary notes gratuitously that the unicorns and bulls of verse 7 are "a Metaphor onely of Great Tyrants, and men of the mightiest power." Equally provocative was his handling of the sword of divine justice in verse 2. "I see the Scabbard cast away," Isaiah was made to say, without any basis in the original; the note reads:

> As not intending to put it up again, or to be ever reconciled, in which sense it was said, as I take it, to the great Duke of Guise, that he who draws his sword against his Prince, should fling away the Scabbard. (p. 51)

In the context of Cowley's other allusions to tyranny in the odes, and in the light of his controversial preface to the entire 1656 volume, this note cannot be innocent. On the other hand, its topical reference cannot be ascertained, prince and tyrant being equally relative terms in the unstable lexicon of shifting allegiance. Hermeneutical difficulty is everywhere stressed, not only in the commentary ("in which sense it was said, as I take it") but in the nature of the prophetic imagination, which in turn reflects the greater, more absolute mysteries: the heavenly bodies, "beauteous Characters" written "With such deep Sense by Gods own Hand . . . / whose Eloquence though we understand not, we admire" (p. 49).

This, as I take it, was Cowley's program in the *Pindarique Odes:* to develop a figurative response to the extraordinary events of the past decade that would be true to both their grandeur and their horror; to be admired for his eloquence (and his scholarship) without being precisely understood; to make strong claims, nevertheless, for the imagination as being as vital for its purchase on a new era as Hobbes's analytical philosophy, as salutory in its effect as Scarborough's medical research; and, above all, to show what could safely be written and published in 1656. Habits of mind induced by years of living with conspiracy, with necessarily encoded documents, were surely part of his structure of motivation, not to mention the psychological trauma of imprisonment and interrogation; but more important still was his *conscious* grasp of the political indeterminacy of the Engagement. Everywhere evident in the odes and their commentary is a sense that poetry should not take sides, could not legitimize when the very bases of legitimacy were still in dispute. This account of his intentions would hold whether or not he began his work on Pindar in Jersey in 1651 (for which we have only Sprat's testimony). It places the odes in close relation to the offending preface, which might best be described as a statement of literature's *temporary* neutrality; and it certainly helps to explain why Cowley, like Hobbes, whose "Gigantique Sense" (p. 27) he praised, continued to be misunderstood by both sides.

It is also significant that Cowley's Restoration odes, to Dr. Harvey, to the Royal Society, and to Charles himself, have none of the characteristics and make none of the claims of the interregnum pindarics. The *Ode upon the Blessed Restoration and Return of his Sacred Majesty* not only abandons neutrality and equivocation, but also discards the poetics of transport, with its esthetic of radiant terrorism. "Vain men!" wrote Cowley a decade wiser,

> . . . who thought the Divine Power to find
> In the fierce Thunder and the violent Wind:
> God came not till the storm was past,
> In the still voice of Peace he came at last.[55]

If we return, finally, to Wallace Stevens's *Of Modern Poetry,* it should be easier to see how deep was its elegant injustice (however historically explicable) to earlier theories of lyric. The claim that lyric "has not always had / To find" because it could repeat old forms and formulae—"what was in the script"—is clearly refuted by what we have seen of Jonson and Cowley, and intimated of Marvell and Fanshawe. In its struggle with historicity, its determination to "face the men of the time" and to "think about war" without abandoning the *literary* history of lyric, seventeenth-century lyric made a contribution to genre theory that was better understood by Yeats and Auden, for example, than by Eliot and Stevens. Cowley himself, in *The Muse,* defined the ode in historicizing terms, describing its responsibility to preserve the past, imagine the future, and grasp "this slippery Snake," the present. What he said of lyric's memorial function:

> Thou fadom'est the deep Gulf of Ages past,
>> And canst pluck up with ease
> The years which Thou dost please.
> Like shipwrackt Treasures by rude Tempests cast
>> Long since into the Sea,
> Brought up again to light and *publique Use* . . .
>
> (pp. 23–24; italics added)

contemporary theory ought surely to be able to incorporate.

4   The Royal Romance

In his 1608 tribute to Queen Elizabeth I, Sir Francis Bacon addressed himself to certain weaknesses in the ideology she had created, the myth of the Virgin Queen:

> As for those lighter points of character,—as that she allowed herself to be wooed and courted, and even to have love made to her; and liked it; and continued it beyond the natural age for such vanities;—if any of the sadder sort of persons be disposed to make a great matter of this, it may be observed that there is something to admire in these very things, which ever way you take them. For if viewed indulgently, they are much like the accounts we find in romances, of the Queen of the blessed islands, and her court and institutions, who allows of amorous admiration but prohibits desire. But if you take them seriously, they challenge admiration of another kind and of a very high order; for certain it is that these dalliances detracted but little from her fame and nothing at all from her majesty, and neither weakened her power nor sensibly hindered her business.[1]

The emphasis here on interpretive choice is significant. The possibility that Elizabeth could be criticized for amorous gamesmanship lends support (looking backward to Chapter 1) to my reading of Sidney's *Arcadia;* but Bacon offers his readers a choice between a light (*mollius*) or romance perspective of her behavior and a serious (*severius*) acknowledgment of her actual political accomplishments. Bacon's insight, that political behavior could be interpreted in literary terms, and his selection of romance as one of the possible terms, constituted

167

an early phase of what became, under Charles I, a general under-standing. Bacon's view of romance, however, was gradually displaced during the Caroline period by a more complicated genre theory, in which the alternatives he offered were gradually subsumed into a new, more subtle concept. From being an attractive but untrustworthy al-ternative to the serious, romance itself came to be redefined as seri-ous, as a way of perceiving history and even a means of influencing it. By the time of the Restoration, there had evolved in England a new subgenre of prose narratives, derived from Barclay's *Argenis* and the French historical *romans à clef*, particularly those by Madeleine de Scudéry. Their authors called them "new," "modern," or "serious" in their titles, and often devoted their prefaces to rather sophisticated discussions of romance as a genre, to fictionality as a means of medi-ating historical fact; and two of them, in a highly interesting develop-ment of Bacon's insight, built into their titles the concept of "the royal romance." *Panthalia; or, The Royal Romance* (1659) and *The Prin-cess Cloria; or, The Royal Romance* (1661) are, however, only the most explicit statements of this generic evolution. And here too censor-ship was a significant factor in developing generic self-consciousness. The *roman à clef* did not employ its disguises frivolously.

Renaissance romance theory

Romance theory before the seventeenth century was organized, though in a loose and fragmentary way, around the distinctions between light and serious, fictive and truthful narrative. Medieval writers claimed or disputed the historicity of the three great branches of narrative (the Matter of Britain, the Matter of France, and the *romans d'an-tiquité*); from an ecclesiastical perspective all three were to be avoided as "Mençonge e fable e falseté."[2] The Matter of France claimed a cer-tain authenticity from an eyewitness, Archbishop Turpin of Rheims, whose credibility was supposed to unite both cleric and lay audiences.[3] The claim was, of course, itself a fiction; and during the late Middle Ages even the distinction between the Matters disappeared. The Ro-land of the great *Chanson* was transformed into an Italianate hero, culminating in Boiardo's *Orlando innamorato* (1483); while in En-gland, Sir Thomas Malory repatriated Arthurian legend and gave it, in the context of the Wars of the Roses, a new historical seriousness. By the late fifteenth century, the *romans d'antiquité* had vanished, and the others had merged into a single genre, the chivalric romance, of great appeal but dubious epistemological status.

With the publication of Ariosto's *Orlando furioso* in 1516, romance theory as such was properly inaugurated. What *was* that infuriating but fascinating mixture of magic, erotic fantasy, Carolingian personnel, Vergilian allusion, and ironic deflation? Ariosto's contemporaries divided. Some, taking the lead from the *Furioso*'s patches of overt allegory, wrote elaborate moral interpretations. Others censored it for nonconformity to the newly discovered standards of Aristotle's *Poetics*—unity, verisimilitude, epic seriousness.[4] Others defended it as a primary example of a genre unknown to Aristotle, namely, the romance. In 1554 both Pigna and Giraldi Cinthio attempted to define the new genre.[5] In response to them as well as to Castelvetro, Robortello, Mazzoni, and other neo-Aristotelians, Torquato Tasso developed a theory of narrative poetry that resisted attempts to separate romance and epic, fusing them in a single genre, the heroic poem, that justified his own practice in the *Gerusalemme liberata*.[6]

Central to Tasso's compromise solution was the old question of truth content, updated in the light of Aristotelian verisimilitude. In his revised *Discorsi del poema eroico* (1594), Tasso declared that the poet should work with a base of historical truth, preferably with Christian history, especially that of the Crusades; but that he should also intermingle fiction with fact. History is needed in order for the poem to be taken seriously; the poet "makes an effort to gain . . . belief and credit through the authority of history and renowned names"; but "whoever does not invent or imitate . . . would be no poet but rather a historian." That which distinguishes "literary" experience—in other words, pleasure, novelty, wonder, the effect of *meravigliose*—depends on "mingling" the true and the fictitious:

> This example Homer gave, teaching us with both history and fable (as Dio Chrysostom said, and Strabo before him) that poets intermingle fictions among true things and fables among true thoughts, like the man who fuses gold with silver. . . . history aims at truth, arrangement at expression, fable at delight.[7]

On the two other issues raised by his contemporaries, Tasso also took compromise positions. If Aristotelian unity of structure contrasted with the Ariostan web of interlaced narrative, with "variety and multiplicity," Tasso argued for variety *within* unity:

> One may read here of armies assembling, here of battles on land or sea, here of conquests of cities, skirmishes and duels, . . .

> here tempests, fires, prodigies, there of celestial and infernal councils, there seditions, there discord, wanderings, adventures, enchantments. . . . Yet the poem that contains so great a variety of matters none the less should be one, one in form and soul. (p. 78)

And on the legitimacy of the supernatural or fantastic element in Ariosto and his predecessors, Tasso observed prudently that an author needs "wonders" to "move not only the unlearned but the judicious as well":

> I mean enchanted rings, flying steeds, ships turned into nymphs. . . . But if these miracles, or rather prodigies, cannot be accomplished naturally, they must be caused by some supernatural force or diabolical power. (p. 35)

Tasso, in other words, rationalized the supernatural by appealing to a principle of agency, and suggesting that even wizards and fairies may be conceived as "granted power by God or by demons" (p. 38).

For all its evasions and ambiguities of motive (self-justification), Tasso's genre theory was far more influential in England than were the arguments he disputed. The *Discorsi,* by refusing to allow romance a separate and popular existence, kept it in contact, at least, with serious literature, if only by incorporation. Clearly a force in Spenser's conception of *The Faerie Queene,* Tasso's theory deeply influenced Milton, who came ultimately to reject it;[8] and it acquired a surprising new currency among the writers of romance in the 1650s and 1660s, when the interface between romance and history became again a central issue.

While the sixteenth century clarified some generic thinking about romance, it also complicated matters by producing new forms to think about. One of the more obvious attachments to the genre, if it were one, was the Spanish revival of chivalric romance, inaugurated by *Amadis de Gaula* in 1508, and, compared with Ariosto, old-fashioned in its appeal, totally without irony, to the popular taste for fantastic adventure. Sannazaro's *Arcadia,* on the other hand, introduced in 1504 a type of romance (if it was one) that required generic adjustment and blending. Proof that the *Arcadia* was later perceived as a pastoral romance, rather than a narrative expansion of Vergil's *Eclogues,*[9] comes in its imitations: the *Diana enamorada* of Jorge de Montemayor, Gil Polo's continuation, and above all Sidney's *Arcadia,* all

of which incorporate elements from the chivalric tradition. The third
new entry to the genre was Greek romance, represented most promi-
nently by Heliodorus. When Jacques Amyot produced the first Renaissance version, he called it *L'Histoire aethiopique;* but he offered
it to his audience with an elaborate defense of fiction, "au default
de la vraye histoire," citing, like Tasso, Strabo on the tripartite nature
of narrative art:

> Premierement en histoire, de laquelle la fin est verité . . . Secon-
> dement en ordre, & disposition, dont la fin est l'expression, &
> la force d'atraire & retenir le lecteur. Tiercement en la fiction,
> dont la fin est l'esbahissement, & la delectation, qui procede de
> la nouvelleté des choses estranges, & plaines de merveilles.[10]

The peculiar characteristics of Heliodoran romance were well-
understood: the survival of chaste and faithful love in the face of all
odds; wild adventure and coincidence in an uncivilized environment,
where piracy and shipwreck symbolized human and natural anarchy;
and a significant difference from chivalric romance, with its casual
adulteries and elaborate rituals. Yet Heliodoran and chivalric romance
could also be combined; or so at least Sir Philip Sidney had thought
when he began to revise the *Arcadia.*

There was, then, by the beginning of the seventeenth century, a
body of texts, connected by visible lines of influence, and attached
rather uncertainly to certain problems in epistemology and ethics, to
which the term "romance" might apply. And just after the turn of
the century, there occurred a major event in the evolution and self-
definition of the genre, with the publication of Cervantes's *Don Quixote.* From its first introduction into European culture, *Don Quixote*
has demanded from its readers a high level of interpretive skill; and
in *The Order of Things,* his first major essay in the archeology of
culture, Michel Foucault claimed that *Don Quixote* is the very emblem of textuality itself, and hence the subject of all our frustrated
interpretive energies:

> With all their twists and turns, Don Quixote's adventures form
> the boundary: they mark the end of the old interplay between
> resemblance and signs and contain the beginnings of new rela-
> tions. . . . *Don Quixote* is the first modern work of literature,
> because in it we see the cruel reason of identities and differences
> make endless sport of signs and similitudes.

But with all its late-twentieth-century resonances, Foucault's reading of the romance, or the antiromance, whichever it be, is grounded in the perception that this is a work of epistemological force. Don Quixote's fictional adventures, motivated by the reading of fictions, are in some deeply moving way a study of fictionality itself:

> The chivalric adventures have provided once and for all a written prescription for his adventures. And every episode, every decision, every exploit will be yet another sign that Don Quixote is a true likeness of all the signs that he has traced from his book. But the fact that he wishes to be like them means that he must put them to the test, that the (legible) signs no longer resemble (visible) people. All those written texts, all those extravagant romances are, quite literally, unparalleled: no one in the world ever did resemble them; . . . If he is to resemble the texts of which he is the witness, the representation, the real analogue, Don Quixote must also furnish proof and provide the indubitable sign that they are telling the truth, that they really are the language of the world.

For Foucault, it is not until the second part of the romance, when Don Quixote meets "real" characters who have read the first part and see him now as a fictional one, that the epistemological dilemma is resolved — in favor of a textuality that is sufficient unto itself:

> Between the first and the second parts of the novel, in the narrow gap between those two volumes, and by their power alone, and which resides entirely inside the words . . . the hollow fiction of epic exploits has become the representative power of language.[11]

I certainly do not intend to offer here a competing interpretation of *Don Quixote* as a whole. Yet I think it not without significance that the romance begins, or almost begins, with what is in effect a formal discussion of the differences between truth and fiction, and of the nuances between the two; and that this discussion is framed in terms of a scene of censorship. In the fifth chapter, the priest and the housekeeper, emblems respectively of the church and common sense, destroy selectively the old knight's library of romances; and in the process they articulate several theoretical distinctions about the genre and its subsets.

For Cervantes's fictional censors, the most dangerous type of ro-

mance was that descended from *Amadis de Gaula,* naive, chivalric
tales with a high fantasy content. Although style played some part
in the priest's judgments, the principal criterion by which the romances
were sorted was that of verisimilitude. The original *Amadis,* as the
best of its kind, was saved; but its "mendacious" ("mentiroso") off-
spring, *Amadis of Greece, Esplandian, Palmerin de Oliva,* were
burned. When he came to *The Mirror of Chivalries (Espejo de prin-
cipes y cavalleros)* the priest hesitated — and compromised:

> Therein are Lord Reynald of Montalban with his friends and
> companions, worse thieves than Cacus; and the Twelve Peers,
> and that faithful historian Turpin. But I am for condemning
> them to nothing worse than perpetual banishment, if only be-
> cause they had a share in inspiring the famous Mateo Boiardo,
> from whom the Christian poet Ludovico Ariosto also spun his
> web. . . . In short, I say that this book and every one we find
> that deals with these affairs of France, shall be thrown out and
> deposited in a dry well till we see, after further deliberation,
> what is to be done with them. [12]

Vestigial in this passage is the old medieval respect for the Matter of
France, although the allusion to "that faithful historian Turpin" ("el
verdadero historiador") is not without irony; but Cervantes also reveals a sophisticated understanding of Ariosto, both formally, in the
reference to his "web" ("tela"), and theoretically, in his recognition
of the superior claims, in terms of truth content, of a chivalric poem
whose background was the Carolingian crusades.

    Don Quixote also formally recognizes the subcategory of pastoral
romance. Finding them in a separate pile, the priest was originally
for sparing all the pastorals, on the grounds that they "do not and will
not do the mischief those books of chivalry have done" (p. 61); but
the Don's niece points out that there are illusions other than heroic:

> For once my uncle is cured of his disease of chivalry, he might
> very likely read those books and take it into his head to turn
> shepherd and roam about the woods and fields, singing and pip-
> ing and, even worse, turn poet, for that disease is incurable and
> catching, so they say. (p. 61)

Even so, the priest insists on sparing Montemayor's *Diana* and Gil
Polo's continuation. It is the romance of chivalry, particularly in its
Spanish second childhood, that gives the genre a bad name.

In England twenty years later it was still possible to make similar statements, especially when the inspiration was Cervantes. *Don Quixote* was translated into English by Thomas Shelton in two stages, in 1612 and 1620. When Ben Jonson's library was burned out in 1623 he wittily recalled the burning of that other famous library, and complained of injustice to the god of fire. Being neither an obsessive reader of romances, like Don Quixote, nor a writer of them, he had not deserved such punishment. The conflagration would only have been intelligible, Jonson complained in his *Execration Upon Vulcan*:

> Had [he] compil'd from Amadis de Gaule,
> Th' Esplandians, Arthurs, Palmerins, and all
> The learned Librarie of Don Quixote
>
> . . . the whole summe
> Of errant Knight-hood, with their Dames,
>   and Dwarfes,
> Their charmed Boates, and their inchanted
>   Wharfes;
> The Tristrams, Lanc'lots, Turpins, and the Peers.
> All the madde Rolands, and sweet Oliveers.[13]

In fact, Jonson here goes well beyond Cervantes as an antiromancer. The careful distinctions have disappeared. There is no contrast between the Matter of France and other chivalries, no exception made for Ariosto, no special mention of the pastoral romances as potentially more innocent. Romance is epitomized as "the whole summe / Of errant Knight-hood," with a moral emphasis on "errant"; and the only surviving ambivalence is in Jonson's recognition of a symbolic pairing. "Madde Rolands" are accompanied by "sweet Oliveers," irrationality with an alluring, if fatal, idealism. There is no great difference, except in its poise, between this elegant devaluation and Beaumont and Fletcher's mockery of chivalric romance in *The Knight of the Burning Pestle* a decade earlier. It will be all the more interesting, then, to consider why Jonson agreed to translate Barclay's *Argenis* and publish it (as he is recorded as having done) in 1623, the very same year as his *Execration*.

Charles I as romancer

The year 1623 also marked the first moment of what even in its inception observers perceived as the Caroline romance. Acted out in "real life," in events that would later be "read" in terms of various narrative conventions, some more explicitly fictionalized than others, the royal romance originated in the personality of Charles I, in which sentimentality and idealism were dangerously potent. Charles was not yet king. James I, who had been trying for several years to negotiate, through marriage, a major alliance with Spain, intended his son for the Spanish infanta. His own favorite, George Villiers, duke of Buckingham, had turned from James in his dotage and attached himself, with all his irresponsible charm, to the heir apparent. In the spring of 1623, Charles and Buckingham got themselves up in disguises and took ship for Spain, in order to woo the Spanish infanta personally. James, hearing of the adventure, called them his "sweete boyes, and deare ventrouse knights, worthie to be putte in a new romanse."[14] James Howell (whose generic innovations will be described in Chapter 5) wrote from Spain that negotiations had been going smoothly "when, to the wonderment of the World," the prince and Buckingham arrived, and changed the tone of the whole affair. "The People here do mightily magnify the Gallantry of the Journey, and cry out that he deserved to have the Infanta thrown into his Arms the first night he came."[15] In England, on the other hand, fears for the prince's safety only increased public pressure against the match. James lost his nerve, and the negotiations foundered. When Charles was asked whether he "intended to go away disguis'd as he came," the prince made a "brave Answer . . . That if Love brought him thither, it is not Fear shall drive him away."[16] But the romantic gesture ended in retreat nevertheless, James covering his own humiliation by insisting, at the last moment, on the return of the Palatinate as a condition of the match, Charles and Buckingham dealing with theirs by immediately becoming anti-Spanish militants.

These tendencies in Charles's character were to reappear, in a different form, after Buckingham's assassination in 1628. Buckingham's removal allowed Charles to abandon his unsuccessful war policy, and encouraged a rapprochement between the new king and Henrietta Maria, whom he had married in 1625 on the rebound from the infanta, and been instantly disappointed in. Now there suddenly developed the first really convincing royal marriage in well over a century. After Henry VIII's excesses, Mary's barren yearnings for Philip of Spain, Elizabeth's tactical virginity, and James's blatant homosexuality, the English had at last acquired a pair of rulers genuinely attached to each other, and fruitful. Their first son, Charles, was born in 1630; other healthy children followed. Everything pointed to a new respectability for the idea of romantic love.

But Charles had, in addition, political reasons for developing his own image in romance terms, in contrast to the Solomonic typology favored by his father. Given his difficulties with the parliament of 1628, the unpopularity of his peace settlement with Spain, and suspicion of Laud's counterreforms of the church, given his own determination, after March 1629, to rule without Parliament, Charles needed an image that would authorize and sanction, simultaneously, his new pacificism, his commitments to spiritual reform and monarchical absolutism, and his isolation. He chose a version of chivalry, but one carefully selected to avoid such criticisms as had been voiced by Cervantes and Jonson. He chose the figure of St. George, as combining the ideals of warrior and saint, in an inarguably English embodiment. He commissioned one of his chaplains, Peter Heylyn, to establish the historicity of St. George—that is, to rescue him from the Puritan charge of being a fiction. Heylyn's *Historie of that most famous Saint and Souldier of Christ Jesus, George of Cappodoccia* appeared in 1631, and was "corrected and enlarged" in 1633. In 1629 the painter Rubens had also been employed to authenticate the legend, but differently. His painting *St. George and the Dragon* (Fig. 3) shows a medieval knight who is clearly recognizable as Charles, with Henrietta Maria as the rescued maiden. The painting was executed during Ruben's visit to England as an envoy for Spain and the Spanish Netherlands, in connection with the peace treaty.

It appears, then, that Charles was not merely concerned to renovate the Order of the Garter, but that he deliberately chose to identify himself with a romance figure, an emblem not only of his nation, but of a spiritualized and pacific chivalry. Proof of the identification appears almost casually throughout the reign, but especially at moments when its political efficacy was in doubt. In 1634, we remember, Thomas Carew had proposed some reforms in Caroline iconography. In *Coelum Britannicum* the new British heaven would actually be improved by retaining some of the old constellations, "as the Skales and Sword (Libra) to adorne the statue of Justice, since she resides here on earth onely in Picture and Effigie. . . . and then had you but clapt Perseus on his Pegasus . . . *there had beene a Divine St. George for this Nation*" (italics added). The implication seems fairly strong that the nation did not have its patron saint firmly in place at the moment, that the king, in his confrontation with Prynne,

Figure 3. Rubens, St. George and the Dragon. By permission of Her Majesty Queen Elizabeth II.

had been less than chivalrous, except perhaps toward his wife. In 1642 Sir John Denham presented Charles as St. George in *Coopers Hill,* a poem now recognized as a carefully mediated political comment on Charles's temperament, his marriage, his confrontation with the Long Parliament, his unheroic campaign against the Scots, and recent capitulation in the Treaty of Berwick. Doing his best to make weakness into sanctity, Denham wrote nervously that in the king he saw "the Saint / Better exprest, then in the liveliest paint."[17] The reference to painting would surely have recalled the Rubens *St. George and the Dragon* and reminded Denham's countrymen of that earlier, more hopeful peace settlement in 1629. But even when mediatorial voices like Denham's had given place to strident polarization, the meaning of the icon was remembered. Richard Lovelace's *Posthume Poems* (1659) contain *A Mock Song,* supposedly a rallying cry for the revolutionaries written shortly after the king's execution in January 1649:

> Now the Thighs of the Crown
> And the Arms are lopped down,
> And the Body is all but a Belly;
> Let the Commons go on,
> The Town is our own,
>   We'l rule alone;
> For the knights have yielded their Spent-gorge;
> And an order is tane
> With *HONY SOIT* profane,
>   Shout forth amain
> For our Dragon hath vanquish'd the St. George.[18]

If Charles had self-consciously identified himself with a spiritualized version of chivalric romance, Henrietta Maria had, as is well known, chosen the pastoral romance as her personal genre. In this she partly followed in the footsteps of Anne of Denmark, for whom Samuel Daniel had written a masque, *The Queen's Arcadia,* derived from Sidney's romance. As John Donne noted, writing to Sir Henry Goodyere in 1625:

> They continue at Court, in the resolution of the Queen pastorall; when Q. Anne loved gamboils, you loved the Court; perchance you may doubt whether you be a thorough Courtier, if you come not up to see this, the Queen a Shepperdesse.[19]

But the contrast in this letter between the preparations for *Florimène* and Donne's stark accounts of the plague in London and the wars in Europe was premonitory. The especially political coloring that the vogue for pastoral romance acquired under Henrietta Maria, the focus by her critics on the frivolity of her forms of self-expression, led to a change in the national understanding of the genre itself, to its penetration, in effect, by ideology.

One of the signs of this shift in generic consciousness was what happened to Sidney's *Arcadia*. Although still read in James's reign and occasionally adapted to Jacobean uses, as in Lady Mary Wroth's *Urania* (1621), the *Arcadia* became, for the Caroline court, the center of a little renaissance. It was republished in 1627, 1628, 1629, 1633, and 1638, and dramatized by James Shirley in 1632 and by Henry Glapthorne in 1634. Francis Quarles's *Argalus and Parthenia* (1628), described in the preface as "a Ciens taken out of the Orchard of Sir Philip Sidney of precious memory, which I have lately graffed upon a Crab-stock, in mine own," was also a publishing success;[20] quite remarkably so, given that it consists of one narrative thread only of the original *Arcadia,* retold at great length, in execrable verse. That Sidney's complex text could have been reduced to this sentimental tribute to marital fidelity suggests an effort of cultural revisionism; and it is hard to see how Sidney's critique of English arcadianism could have been assimilated to Caroline thinking, except by such extreme selectivity. Nevertheless, the *Arcadia* flourished to the point that it almost became its own genre. When William Prynne extended his critique of Caroline culture to include all types of fiction, he specified "Arcadiaes, and fained Histories that are now so much in admiration."[21] When Prynne was brought to trial for sedition libel, the stated issues were that he had insulted the queen and incited the king's subjects to insurrection; but the more subtle, unstated charge was that he had challenged Caroline culture at its heart, attacking as decadent and unchristian the genres in which the court read itself.

Prynne was imprisoned, fined exorbitantly, deprived of his university degree, and half of both his ears. But to complete its public refutation of Prynne's criticisms, the court needed to restate its cultural assumptions. Shirley's *Triumph of Peace* and Carew's *Coelum Britannicum* both, as we have seen, proclaimed the public importance of the masque as a medium of amelioration, a position that Prynne had vehemently denied, and both, more subtly, offered the court a less than fully congratulatory view of itself. But the most complicated theatrical event of 1634 was probably the new production of John Fletcher's *The Faithful Shepherdess,* staged in the same costumes that had been used the previous January for Walter Montague's production of *The Shepherd's Paradise,* the very play that had made the appearance of *Histriomastix* a few days later seem so untimely, so obtrusively relevant. The reuse of last year's costumes was a prudent response to Prynne's complaint that the "over-prodigall disbursements upon Playes and Masques . . . have been wel-nigh as expensive as the Wars" (p. 321); but the *choice* of play was another sort of answer to *Histriomastix.*

In order to understand this event, and its ideological content, we need briefly to consider its origins, especially in Guarini's *Il pastor fido,* to which Fletcher's play was, of course, a sustained allusion. *Il pastor fido,* published in 1590, was in part a critique of Torquato Tasso's *Aminta,* particularly on the subject of sexual ethics. In the *Aminta* the Golden Age is defined not as a lost national culture, but as an era of sexual freedom, where "s'ei piac' ei lice," you might do whatever you pleased. Guarini, however, warned young lovers not to obey "Nature's Law . . . , Love where thou Wilt: / But that of Men and Heaven, Love without guilt."[22] More important, he relocated the debate on chastity within a sociopolitical framework. Past failures in sexual mores are presented as the cause of Arcadia's degeneration, so that Guarini's own persona, Carino, returning to his homeland, can complain, "I for Arcadia in Arcadia hunt" (p. 131). But Guarini's play offers a myth of restoration. Diana's curse is to be lifted by the chaste love of Amarilli and Mirtillo, the Faithful Shepherd himself, a myth, moreover, to be literally enacted in sixteenth-century Italy. When the play was presented to Charles Emmanuel, duke of Savoy, in honor of his marriage in 1585 to Catherine of Austria, it acquired a prologue spoken by the River Alpheus, traditionally a figure of chaste and faithful love. Alfeo discovers that Arcadia has mysteriously been "transported" to Turin, a "transplant" or *translatio studii* effected by the influence of Catherine, whose marriage to Charles will bring peace.

Il pastor fido would, then, have been a perfect text for another *translatio,* an adaptation for an English Charles and his foreign wife, expressive both of Caroline arcadianism in foreign policy and the concept of an ethically purified court. But *Il pastor fido* was not immediately available in a decent translation. Sir Edward Dymocke's blundering version of 1602, reprinted in 1633, and Jonathan Sidnam's unpublished version of about 1630 spoke to the same interest, but both were poetically inept. *The Faithful Shepherdess* was, however, available, in a new quarto published in 1629, along with various explanations by Fletcher's fellow dramatists for the play's failure on the Jacobean stage. Beaumont attacked the public audience's lack of judgment, even illiteracy; but Nicholas Field and Ben Jonson had combined with that excuse the suggestion that the play was too moral for its audience. They came looking for decadence and found "innocence." The word "innocence" appears in both commendatory poems, and connects also with Chapman's, which argued that the play displeased because it

> Renews the golden world; and holds through all
> The holy lawes of homely pastorall.[23]

Here, then, was a chastity play, with unassailable character references, and a history of having been misunderstood by James's theatergoers. Its acceptance and reinterpretation in 1634, then, would be simultaneously an indictment of the earlier age, a proof of the new court's finer morals and esthetics, and a handy answer to Prynne. As the poet Shakerley Marmion wrote to Joseph Taylor, the actor chiefly responsible for the revival:

> When this smooth Pastorall was first brought forth,
> The Age twas borne in, did not know it's worth.
> Since by thy cost and industry reviv'd,
> It hath a new fame, and new birth atchiv'd.
> Happy in that shee [the play] found in her distresse,
> A friend, as faithful, as her Shepherdesse.
> For having cur'd her from her courser rents
> And deckt her new with fresh habiliments,
> Thou brought'st her to the Court, and made her be
> A fitting spectacle for Majestie.
>
> (3:498)

In this poem, published in the third quarto in 1634, we have, in effect, the lexicon of the Caroline idyll as Charles and Henrietta Maria wished it defined, the lexicon of the reformed court and the halcyon days: "smooth," "happy," "fresh," "faithful," and above all "new," three times "new," a cultural and ethical renaissance.

Unfortunately, Fletcher's play was not quite as innocent as it was advertised to be, and certainly not a faithful *translatio* of Guarini.

The Priest's rebuke to the Sullen Shepherd ("Yee are better read then I, / . . . in Blood and Letchery," 3:574) confirms what many readers have felt, that for all its *talk* of chastity, this is, after all, a play of sex (merely deferred or interrupted) and of sexually motivated violence — the very stuff, or so we tell our students, of Jacobean drama. It is extremely interesting to reread W. W. Greg on this point. Greg took umbrage at the play's ethical instability, and assumed that Fletcher, "obsessed by some Platonic theory regarding the ethical aim of the poet," had decided to write a serious chastity play. This was an object, wrote Greg ironically, "to which no self-respecting person can take exception. There was, however, one point the importance of which the author failed to realize, namely, that this ideal which he sought to honour was one with which he was himself wholly out of sympathy."[24] Greg then identified, and rejected, the "one other rational solution . . . namely that [Fletcher] intended . . . an elaborate satire on all ideas of chastity whatsoever." It is fascinating to see this great late-romantic scholar and critic articulating the problem, but protecting himself from his own insight. He preferred to posit artistic failure rather than admit the possibility of parody. Yet *we* may surely admit this possibility; and we may admit also that a play written sardonically in 1608 or 1609 could be read straight, as Greg desired to read it, in 1633/34. If Fletcher was not "obsessed by some Platonic theory," Henrietta Maria certainly was, as even her own court poets were capable of noting with irony; and in the context of her own psychological and sociopolitical needs, she reinvented *The Faithful Shepherdess,* or caused it to be reinvented on her behalf, translating it from Jacobean camp into the queen's pastoral, making it "new."

As allusions to the St. George iconography tended to appear in defensive or elegiac postures later in the reign, so too the political meaning of pastoral romance was most conclusively demonstrated when its disastrous effects were known. In 1647 and again in 1648, Sir Richard Fanshawe published a translation of Guarini — *Il Pastor Fido, The Faithful Shepherd* — that was ironically the fine translation that would have served the court's purposes in 1634. An equally tragic irony pervades the dedication of the work, not to the king or queen, but to "the Most Hopefull Prince, Charles, Prince of Wales." In the 1647 edition, Fanshawe presented his audience with a political rationale for its appearance at this dark moment in the civil war. According to Fanshawe, Guarini had intended his play to offer advice to Charles Emmanuel, with respect to "the troubles that had formerly

distracted that State." So, in "exposing to ordinary view an Enter-
lude of Shepherds, their loves, and other little concernments, with
the stroke of a lighter pencil," Guarini actually presented, "through
the perspective of the Chorus, another and more suitable object to
his Royall Spectators. He shews to them the image of a gasping State
(once the most flourishing in the world). A wild Boar (the sword) de-
populating the Country," and a number of other calamities that are
all happily resolved "by the presaged Nuptials of two of Divine (that
is, Royall) extraction."[25] We should immediately recognize in this
passage a double act of generic criticism: on the one hand, the assumption that Renaissance pastoral carries a hidden message, the ancient
Servian distinction between reading *simpliciter* ("to ordinary view")
and *allegorice* ("through the perspective of the Chorus"); and on the
other, the late medieval distinction between vain and serious fictions,
the "lighter pencil" and "the more suitable object."

What made the pastoral romance serious, for Fanshawe, was its
political relevance, not only to Guarini's Italy, but to his own country in 1647. He provided a principle of interpretation for Guarini's
text, claiming (as Greville did for Sidney) a knowledge of Guarini's
intentions; and he extended the metaphor to England, and his own
Charles:

> Because it seems to me (beholding it at the best light) a Lant-
> skip of these Kingdoms, (your Royall Patrimony) as well in the
> former flourishing, as the present distractions thereof, I thought
> it not improper for your Princely notice at this time, thereby
> to occasion your Highness, even in your recreations, to reflect
> upon the sad Originall, not without hope to see it yet speedily
> made a perfect parallel throughout.

The conventional interplay between "recreations" and "sad" reflections, the wish-fulfillment structure of *any* romance, and the gap between a complete and an as yet incomplete example of the genre, are
all finely calculated to accord with *Il pastor fido*'s new historical context. All optimism residual in the genre must, Fanshawe suggests most
clearly, depend on "the Most Hopefull Prince" who now, with his
father a prisoner in Hampton Court, must become Mirtillo, the Faithful Shepherd. The royal romance must survive, if at all, in the next
generation. Fanshawe was not to know that his own hopes for a "perfect parallel" between original and translation, as between text and
context, would not be fulfilled until 1660, when the "Patrimony" could

be reclaimed; but even in 1648, the year that began with the Vote of No Addresses to Charles I, he seems to have thought better of his allegorical preface, which did not appear in the second edition.

John Milton: romance in disgrace

During the civil war, the role of Ben Jonson as self-appointed arbiter of the national culture was taken by John Milton; and as his political thinking evolved, certain shifts in his esthetics and poetics became necessary. Among them was a perceptible alteration in his attitude to romance *as a genre,* despite his loyalty to certain authors, most notably Spenser. In *Il Penseroso,* reading Chaucer and other chivalric romances "where more is meant than meets the ear" is declared to be a "sage and solemn" literary experience, dependent (presumably) upon the presence of allegorical meaning. And in September 1634, the year after the *Histriomastix* crisis, Milton produced a work that seems designed in part to refute Prynne, while distinguishing itself in certain obvious ways from court productions. Echoing *The Faithful Shepherdess,* which in January of that year could not have escaped his attention, Milton explored in *Comus* the generic possibilities of masque and pastoral romance, the thematic limitations of chastity. It was surely no coincidence that *Comus* also asserted the moral probity of an aristocratic family, the Bridgewaters, who were still reeling from the family scandal: in *Histriomastix* Prynne had mentioned, as an illustration of the depravity encouraged by "lascivious, amorous, whorish, Love-sicke" plays, the "late example of a memorable act of justice on an English Peere" (pp. 208, 214), namely, the earl of Castlehaven, who had debauched his wife and daughter with his servants, and been executed in May 1631 by order of the House of Lords.[26] Milton's position, implicit in *Comus,* was exactly what Prynne had denied; that there can be morally improving fictions, even theatrical ones.

In the early 1640s, however, there are signs that Milton was reconsidering his loyalties, generic and political. In both the *Reason of Church Government* and the preceding *Of Reformation,* Milton used chivalric metaphor to dignify the revolution against formalism in the church. He praised the refusal of Parliament to fight the Scots over the prayer book, to "ingage the unattainted Honour of English Knighthood, to unfurle the streaming Red Crosse . . . for so unworthy a purpose;"[27] and he urged them, instead, to take on the dragon of episcopacy:

And if our Princes and Knights will imitate the fame of that old champion, as by their order of Knighthood solemnly taken, they vow, farre be it that they should uphold and side with this English Dragon: but rather to doe as indeed their oath binds them, they should make it their Knightly adventure to pursue & vanquish this mighty sailewing'd monster. (1:857)

Conditionally, Milton still reserved a place for Charles in the chivalry of reformation, but his use of the St. George legend contrasted dramatically with Denham's in *Coopers Hill,* also published in 1642, and referring to the same events. Milton, it appears, was attempting to reclaim for his nation at large its patron saint, as an icon that the king had no right to monopolize.

At the same time, in his *Apology for Smectymnuus,* Milton chose to assert his early devotion to romance tradition. It is not always remembered that this much-quoted passage is a *retrospective* account of his own youthful reading, written in the heat of controversy, with the avowed purpose of defending his own character. Milton claimed to have proceeded from the lyric (Dante and Petrarch), to narrative fiction, to "those lofty Fables and Romances, which recount in solemne canto's the deeds of Knighthood founded by our victorious Kings; & from hence had in renowne over all Christendome" (1:891). The romances were defended as "solemne" (that is, serious), based on national history ("*our* victorious Kings"), and compatible with Christian values. Significantly, he cited no examples of this Tassonian ideal; and he then immediately proceeded to undermine it:

> From whence even then I learnt what a noble vertue chastity sure must be, to the defence of which so many worthies by such a deare adventure of themselves had sworne. And if I found in the story afterward any of them by word or deed breaking that oath, I judg'd it the . . . fault of the Poet. . . . So that even those books which to many others have bin the fuell of wantonnesse and loose living, I cannot thinke how unlesse by divine indulgence prov'd to me so many incitements . . . to the love and stedfast observation of that vertue. (1:891)

What Milton gave with one hand he took away with the other. Granting the gap between an ideal theory of fiction and actual texts, granting even Prynne's position that romances deprave their audiences, Milton asserts solely the principle of Cervantes, that selective reading is possible. Even then, it is a privileged and somewhat mysterious reader response ("I cannot thinke how unlesse by divine indulgence") claimed only for himself.

In 1644 Milton's ambivalences and uncertainties in genre theory were reactivated by confrontation with censorship. Outraged by the licensing act passed by the Long Parliament, convinced that the Presbyterians, by becoming more repressive than the Laudians, were improper allies for an intellectual of his calibre, Milton asserted in *Areopagitica* a much more confident defense of the principle of selective reading. Romance was still at the heart of the issue. Censorship cannot possibly work, Milton argued, unless you close down every pleasurable activity, every form of entertainment. There can be no more country songs and dances, for these are the equivalent of courtly romances, these are the "Countrymans Arcadias and his Montemayors" (2:525). His accompanying sonnet *On the New Forcers of Conscience* threatened the Presbyterians with a more liberated Parliament, one that would "Clip ye as close as marginal P[rynne]'s ears." This brutal jeer would, we know, be revised out of the published text of 1673; for by that time Milton had moved again, closer toward Prynne's position.

What moved him was the king's execution, in January 1649, and the threat posed to the emergent commonwealth by the immediate appearance of a royal best-seller — *Eikon Basilike,* supposed to be the text of Charles's final meditations. Milton took upon himself the task, in *Eikonoklastes,* of destroying the royal iconography. Among his strategies was the discovery of plagiarism: the use of a prayer from Sidney's *Arcadia,* as if it were the king's own. It has been argued that Milton's response, which was to jettison the *Arcadia,* was only temporary, untypical of his normal literary attitudes;[28] but if one follows his text closely it is remarkable how he broadened the issue, to include in one scathing critique the morals, politics, and esthetics of the king *and of the romance tradition,* since the two had become inseparable. Charles had "so little care of truth," wrote Milton,

> as immediately before his death to popp into the hand of that grave Bishop who attended him . . . a Prayer stol'n word for word from the mouth of a Heathen fiction praying to a heathen God; & that in no serious Book, but the vain amatorious Poem of Sir Philip Sidneys *Arcadia;* a Book in that kind full of worth and witt, but among religious thoughts, and duties not worthy

to be nam'd; nor to be read at any time without good caution.
(3:362)

The conception of a Christian romance, as Charles had tried to define it, is a contradiction in terms. The *Arcadia* is "no serious Book" but a dangerous fiction; and even that minor concession, such as Cervantes would have made, that the text has "worth and witt," is qualified by the damning generic classification "in that kind." In the 1650 edition of *Eikonoklastes,* Milton expanded this passage to attack romance at large, or, more accurately, abroad; taking in, at one fell swoop, most of the European tradition:

> For he certainly whose mind could serve him to seek a Christian prayer out of a Pagan Legend, and assume it for his own, might gather up the rest God knows from whence; one perhaps out of the French *Astraea,* another out of the Spanish *Diana;* *Amadis* and *Palmerin* could hardly scape him . . . so long as such sweet rapsodies of Heathenism and Knighterrantry could yeild him prayers. (3:366–77)

Charles is associated both with "heathen" (Roman Catholic) cultures, and with the dubious epistemological status of romance in previous genre theory. Fiction has, in effect, become political fraud: "How dishonorable then, and how unworthy of a Christian King, were these ignoble shifts, . . . this deception . . . [of] the cheated People" (3:367).

In *Paradise Lost* and *Paradise Regained* Milton would have to work out for himself the consequences of this rejection, to see whether the genre so lost to him could in any way be regained. In the interim, there occurred an extraordinary renovation of romance, both in theory and practice. In the 1650s and early 1660s, there was a sudden vogue in England for a new kind of romance, one that was neither pastoral nor chivalric. Their authors gave great emphasis to the historical dimensions of the new genre, or subgenre, a fact which seems to have been largely ignored by modern criticism. Usually mentioned in histories of the novel, which have a natural bias toward realistic fiction, they tend to be disparaged on one or more of these grounds: excessive length, preciosity, mere trendiness (a fashion set in France), and lack of seriousness, precisely that quality their authors claimed. In a fairly typical study, significantly entitled *The Light Reading of Our Ancestors,* one critic accounted for the popularity of these books during the Protectorate as follows: "An escape from the grim actualities of life was needed, and publishers gauged the public taste more accurately than painful preachers."[29] When combined with the view that the public taste was defective, the result has been a form of critical taboo.

Some of these criticisms are based on fact. The fashion *was* set in France, especially by Mlle. de Scudéry. Even John Barclay, the Scot whose *Argenis* was the true progenitor, had a French mother, married a Frenchwoman, and lived all of his life in France. Much of what the English read as romance in the 1650s was translated from French texts. Complaints about excessive length or affected style are matters of taste, with which it is foolish to argue. But the claim that these "historical" romances were written and read purely as entertainment is surely a misconstruction. What made them interesting was their new seriousness of purpose, their program of generic innovation, and the message they were intended to carry to their audience—a group considerably more select, I shall argue, than the term "public" supposes.

Barclay's *Argenis*: the Key and the Cabinet

To understand the Protectorate genre and its reception, we need to go back to *Argenis,* published in Latin in 1621, and translated into English in 1623 by Ben Jonson (in that nonextant version), in 1625 by Kingsmill Long, and in 1628 and 1629 by Robert Le Grys, with Thomas May as partial collaborator. In its Latin version, *Argenis* was clearly addressed to an educated European audience, and quickly recognized as an encoded and fictionalized account of European history in the late sixteenth century, in the guise of Heliodoran romance. When Robert Le Grys produced his translation for Charles I, he appended a "clavis" or key to the text, identifying as best he could the principal characters in the political allegory; and he also pointed to the second book in which Barclay himself discussed the principle of encoding with its motives. Both the "clavis" and the section of text so identified carry generic and hermeneutical import. In the "clavis," Le Grys offered not only to satisfy his readers' curiosity, but to allow them to draw from the text "what profitable knowledge they may, not slightly passing it over as an idle Romance, in which there were no other fruit conteined, but fantasticall tales, fit onely to put away the tediousnes of a Winter evening";[30] and, cautiously, he proposes to "unlocke the *intentions* of the Author in so many of the parts of it, as I could conceive he had any aime in at all" (italics added). His hesitation as an interpreter, as an intentionalist, derives from the second book, where "under the name of Nicompompus (by which, thorow the whole worke he doth personate himself)" Barclay discusses his strategy of mixing fact with fiction *so as to avoid interpretive certainty.*

The crucial passage in Book II is a dialogue between Nicompompus and a priest as to whether literature can possibly effect political persuasion, and what kinds of audience it may hope to reach. Nicompompus declares his determination to speak out: "I will . . . with a free hand guide my Pen; wherein the King hath erred, I will set downe; and what anchor to save him, that now is neere wrackt, the history of former Ages doth offer." But the priest replies:

> To what end, or to whom will thou thus write? Is it then the King that in this sort thou meanest to admonish? If thou didst in private, yet not amiss. But now what a brave way of counselling will this be, that what thou beleevest he hath erred, thou shouldest divulge by thy writings; . . . But suppose thou couldst deliver documents of so effectuall wisedome, as they were able to allay the rage of such as should reade them; . . . how few would have leasure to reade thee? Onely those, who being with their perpetuall spite apt to speake ill, doe reckon that above eloquence, if thou doest ierke the greatest men with bitter language. Or perhaps meane gowne-men in the Schooles, who not accustomed at all to affaires, doe onely contemplate Precepts of state in their bookes. Wilt thou write to these kindes of men? . . . I say nothing of the danger of that liberty which thou takest. (pp. 129–30)

The alternative modes of political self-expression, as the priest sees them, are private advice to heads of state, satirical invective, which will appeal only to malcontents, or abstract political theory, which can reach only a leisured, academic audience and can have no practical effect. Any or all of these may be dangerous for the writer.

The dilemma resembles Sidney's in the *Arcadia;* and Barclay's solution is likewise to approach the problem of communication by displacing contemporary history into romantic fiction, a strategy made explicit by Nicompompus:

> So I, with a sudden and bitter complaining, will not, as guilty men, call them which trouble the Common-wealth to a pub-

> lique triall. . . . But I will leade them, *ignorant of my intention,*
> about with so delightfull mazes, as even themselves shall be
> pleased to be blamed under other names . . . I will . . . write
> *a Fable like a Historie.* In it I will wrap up strange events: armes,
> marriages, bloud, and contentments, I will blend together with
> successe that could not be hoped for. (italics added)

Having attracted his audience by their curiosity, he will win their assent to his ethical system, so that "they will bee ashamed to play any
longer that part upon the Stage of this World, which they shall perceive in my Fable to have beene duely set out for them"; but (lest anyone confuse this strategy with the generalized didacticism of Renaissance poetics), Nicompompus explains the new principle of encoding
that he plans to exercise:

> Lest they should complaine that they are traduced, there shall
> be no mans picture to be plainely found there. To disguize them,
> *I will have many inventions that cannot possibly agree to those
> that I entend to point at.* For this liberty shall bee mine, who
> am not religiously tyed to the truth of a History . . . That in
> this my Booke, *he shall erre, as well, that will have it all to be
> a true relation of things really done, as he that takes it to be
> wholly fained.* (p. 131; italics added)

We should recognize here the same attitude to history as that invoked
by *Sejanus* and *King Lear,* the same tantalizing because inexact fit
between the past and the present; but the textual stress on authorial
intention here is an important development, which shows how far the
hermeneutics of censorship has already acquired formal recognition.

The reader's cognitive attitude to *Believe As You List* was contrasted above, in passing, to Shakespeare's *As You Like It.* It is worth
noting that *Argenis,* set in Sicily, was implicitly contrasted by Le Grys
to *The Winter's Tale.* The new historical romance is neither "idle"
nor one of those "fantasticall tales, fit only to put away the tedious-
ness of a Winter evening." Its Sicily is France, its intended audience
the leaders of the major European nations, its message not only
"wherein the King hath erred," but also "what anchor to save him
. . . the history of former Ages doth offer." Not that there is not fantasy in *Argenis.* Queen Hyanisbe of Mauritania, for example, who
represents Elizabeth I, has, or appears to have, a son, Archombrotus,
ultimately revealed as the long-lost heir of Meleander (Henry III of

France). But the function of Barclay's imaginative license is different. Where the end of *The Winter's Tale,* the apparent resurrection of Hermione, stresses the saving grace of fiction in a spiritual if not fully Pauline sense, the conclusion of *Argenis* depends on the reception of a "little Cabinet, which . . . Poliarchus had recovered from the Pirates. . . . There was in the Letter a little key: the same indeed which was to open the Cabinet" (p. 469). The metaliterary force of this image is unavoidable. The "Cabinet" of Barclay's fiction both resists and requires opening, if its reading is to be completed. The "letter" of the text contains its own key, not, as in the translator's "clavis," to the cast of historical characters, but to the intentions of its author and his innovative genre theory.

A standard history of English literature relegates *Argenis* to a footnote, with the comment that this "most important derivative of the *Arcadia* . . . achieved great popularity . . . but it hardly belongs to English literature."[31] Presumably this exclusion is based on the fact that *Argenis* was written in Latin (a principle that has not been equally applied to More's *Utopia*). But in addition to raising the canonical question, we need to ask whether the phenomenon of three different English translations of the *Argenis* in eight years can really be dismissed in this way. There appears to be something more than "popularity" implied in Robert Le Grys's account of his own motives in embarking on the Caroline translation. His title page twice asserts that the work was "by his Maiesties Command"; the preface "To the Understanding Reader" stresses that it was "imposed" upon him, and that "if his Majesty had not so much hastened the publishing it," he would have had more opportunity for revision. The dedication to Charles, as altered for the 1629 edition, meditates out loud upon the "interest" that the king has shown in this text, and speculates that it was Barclay's connections with James I that "moved your Majesty to cherish it." Such a display of nervousness suggests that there is more to *Argenis* than meets the eye, especially to an English audience at this particular moment.

Now, the most significant events with which Charles was concerned in 1628 were, inarguably, his struggles with Parliament, and the passage of the Petition of Right, which asserted, among other "rights" of the subject, the illegality of taxation without parliamentary consent. In *Argenis* there happens to be a long debate between Hyanisbe and Poliarchus on the king's right to levy taxes without the consent of Parliament. Poliarchus cites, in defense of such a prerogative, the value of taxation in stimulating labor, the need of sudden and secret action in international affairs (calling a parliament might alert an enemy and prevent a preemptive strike), and the model of "Republikes" where the Senate had authority to impose taxes without consultation (pp. 359–61). At the end of his argument, "Hyanisbe was ashamed to confesse, that shee had so suddenly changed her opinion. For Poliarchus had with no great difficultie perswaded her, that Right [of taxation] did belong to Kings." Given a cultural understanding of the ways in which contemporary affairs could be displaced into fiction, given the fact that *Argenis* was already established as a roman à clef, it seems plausible to suggest that Charles had perceived the relevance of this debate to his own situation in 1628 and 1629, and chose this oblique and rather laborious method (laborious, certainly, for Le Grys) to have his case argued in print. Parliament was, however, considerably less easily "perswaded" than Hyanisbe. In the debacle of 2 March 1629, when the Commons preempted Charles's right to dissolve them by doing it themselves, they passed at the very last moment defiant resolutions against tunnage and poundage.[32]

To read the 1628/29 *Argenis* in the light of such motives would have been, of course, a reinterpretation. It also suggests interesting (but completely unverifiable) motives for the translation that James had commissioned from Ben Jonson in 1623, another time of constitutional crisis. It is much to the point that Argenis, the titular heroine, was recognized by Le Grys as no specific historical personage, but as an allegorical concept, the crown of France, the principle of sovereignty and hereditary rule.

In the romances that Barclay inspired, there is evidence that the genre he had founded was well understood. Its matrix was Heliodoran romance, a form that allowed for adventure and coincidence but not for the improbable supernatural "marvels" of the old chivalric narratives. Its real subject was European history, presented as an allegorical subtext, but deliberately made resistant to any neat, consistent decoding. Included among its formal properties were passages of explicit commentary upon the author's intentions, especially with respect to the mixing of fact and fiction, and the principles of interpretation required by that compound. And those who read it were fully aware of the causal connection linking all of these characteristics with what we have been calling the hermeneutics of censorship. It was this that made it ethically superior to previous phases of romance. Charles Sorel, an important exponent of antiromance theory, exempted it from many of the criticisms that he made against the genre in *Le berger extravagant,* published in France in 1628, and translated into English by John Davies in 1653 with a dedication to Mary, countess of Winchelsea:

> You do well to tell us that the true customes of Sicily are not observed in this History, every one confesses it . . . , since it was only the Authors design, to represent divers accidents hapned in France. If you esteem not his intention because he treats of these things with some obscurity, should you not consider that he was obliged to carry himself with that caution, it being a thing not a little dangerous to speak openly of the affairs of great ones? As for the discourses of State which are so seasonably introduced, 'tis a black malice to blame a thing so noble.[33]

Mlle. de Scudéry and the "Wars of the Closet"

When Madeleine de Scudéry began to publish her own romances, initially under her brother's name, she first directed her readers' attention to genre theory. *Ibrahim* (1641) appeared with a long preface attributed to Georges de Scudéry, in which the question of historicity is paramount. Mlle. de Scudéry had obviously been reading Tasso, whose *Gerusalemme* she refers to. Her description of the new historical romance is, in places, virtually quoted from Tasso's definition of the ideal heroic poem. She argued for a narrative in which "falsehood and truth are confounded by a dextrus hand," because when "falsehood is produced openly, this gross untruth makes no impression in the soul, nor gives any delight. As indeed how should I bee touched with the misfortunes of the Queen of Gundaya, and of the King of Astrobacia, when as I know their very Kingdomes are not in the Universall Mapp"; and she complained of the misuse of the Marvellous in previous romances, "for we have at other times seen Romanzes, which set before us monsters, in thinking to let us see Miracles; their Authors by adhering too much to wonders have made Grotesques, which have not a little of the visions of a burning Feaver."[34]

In fact, de Scudéry went considerably beyond Tasso in her commitment to probability. "As for me," she wrote, "I hold, that the more naturall adventures are, the more satisfaction they give; and the ordinary course of the Sun seems more mervailous to me, than the strange and deadly rayes of Comets" (A4r). Her realism even caused her to be chary of shipwrecks, those popular agents of Heliodoran adventure, although she was fully aware of the deep metaphor beneath such strategy: "The Sea is the Scene most proper to make great changes in, and . . . some have named it the Theater of inconstancie." But her chief objective was to shift the emphasis from external to internal action, the true test of a modern hero. "It is not by things without him, it is not by the caprichioes of destinie, that I will judge of him, it is by the motions of his soul, and by that which he speaketh" (A4v). This is the justification for all that talk, the narrative *de longue haleine,* which modern readers have found impenetrable. In the new historical romance, as de Scudéry saw it, veracity and loquacity explained each other.

However, this statement is a half-truth, and has something of the function of a protective disclaimer. The action of her romances is by no means purely psychological. In *Clélie,* for example, published in installments between 1654 and 1661, de Scudéry constructed a massive fictionalized account of the expulsion of the Tarquins from Rome, based in the loosest possible way on the old Roman legend of the maiden Cloelia, who was given as hostage to the Etruscan king Porsenna, and escaped by swimming the Tiber. Leading figures in contemporary France—Louis XIV, Fouquet, and Ninon de Lenclos—have been recognized in their pseudoclassical disguises; and there is reason to suspect that Tarquinius Superbus, the dictator figure, represents Cromwell, and that the various debates by the Romans as to how to respond to his regime are active, urgent political theory. In October 1650, Mlle. de Scudéry wrote to Bishop Godeau, "God grant that those who design to make of France what Cromwel and Fairfax have made of England may never gain control";[35] and in *Clélie,* she concluded a retrospective account of Tarquin's usurpation: "It must be said to the shame of all Romans, that they all did sit still, with their hands in their Pockets, and all submitted themselves."[36]

In *Artamène, ou le Grand Cyrus* (1649–53), her *sous-texte* was the career of Louis de Bourbon, prince de Condé, who in the first phase of the Fronde had commanded the troops of the queen regent against the rebellious Paris *parlement,* although he was later, in 1650, imprisoned by the queen for opposing Cardinal Mazarin. This story also had implications for English history, given the negotiations of both Mazarin and Condé with Cromwell's government, the uncertainties of the Fronde in its attitude toward the English revolution, and the French policy of "official neutrality (but unofficial partiality) toward the English royalists."[37] The English exiles in France had to plan their

return to power in England in the face of the Fronde, and many of
them, especially the "Old Royalists," Hyde and Sir Edward Nicholas,
were skeptical of French assistance, and deeply suspicious of Mazarin,
who had so conspicuously failed to intervene on behalf of Charles
I. Yet Henrietta Maria's brother, the duc d'Orléans, eventually joined
the Fronde; and in the autumn of 1651, when Charles II returned to
France after the disastrous battle of Worcester, there was talk of two
marriages, one between Charles and the daughter of the duc d'Orléans, the other between James, duke of York, and the daughter of
the duc de Longueville. French history and English history were, in
other words, inextricably intertwined.

It is in the context of this network of negotiation and intrigue that
we can best understand the literary program of Mlle. de Scudéry, and
the special modifications that she made in the new romance, her differences both from Tasso and from Barclay. The most important adjustment that she makes is in relating the truth/fiction problem both
to the actualities of history as she felt it operating in her environment
and to the question of readership, the audiences to which romances
were thought to be addressed. At the heart of her theory is a decid-
edly feminist impulse. In *Clélie* (Part IV, Book II) she introduced a
debate on romance theory, which repeats most of the major propositions made in the preface to *Ibrahim,* but which not only dramatizes
literary theory, but also, in salute to the female protagonist, involves
her and other women in the debate. It encompasses the paired propositions that romance is not a serious form, and that women are
not serious readers.

A male speaker, Herminius, is made the spokesman for the Tassonian compromise on historicity:

> Nothing more commends a well-invented Fable, than those
> historicall foundations which are interweav'd throughout in it,
> and cause the Fiction to be receivd together with the truth. But
> to speak unfeignedly, 'tis more difficult than is believ'd, to min-
> gle those two together aright: for they must be so handsomely
> blended, as not to be discerned one from another, and that
> which is invented, must generally seem more likely than the
> true.

But a female figure, Plotina, then takes up what appears to be a female and contrary position, resembling earlier Renaissance defenses
of the romance as the genre that is permitted to exploit the fantastic:

> Were I to invent a History, I think I should make things much
> more perfect than they are. All Women should be admirably
> fair . . . all my Heroes should slay at least a hundred men in
> every battle . . . I would make prodigies fall out every moment,
> and without troubling myself to invent with judgement, I should
> suffer my fancy to act as it pleas'd . . . I should certainly make
> very extraordinary things, as continuall shipwracks, burning of
> Cities, and a thousand other like accidents. (p. 201)

The reader is therefore tempted to identify the excesses of this position with the female imagination, and hence with an attitude to romance as the marginal, the nonserious; but de Scudéry corrects this
assumption. Plotina is described as having spoken "with a certain
sprightly air, which made it apparent, *she knew sufficiently, what she
said was not that which ought to be done*" (italics added). What the
reader had not been previously trained to recognize—the seriousness
that sometimes only irony can convey—is supplied editorially by the
female author. The strategy should remind us of Sidney's precautionary descriptions of his "toyfull" *Arcadia,* and Greville's explanation
of the circumstances that leads writers to make "toies of the utmost
they can do."

It is also a woman, Clélie herself, who defines the intellectual
qualifications of the modern romancer:

> He must have an universall knowledge of the World, of the in-
> terests of Princes and the humours of Nations, policy must not
> be unknown to him, nor the art of War; he must understand
> to describe battles; and, which is most of all necessary, he must
> be able perfectly to represent those Wars of the Closet which
> are met with in all Courts, which consist in intrigues, delusions,
> and negotiations true or feign'd, and which notwithstanding are
> of such importance, that 'tis in them the seeds are sow'd of the
> most considerable Wars, and on which the ruin or felicity of
> Nations as well as the verity of History depends. (p. 203)

As in the *Ibrahim* preface, the movement of the new romance is
inward, into the mind; but here the connection between external and
internal action is made explicit. The "verity of History" is especially
to be found in "the Closet," in the secret places behind recorded events,
where character breeds action, where "delusions" and the motives,
more critical than public documents, provide interpretive keys to
known facts. It is the unwritten events, in effect, to which the modern

romancer must have imaginative access. It is not hard to see how this provides a role, both in political life and in the new literature, for women, despite (or perhaps because of) the male personal pronouns in this passage.

It is these special characteristics of the de Scudéry romances that we need to take into account in revaluing their "popularity" in England during the Protectorate. And here again, we need to look more carefully at the apparatus introductory to English translations of her work, and that of de la Calprenède, which became part of the same ambience. The translation of *Ibrahim* by Henry Cogan cited above appeared in London in 1652, dedicated to Mary, duchess of Richmond, daughter of Buckingham. The first installment of *Clélie* was translated by John Davies of Kidwelly in 1656 as *Clélie: An Excellent New Romance,* and dedicated to Mlle. de Longueville, a clear indication of a more than literary "French connection." When *Artamenes* appeared in translation in 1653, discreetly attributed only to F. G., it carried a message from "the Stationer to the Reader":

> If you ask why this should have any Precedence before other Romances, 'tis soon answer'd, that our Author in this hath so laid his Sceans, as to touch upon the greatest Affairs of our Times: for, Designs of War and Peace are better hinted and cut open by a Romance, than by downright Histories; which, being bare-fac'd, are forc'd to be often too modest and sparing; when these disguiz'd Discourses, freely personating every man and no man, have liberty to speak out.[38]

This is clearly an echo of Barclay's defense, on precautionary grounds, of fictionalized history. In the period of Cromwell's Protectorate, the censors had changed sides, but the strategy of oblique communication continued to operate as it had under Elizabeth, James, and Charles I. Ambiguity remains the key to intellectual freedom, "disguiz'd Discourses" paradoxically "have liberty to speak out."

Even when there was not, as in de Scudéry, a roman à clef to elucidate, the principle of "relevance," of reading "our Times" into the text, was asserted. When the royalist historian Sir Charles Cotterell published his 1652 version of de la Calprenède's *Cassandre,* his preface suggested a local interpretation of its Eastern history:

> Yet neither can the strange successe of the Graecian Conqueror, the fatall destruction of the Persian Monarchy, the deplorable end of unfortunate Darius, the afflicted estate of his Royal Fam-

ily in exile and Captivity, the easie compliance of his subjects with the prevailing Party, nor any other passage in it seem improbable to us, whose eyes have in as short a space, been witnesses of such Revolutions, as hardly any Romance, but sure no History can parallel.[39]

The original text, published 1642–45, was obviously innocent of any allusion to the English revolution; but the translator's intention is explicit. The function of the 1652 *Cassandra* was to consolidate sympathy for the English "Royal Family in exile," and to reproach those who had taken the Engagement for their "easie compliance . . . with the prevailing Party." The English *Cassandra* thus took its place, along with Cowley's *Pindarique Odes* and Milton's defenses of the republic, in the literature of Engagement politics.

French romances were, therefore, being taken seriously, in more ways than one. Certainly not regarded as escapist literature, they became a medium of cultural reinforcement, an expression of esprit de corps for their preselected audience, selected both by their royalist sympathies and their literary alertness, their knowledge of what the French connection meant. The generic comments on romance in these works are themselves keys to a *kind of thinking,* as well as its medium; while there are also hints of finer ideological distinctions — the dedication to Mlle. de Longueville implying a pro-Fronde policy; the reproach of "easy compliance," disagreement with the policy of Hyde and the moderates.

The Royal Romances

In dealing with these translations we must work in part with hypotheses. Not so with two remarkable texts that nationalized the historical romance tradition in England. In both of them the concept of a specifically "Royal Romance" was made articulate, and further advances were made in the art of encoding ideology. Richard Brathwaite's *Panthalia; or, The Royal Romance* was published under a pseudonym in 1659. We will consider it in second place, because it was preceded by another, anonymous romance with a complicated textual history. Since the history of the text is crucial to understanding its function, we must look at those bibliographical details with some care, though not merely with a bibliographer's aim.

In 1653 there appeared a small quarto volume entitled:

> Cloria and Narcissus. A Delightfull and New Romance, Imbellished with divers Politicall Notions, and singular Remarks of

Moderne Transactions. Written by an Honourable person . . .
London . . . 1653.

The printer was identified only as S. G., and someone equally anonymous had included an address "To the Reader," as follows:

> It was my chance being beyond-sea, to have the perusing of some
> of this story which, according to my sense and understanding
> then appeared not only delightfull in the reading, but seemed
> to my capacity to containe in many places mysteries, belonging
> to the transactions of forraine parts either at present, or not
> very long before put into execution. (A3r)

He was unwilling to let the matter drop, he continues, "since for many
years past, not any one Romance hath been written in the English
tongue; when as daily from other Nations so many of all sorts fly
into the World," but had great difficulty in persuading its author to
release it, "whether out of any diffidence in apprehension, or for other
secret causes, I cannot tell." The preface concludes by stressing the
importance to the author of anonymity, and explaining that the text
is only the first installment of a three-part romance. In 1654 the second part appeared; I have found no trace of a separate Part 3; but
that there was one is established in an edition of 1658, adding a
fourth part, and referring in its preface to "the three first Parts of
this History."

The 1653 preface had clearly established a set of reader expectations in the Barclay-de Scudéry tradition. The titular emphasis on
"new," "modern," and "political" materials, the allusions to "mysteries" and "secret causes" alerting readers to their responsibilities, all
suggested a text of peculiar interest to those inhibited by the terms
of Cromwellian culture. But in April 1661, when that environment
had been replaced by the initially more liberal culture of the Restoration, a new version appeared. This was a substantial folio volume,
with an additional part, and a great deal of information besides. The
title now read:

> The Princess Cloria: Or, The Royal Romance. In Five Parts. Im-
> bellished with divers Political Notions, and singular Remarks of
> Modern Transactions. Containing The Story of most part of Eu-
> rope, for many Years last past. Written by a Person of Honour.

Facing the title page was an elaborate engraved frontispiece, showing
the Princess Cloria herself, and over her head the unmistakable fig-

ure of Charles I, iconographically derived from Van Dyck's portraits, with the medal of St. George on his breast (see Fig. 4). The figure of the girl is emblematic, yet only partially enigmatic. She appears profoundly meditative, but the subject of her meditation appears above her head for all to see. The setting is a natural landscape, but seen through the columns of some monumental structure. The sea behind the monument is calm; but beneath her feet is a pile of weapons, partially veiled by the motto that explicates the whole: "What Sacrifice can Expiate? past Crimes / Are left to Jove; Our King must bless the Times." The fact that this is a Restoration text is thus established unequivocally; but the relationship between past and future is left partly undecided, the girl herself mediating between "past Crimes" and Restoration amnesty.

Following the title page was a long, new, explanatory preface, interpreting, among other things, both title and frontispiece:

> You have now the whole work, some of it being printed formerly in the worst of times, that is to say, under the Tyrannical Government of Cromwel; when but to name or mention any of the Kings concernments, was held the greatest crime, almost could be committed against that Usurpation. (A2r)

The Restoration text, in other words, is "whole," both in having reached its conclusion and in being explicit. Its subject is now revealed to be not the "transactions of forraine parts," but "the Kings concernments"; that is, recent European history as it particularly affected Charles I and Charles II. As for the Princess Cloria, she is "not only to be taken for the Kings Daughter, but also sometimes for his National Honour; and so consequently appearing more or less in prosperity as accidents increased or diminished; by reason of the unnatural Differences, and Rebellions." (A2r) In other words, she is an allegorical concept in the tradition of Barclay's Argenis, emblem of the crown of France.

Reading backward, then, we can deduce the original function of the Protectorate versions. They offered, as an English roman à clef, an account of the revolution from its origins up to the battle of Worcester and its aftermath. The text would have been either inscrutable to Cromwell's censors, or sufficiently oblique to avoid direct confrontation. Its function would have been to consolidate and direct the loyalties of its royalist readers; but its message was, as we shall see, by no means simple propaganda.

Figure 4. Frontispiece, The Princess Cloria: Or, The Royal Romance *(Anon., 1661). By permission of the British Library.*

It is obvious, to begin with, that the text is to be read in the context of Sidney's *Arcadia,* since the narrative opens with a monarch named Evarchus considering political action, or rather inaction. The occasion is the arrival in the Lydian (English) court of Cassianus, a figure for Prince Frederick of the Rhine, son of Elizabeth of Bohemia, who appeals to Evarchus for assistance in regaining his lost rights. The theme of the lost Palatinate is thus presented as the first cause of the revolution, the original fall from grace of the Stuarts, a proposition developed with remarkable subtlety and dialectical force. Echoes of Jacobean criticism of James's insularity combine with Sidneian allusions to create a text whose heredity is obvious but whose genes are provocatively mixed. The identification of Charles I with Sidney's normative "good governor" leads in one direction; the subsequent debate on English arcadianism in another. Pacificism is represented by Pollinex (Weston) whose "advice extreamly pleased the King" and activism by Dimagorus (originally a Sidneian villain) who speaks of his care for "the present and future honour and glory of our Nation, now almost adulterated by ease and quiet," and his embarrassment by his king's "cold newtrality," which makes him in Europe "esteemed if not an enemy at leastwise no friend to any, but his own concernments" (p. 17).[40] And Evarchus's character is clearly that of Sidney's Basilius, one

> who aimed rather at present content than future glory, although his courage might pretend to the greatest honour, not onely for that it took away the occasion of exhausting his treasury, but was also as he thought, a principal means still to maintain his State in tranquility, and his Government without perturbation. (p. 8)

Given this debate, given the potential for criticism of Caroline arcadianism, it cannot be a coincidence that the Princess Cloria is "sometimes" to be taken for the "National Honour," that the romance was written by "a Person of Honour." What more appropriate theme for a modern historical romance could there be than "National Honour," a descendant of the old debased chivalric idealism? But it appears here that its maintenance is problematic from the start, that this romancer is, like Barclay, quite prepared to indicate "wherein the King hath erred."

There is also a strange echo between the charge that Evarchus is "no friend to any, but his own concernments," and the stress in the

1661 title on "the Kings concernments." One might be tempted to dismiss this as lexical coincidence, were it not for the fact that the romance tends to focus on episodes in Caroline history that support the charge. Discussing the execution of Strafford (also figured in Pollinex), the narrator remarks:

> Evarchus was also constrained, by the cries and exclamations of the enraged people, to give his unwilling consent to this unfortunate and cruel judgement, though long he disputed with his Flamins about it, who all persuaded him to the compliance, rather than hazzard his own Person and the Kingdoms ruine. (p. 47)

When the revolution has progressed to the point where the king's cause seems lost, shortly before the Vote of No Addresses, two characters debate the question of his courage, and whether his passivity might not be strategic. It is suggested that if the king "sit quiet sometime under his injuries," his enemies may fall out among themselves, which is probably "the reason, that he hath in outward appearance yielded so much to their demands" (p. 204). When the news comes that the Myssians (the Scots) are preparing to invade on the king's behalf, and Cloria's brother Ascanius (James, duke of York) determines to seek his "honour" in this campaign, her confidante Roxana proposes a significant compromise between activism and passivity:

> When with a wise (though not a base) complyance, we can avoid both the inconvenience and hazard to ourselves, with more ease and no dishonour, I see no reason, why we should go about to strain nature to no purpose? especially if we be not well assured to gain a beneficial victory. . . . In fine, the best mixture must be so to moderate our actions, that as precipitately we put not our selves upon vain and needless sufferings, without necessity, so ought not we too much to yield to the inconstant strokes of fortune and oppression, when either Honour or Religion, calls us to a publick demonstration of our bravery and courage. (pp. 230–31)

The 1654 installment concluded here, making as it did so a manifest contribution to Engagement politics. The "wise (though not a base) complyance" here recommended is distinct from the "easie compliance" rebuked by the 1652 *Cassandra*. It is an enabling compromise, anticipating the Restoration. Recognizably in the tradition of chivalric codes of honor, it is a "mixture" of courage and prudence, idealism and political realism, as the historical romance is itself a mixture of historical fact and imaginative license.

When the 1661 *Princess Cloria* appeared, the problems of reception from which the Protectorate version derived its force and function were solved; the ending was happily known. The new Part V brought its readers from 1658 with an account of the death of Hercombrotus (Cromwell) to the new king's triumphant return and coronation in 1660. But the 1661 text did have a great deal to add on the subject of genre and interpretation. On the question of veridicality, the author poses the rhetorical question:

> why the perfect History might not have been as well undertaken for their Honour, as to be thus mixed with several sorts of Invention and Fancies, that rather leades peoples thoughts into a dark Labyrinth of uncertainties, then instructs their knowledges how matters passed indeed?

There are three answers offered. One is from de Scudéry: the importance of inward or cabinet history, since "a bare Historical Relation . . . gives no liberty for inward disputation . . . Counsels for the most part being given in private." One is the more old-fashioned, idealist principle of heightening, "for example, or to stir up the appetite of the Reader." But the third, partly anticipated in Sidney's *Defence of Poesie,* resorts to a more sophisticated notion of historiography, and the epistemological problems inherent in the concept of "history." The romancer has as much authority as the historian proper:

> For Stories [histories] of former Ages are no other, then certain kinds of Romances to succeeding posterity; since they have no testimony for them but mens probable opinions; seeing the Historical part almost of all countrys is subject to be questioned.[41]

In this skeptical view of the interface between history as a written construct and more confessedly structured or subjective discourse, the Person of Honour reminds us that there may be more in common between textual theory then and now than many a modern reader might suppose.

There is also a suggestive account here of the interpretive act, poised as it is in this genre between esthetic and political experience. Despite the fact that the "Tyrannical Government" of Cromwell no longer requires precautionary encoding, the Person of Honour has resisted, so we are told, all requests for "a Key of plainer and more particular intelligence," in which all the historical characters and events would be officially elucidated. Such a guide was "not thought altogether convenient to be printed," partly because "it might seem publickly, too much to determine State particulars and eminent Persons," partly because "too much explanation of Mysterious Conceptions of this nature, would have taken off something from the quaintness of the Design, and left many affected Wits, less matter for ampler Discourse, occasioned after by conjectural Disputes." Even in the Restoration version, the text is still to remain partially encoded; the reader is urged to believe that value still resides in indeterminacy.

What does this mean? For one thing, it suggests that the efficacy of the text as ideology consisted, and still consists after the Restoration, in its ability to present a balanced and not uncritical account of Caroline history, of Charles's behavior as directly contributing to the revolution, and of his son's subsequent negotiations in France and elsewhere. The object of such analysis would have been to reground the nation's loyalty to the Stuarts, by admitting their mistakes and by separating those from the deeper questions of their legitimacy, the constitutional basis of national honor. If so, the need for some tactful indirection would remain even after 1660. But second, and perhaps more interesting, it is suggested that interpretation is its own object, that too much explanation would deprive the text of its intellectual challenge. The point is an important one for any larger evaluation of the literary effects of censorship. The habits of mind, the arts of difficulty, developed out of political necessity are seen to retain their value when the constraints that produced them are removed. What we witness here is the birth of the most characteristically "modern" idea of fiction, that it ought to be artfully difficult, a concept whose ultimate product will be *Finnegans Wake,* with its own scholarly industry and keys published, though not by its author. And what is simultaneously registered here is the demotion, into a second, inferior category, of what had previously been the primary idea of fiction, the light and popular romances that had supposedly diverted medieval and Renaissance readers. The author of the 1661 preface was not prepared to discard this market altogether; but it is clear that mere enjoyment of *The Princess Cloria* will be a quite inadequate response:

> For others of the more vulgar sort, a bare Romance of Love
> and Chivalry, such as this may be esteemed to be at the worst,
> will prove entertainment enough for their leisure.

A distinction between two kinds of readers and two levels of reading
is, of course, commonplace in Renaissance discussions of allegory;
but here the theory is given a new, sociopolitical dimension. The "vulgar sort," who cannot penetrate to the deep structure of the narrative, will be, like Cromwell's censors, excluded from the interpretive
community. The historical romance equates seriousness with intellectual elitism, popularity with misreading; entertainment is the
"worst" function the text is capable of.

We return now to the other "Royal Romance," *Panthalia.* In August 1659, shortly after the abdication of Richard Cromwell, *Panthalia; or, The Royal Romance* appeared on the London market,
showing signs of having been written and revised up to the very moment of its appearance. As Benjamin Boyce points out, the book was
entered in the Stationers' Register on July 1, before Richard's abdication, and addressed itself to "a prudent reassembled Synod," either
Richard's parliament of January 1659, or the restored Rump of May.
The text itself had to be provided with a "historical sequel" taking
account of Cromwell's death and the succession of Richard (Dar-
chirus); and a final "Postscript" incorporating his abdication must
have been added late in July, perhaps even while the book was in
press.[42] Such was the pressure of the historical context, in other words,
that the book's function and primary audience changed in the course
of a few months, as its author deflected his message from a government whose "constant care for constitution and conservation of a Republick" qualified them to receive it, to a monarch whose return
seemed inevitable. The title page bears a portrait of Charles II, wear-
ing the crown. The subtitle placed it firmly in the genre of the new
historical romances: "A Discourse Stored with infinite variety in relation to State Government . . . And presented on a Theatre of Tragical and Comical State, in a successive continuation to these Times."
An "Advertisement to the judicious Reader" explains the relationship
of the work, and especially its *timing,* to Cromwellian censorship:

> So keen and eager were the Talons of our Statizing Censors,
> as this Royal Romance would not upon its first production . . .
> be admitted to the Presse. It came too neer Truths heele to be

entertain'd as a welcome Guest. The Stationer, to whom it was first addrest, though he held close to the Principles of a just Monarchy . . . has never given acceptance nor countenance to any Copy, that might saucily detract from the High Prerogative of his Great Master. (A3)

Only now, in the ambience of a "prudent . . . Synod," has the text achieved its freedom.

In its compliments to the Parliament, the "Advertisement" recalls the strategy of Milton's *Areopagitica;* but there is little other connection between Milton's magnanimous appeal for a free press and this rather specious, self-conscious timeserving. It is impossible to dislike its author, however, who calls himself Castalion Pomerano, but who is generally agreed to have been Richard Brathwaite, a man of many pseudonyms.[43] As compared with Sir James Mackenzie's *Aretina, or the Serious Romance* (1668), another Restoration adaptation of the genre, Brathwaite's *Panthalia* seems deliberately lighthearted, and to exploit the now-recognized features of historical romance rather (to use his own word) "saucily." Thalia, as a muse, presides over both pastoral and comedy; and Brathwaite declared his subject to be recent history in both its "Tragical and Comical State."

Frivolous, however, it was not. The plot begins in the reign of Elizabeth (Bellingeria), includes the reigns of James (Basilius), Charles I (Rosicles), includes the adventures of Charles II (Charicles) at the battle of Worcester, and proceeds through the Protectorate to the death of Cromwell (Climenes). The history is strikingly intersected by the purely fictional tale of Panthalia, the "pretty pedlar" herself, a seventy-odd-page block of Heliodoran material inserted into the center of the work; and this in turn is further intersected by history, as Panthalia, who has sought shelter and peace of mind in a convent, relates to the abbess the civil war in Candy (England) with her own account of its causes (pp. 173–79). Brathwaite makes sure that we realize that this structure is intentional:

> I shall here take occasion to relate some pleasant Passages, varied and interwoven with much delight (as an Alloy to our more serious discourse:) which we shall return to you in modest dress; without the least touch of levity or petulant scurrility: for such light trimming should be out of request and quite estrang'd from the native body of Contexture of an History. (p. 146)

The light and the serious, fiction and history, are now shown to be structurally distinguishable, only to make their interdependence the more marked; while Panthalia, the titular heroine, plays a remarkable role in mediating between them. If Barclay's *Argenis* was the emblem of hereditary monarchy in France, and the Princess Cloria of England's national honor, Panthalia is the emblem of the historical romance itself, the theoretical compromise that enabled those other propositions.

One of the commendatory verses preceding the text is signed "Amadin Barclay," another syncretic gesture. But there is more of Barclay than Amadis here, especially in Brathwaite's willingness to indicate "wherein the King hath erred." Panthalia's own analysis of the causes of the civil war focuses, like so many of the texts we have investigated, on English arcadianism. It is no coincidence that James I is named Basilius after Sidney's escapist monarch, in contrast to his militant female predecessor Bellingeria; nor that his pacificism is reproached in terms that should by now sound extremely familiar:

> This graceful and long-continued habit of peace, as it enricht the State with plenty: so it begot in the Inhabitants an incommodious securitie. For those virile & masculine Spirits, which formerly proclaimed them Heirs of Honour, [had been brought] to that delicacy; that as their Spirits were averse from the Exercises of Arms; so were their intellectual parts and inward abilities . . . weakened, or rather estranged from civil Consultations and affairs of State. (pp. 42–43)

This national effeminacy, Brathwaite argued, undermined the whole political system, making it impossible to elect a decent parliament: "There was not one found of all that conspicuous line capable of such high undertaking: being better known to a Game at Tenis" (p. 43). Although Brathwaite first introduces these criticisms as if they were the Puritan position, the view merely of "those Stoical Censors of the State who profest themselves mortal Antagonists to all Masks, Treats, Balls," he soon, in mid paragraph, and with a revealing "indeed," adopts the critique as his own. It is also noticeable that he moved the origins of arcadianism back to James's court, suggesting that the causes of the civil war could be found rather evenly distributed.

Brathwaite also shows considerable psychological subtlety in his analysis of the Caroline phase of the royal romance, the "unrestrained liberty" of court entertainments, "which Rosicles easily gave way to, because he perceived his young amorous Queen to be a Person of pleasure." "But Habits are dangerous," continued Brathwaite, "when grounded on faulty Principles":

> The Prince became a Subject to his Queens command: and . . . became a Compleat Courtier . . . seing Irina would have it so. (pp. 97–98)

Condensed into this remarkable passage are: sympathetic perceptions about the motives and feelings of real persons; moral and political analysis; an astute connection between the pleasure principle and arcadianism, in the person of Irina, whose name signifies peace; and a new and hitherto unrecognized ingredient in the subject matter and theory of the romance—its domination by the female. It is a short step from here to the comic theme of henpecking, exhibited in Brathwaite's account of Fairfax, "who had more strength in his hand, then sage in his pate," and was subject to lectures in bed from his domineering spouse. As a statement of Brathwaite's sexual politics, this should make us uneasy; but as a contribution to the theory of the romance it is both original and apt. As the English civil war could, from one perspective, be seen to have been caused in part by effeminacy, by the feminization of culture, so romance, in Brathwaite's opinion, was a form that history should *not* have taken.

Panthalia does not come equipped with formal definitions of or debates about genre. It does not need to. Self-consciousness is built into the text, at the level of narrative and editorial comment. The programmatic gravity of the genre's earlier phases is refreshingly absent. It is ironic, however, that though its good humor and readability have been admired, they have been admired for the wrong reasons, reasons of literary teleology. *Panthalia,* we are told, was "a promising experiment" in realism, after which "the respectable historical novel was conceivable."[44] My object has been to show that the historical romance had already acquired respectability in Brathwaite's culture, and to show that it deserved it. If *Panthalia* charms, it is not because the literary system was evolving toward "better" forms, but because a section of that system was already so highly developed that it could admit of a certain play. Years later Sir Walter Scott would predicate *Waverley* on the belief that "a romance founded on . . . more modern events, would have a better chance of popularity than a tale of chivalry."[45] Nobody would dare to question the bases of his enormous success, or think of disturbing his place in the canon. Yet much of the point of *Waverley* is its extreme self-consciousness about genre, its deft (and ideological) manipulation of the relationship between fiction and history; and the historical romances of an earlier "modern" period should surely share in the credit.

5 Letters to Friends

The Self in Familiar Form

Here's what I know about the book so far. Its working title is LETTERS. It will consist of letters . . . between several correspondents, . . . and preoccupy itself with, among other things, the role of epistles — real letters, forged and doctored letters — in the history of History. It will also be concerned with, and of course constituted of, alphabetical letters: the atoms of which the written universe is made. Finally, to a small extent the book is addressed to the phenomenon of literature itself, the third main sense of our word *letters* . . .

— John Barth, *Letters*

In the above late passage from *Letters,* the ultimate epistolary novel, Barth explained both the structural premise of his work and his largest conception of all that "letters" can mean to a theory of literature.[1] To an uncanny degree, this passage encapsulates many of the topics broached in this chapter, including the elusive place that letters (as epistles) have always had in letters (as literature). Recent theory has been especially interested in the letter as a strategy of fiction, its capacity to identify and explore, if not to solve, certain problems of reportage: interiority, privacy, immediacy, authenticity.[2] Yet this focus, inevitable since the development of the epistolary novel, itself depends on fiction's equivocal relationship to history, a major concern of Barth's novel, as also of my previous chapter. In Henry Fielding's "Preface to Familiar Letters of David Simple . . . 1747," written when the epistolary novel was a center of critical interest, letters were described as "the most valuable Parts of History, as they are not only the most authentic Memorials of Facts, but as they serve greatly to illustrate the true Character of the Writer, and do in a manner introduce the Person himself to our Acquaintance."[3] This statement derives directly from epistolary theory as it was evolved during the Renaissance and seventeenth century. It was, paradoxically, the *documentary* status of the letter, as well as its ability to personalize history, that first allured the writers of fiction to it. This paradox is recognized and extended in Barth's three categories, "real," "forged," and "doctored" (or history, fiction, and some compromise between them), which promote meditation on the peculiar ontological status

211

of letters as texts, as generic modules or modifiers, or as members
of a distinct and in some ways unique genre.

Letters could not, I shall here argue, have acquired their later power
in fiction unless they had first been recognized as a genre with models and norms. These were derived primarily from the familiar letters
of Cicero; and the Ciceronian strain of familiar letter became dominant in the seventeenth century primarily because of censorship, taken
in its largest sense as a set of restrictions on discourse. We have already seen, in Chapter 2, how the letters of John Chamberlain and
John Donne recorded their awareness of Jacobean and Caroline censorship, and how this gave their correspondence, especially Donne's,
a self-conscious, nervous intimacy. This self-definition was a product
of political circumstances, a fact that connects the familiar letter to
the lyric, at least in the versions explored in Chapter 3. But even more
urgently than the lyric, the letter poses the problem of how literary
and extraliterary motives intersect in genre formation. Throughout
the seventeenth century, writers reproduced in their own familiar letters features that had previously been perceived in Cicero's; yet they
did so, it appears, out of "real" needs, by the accidents of historical
circumstance and temperament. Do we have here, then, a case for a
natural genre?

We had better begin by determining what Cicero's letters would
have meant to Fielding's predecessors, and why it can be asserted that
Cicero fathered the familiar letter. The coincidences of textual survival and publication history have their part to play in this story. Cicero's letters survived in two major collections, the letters *ad Atticum,*
which he probably never thought of publishing, and the *Ad familiares,* from which the familiar letter takes its name. Two symbolic Renaissance "finds" initiated a legend and started the process of interpretation. When, in 1345, Petrarch discovered a manuscript of the
Letters to Atticus in the Chapter Library at Verona he wept at their
revelation of Cicero's psychological nakedness, his failure to maintain philosophical detachment, his seduction by political life. In 1392
Coluccio Salutati acquired by mistake a manuscript of the *Ad familiares* when he was really looking for the *Letters to Atticus;* and what
he most admired in both collections was their testimony to Cicero's
republican spirit.[4]

Later Renaissance editors observed the distinction between the
two collections and meditated upon it. The 1577 edition of the *Ad
familiares* by Henri Estienne (Stephanus) contains a long commen-

tary by himself on epistolary genre.[5] In it he remarks that not all the letters *Ad familiares* were written to friends, and that few of them show the same degree of intimacy ("quanta familiaritas") as is found in the *Letters to Atticus*. The annotated Amsterdam edition of 1677 by John Graevius opens with a long and somewhat apologetic note on the title, admitting that many letters in the *Ad familiares* collection are on serious subjects and written with much art ("summo artificio"), so that the name "familiar" might with more validity be applied to the *Letters to Atticus:*

> Although in those letters Cicero often spoke of public affairs, yet he used a more open and relaxed style, and they are written with less art and care, as men on intimate terms are accustomed to write to each other.[6]

These distinctions (serious and artful, *not* familiar; political, *yet* familiar) derive, as Estienne's commentary makes clear, from Cicero's own poetics of the letter, as expressed in *Ad familiares,* II, 4. This elegantly evasive letter to Curio begins by reminding his correspondent that although there are many kinds of letter, the primary, original kind is that which carries news:

> A letter of this kind you will of course not expect from me; for as regards your own affairs you have your correspondents and messengers at home, while as regards mine there is absolutely no news to tell you. There remain two kinds of letters which have great charm for me, the one intimate and humorous, the other austere and serious [unum familiare et iocosum, alterum severum et grave].

This apparently useful threefold distinction between the letter of news, of affectionate wit, and of moral or philosophical gravity is, however, immediately subverted. Cicero explains that his present circumstances make his scheme unworkable:

> Am I to jest with you by letter? On my oath, I don't think there is a citizen in existence who can laugh in these days. Or am I to write something more serious? What is there that can possibly be written by Cicero to Curio, in the serious style, except on public affairs? . . . in this regard my case is just this, that I dare not write what I feel, and I am not inclined to write what I don't feel.[7]

His conclusion is, inevitably, that "there is no subject left . . . for a letter" except the compliments with which he concludes. Cicero's dilemma, if we take it as more than a charming gesture, is a formalist one, a consequence of thinking in generic terms, which separate the letter writer from his natural impulses.

What happens in the letters to Atticus is different. In his confidence in the relationship and under situational stress, Cicero allows the notion of "kinds" to disappear, and the functions distinguished in the letter to Curio simply merge. Day after day Cicero writes to Atticus of his own shifting position in the struggle for power in Rome. As self-appointed defender of the republic, at the heart of intrigue, he seeks perspective from his more detached friend. Continually he asks for advice and for psychological support. News of himself is inevitably political news; but political news alternates in tone between the satiric (*iocosus*) and the tragic (*severus*). To Atticus he can write what he feels, even to the point of crying for his mistakes; but the pressure of egocentricity cannot, finally, destroy the ethical structure of the correspondence as a whole. Cicero's attempt to discover the line of rectitude in the tangle of political loyalties which confronted him was symbolized by his successive alignment and disillusionment with the optimates, the "honest men" of Rome. The converse of this ideal was his yearning for the "honestum otium," the high-minded philosophical detachment which Atticus himself could symbolize. During the coalition between Caesar, Pompey, and Crassus at the end of 60 B.C., Cicero retired, he thought, from politics. Writing to Atticus from Antium in April 59, he denied that his requests for news implied regret:

> I have long been sick of holding the helm, even when I was allowed to do so: and now, when I have been marooned and the helm torn from my grasp without waiting for me to surrender it, my only desire is to watch their shipwreck from the dry land. I could wish, as your friend Sophocles says, "in peaceful slumber sunk / To hear the pattering raindrops on the roof."[8]

Another April letter to Atticus ends: "Cicero in his new role of philosopher salutes Titus the politician" (II, 12). Two months later he was back in Rome, up to his ears in political crisis, his sense of public duty balanced by an even greater sense of self-disgust.[9]

During the Renaissance, these features of the *Letters to Atticus* were foregrounded in interpretations of the correspondence as a whole. Ciceronianism in the letter, therefore, as distinct from what we generally mean by that term, was predominantly a matter of content rather than of form, and of content in the largest sense of character, ethos, history. It is true, of course, that in England the letters were initially subsumed by the linguistic programs of humanism. Ascham recommended them, edited by John Sturm, "for the capacitie of children," as a prophylactic against bad Latin,[10] and in John Brinsley's grammar school, boys were taught how to make epistles "imitating Tully, short, pithy, . . . sweete Latine and familiar."[11] Given the assumptions of pedantry, that search for a sweet quotidian style could and did develop into exercises in epistolary form. Gabriel Harvey owned and annotated a copy of the 1563 Aldine edition of the *Epistulae ad Atticum, ad M. Brutum, ad Quinctum fratrem,* a fact which bears on the *Three Proper and Wittie, Familiar Letters* (1580) that passed between himself and Edmund Spenser, and were published as an advertisement of how clever they both were with the classics.[12]

But Erasmus, who represents a more profound version of humanism, perceived that the superiority of Cicero's letters to Seneca's lay precisely in their inimitable realism. "If epistles are wanting in feeling and do not represent a man's real life, they do not deserve to be so called." For Erasmus, the importance of the letters lay in their ambivalent status as historical documents, their access to the secret places behind the official version of events. Cicero's letters, unlike Seneca's, were "of that genuine kind, which represent . . . the character, fortune and feelings of the writer, and at the same time the public and private condition of the time."[13] In the seventeenth century this distinction became a commonplace. Donne distinguished between the "treasures of Morall knowledge" in Seneca's letters, and the weight of "the storie of the time" in Cicero's.[14] The prefatory verses to James Howell's *Epistolae Ho-Elianae* registered the same point in formally balanced couplets:

> In Seneca's rich Letters is enshrin'd
> Whate'er the ancient Sages left behind.
> Tully makes his the secret Symptoms tell
> Of those Distempers which proud Rome befel.[15]

Bacon, in the *Advancement of Learning,* recommended the *Letters to Atticus* as a text for political scientists, though one to be used with caution (II.xxiii.9); and in old age he entrusted his own letters to a

Tiro figure, John Williams, bishop of Lincoln (whose political significance was suggested in Chapter 3), with a request that they should not be published (yet) because "many of them touch too much upon late matters of state." The bishop heard his cue, and in his reply articulated the cultural assumptions they shared. Letters are, he asserted, "the principal pieces of our antiquities":

> For our histories (or rather lives of men) borrow as much from the affections and phantasies of the writers, as from the truth itself, and are for the most of them built altogether from unwritten relations and traditions. But letters written *è re natâ*, and bearing a synchronism or equality of time *cum rebus gestis,* have no other fault than that . . . they speak the truth too plainly, and cast too glaring a light for that age, wherein they were, or are written.[16]

The bishop's skepticism about the veridicality of history proper relates back, of course, to Sidney's *Defence,* and anticipated that of the 1661 *Princess Cloria.* But the most significant coloring in his letter was, perhaps, the note of caution. Erasmus had noted Cicero's frequent fears that his letters might be intercepted, and commented on the hazard of committing such material to paper. In the seventeenth century the issue of confidentiality became central. Personal letters, the most private of all communication except whispers, carried no immunity against censorship. Letters *were* intercepted, and their authors might be dealt with as severely as if they had published a provocative pamphlet. In May 1639, Sir Henry Wotton wrote to his nephew Nicholas Bacon:

> This very morning shall be heard at the Star-chamber the case of Sir Peter Buck . . . an officer (as I take it) of the Navy, who hath lain for some good while in prison for having written to a friend of his at Dover a letter containing this news, that some of the Lords had kneeled down to the King for a toleration in Religion, besides some particular aspersion in the said letter of my Lord privy Seal.[17]

The startling nature of this news shocked Wotton, usually more concerned with court gossip and the state of his own digestion, into epistolary self-consciousness. "I set down these accidents barely as you see without their causes, which in truth is a double fault, writing both to a friend, and to a Philosopher"; yet the momentary preoccu-

pation is really still governed by concern for self, by political hypo-
chondria: "My lodging is so near the Star-chamber, that my pen shakes
in my hand." When the Star Chamber gave way to a revolutionary
government, nothing changed. On 1 January 1644, James Howell, already in prison, wrote to Endymion Porter: "The Times are so ticklish,
that I dare not adventure to send you any London intelligence, she
being now a garrison Town; and you know, as well as I, what danger
I may incur" (I, 363). In another letter "to Sir J. C." published in his
Twelve Treatises (1661), but obviously retrospective, Howell wrote:

> Among many other Barbarismes which like an impetuous Tor-
> rent have lately rush'd in upon us, the interception and opening
> of Letters is none of the least. . . . 'tis a plundering of the very
> brain, as is spoken in another place. We are reduced here to
> that servile condition, or rather to such a height of slavery, that
> we have nothing left which may entitle us free Rationall crea-
> tures; the *thought* it self cannot say 'tis free, much less the *tongue*
> or *pen*.[18]

But the most famous example of intercepted mail during the civil
war occurred in 1645, when Charles's personal letters to Henrietta
Maria were captured at the battle of Naseby and published to discredit
him. The event produced a revolutionary pamphlet, *The Kings Cabinet Opened,* and a satirical poem answering the pamphlet, or rather
attacking its central premise. Significantly, the political defense of the
king's behavior is presented in terms of epistolary theory, which requires a separation between private and public discourse. Since men,
unlike angels, cannot communicate directly from soul to soul, nature provided them with "two close safe Pathes":

> In Presence, Whisper; and at Distance, Penne.
> Publick Decrees and Thoughts were else the same,
> Nor were it to Converse, but to Proclaim.
> Conceipts were else but Records, but by this care
> Our Thoughts no Commons, but Inclosures are:
> What bold Intruders then are they, who assail
> To cut their Prince's Hedge, and break his Pale?
> That so Unmanly gaze, and dare be seen
> Ev'n then, when He converses with his Queen.[19]

The ambiguous status of the letter, meant for the cabinet but just
as likely to end up in a court of trial, was intensified when its author

actually desired a wider audience. To admit that private letters could become historical documents was one thing. To write them *as* historical documents, or, having written them, to publish them for their historical interest, was quite another. How far a correspondence could go into the public domain without losing its Ciceronian qualities is a delicate question. The test case for the seventeenth century is James Howell's *Epistolae Ho-Elianae*.

James Howell: "Doctor of Letters"

Howell published the first installment of his letters, from prison, in 1645. In 1647 a second volume of additional letters appeared, in 1650 a second edition, with a third volume added, and in 1655 a third edition with an additional fourth volume. The question of Howell's motives, and of the authenticity of his correspondence, as "real" letters, was first raised by Anthony à Wood in 1691:

> Many of the said Letters were never written before the Author of them was in the Fleet, as he pretends they were, only feigned, (no time being kept with their dates) and purposely published to gain Money to relieve his Necessities, yet give a tolerable History of those times.[20]

Joseph Jacobs, Howell's nineteenth-century editor, wrestled with this charge, which seemed to be partly supported by the evidence. The dates of the letters, omitted from the 1645 edition and added in 1650, were frequently inaccurate, and, more damning, certain letters were found to combine historical events in chronologically impossible ways. Jacobs's conclusion was, as he himself felt, a "somewhat drab and trimming" compromise: that many of Howell's *Epistolae* originated as genuine correspondence of which he had kept copies; but that for the 1645 edition he had "cooked" some letters "by the insertion of incongruous fragments," and others, especially the series addressed to his father, and containing Howell's autobiography, were probably either entirely fabricated or had the biographical paragraphs inserted, since they "read too continuously."[21] Howell's letters were therefore placed on the interface between genuine and fictionalized correspondence, with his own action in publishing them defined as editing, its only suggested motive vanity, its chief characteristic factual carelessness. Modern criticism has largely accepted these judgments, and focused therefore on the "literary" aspect of Howell's letters, stressing their chatty, entertaining tone, liking those that resemble

philosophical essays: those on the religions, wines, and languages of
the world, the unity of creation, or the habitation of the moon.[22]

Yet these decisions preempt the question of genre, and involve a
degree of misreading or oversight. To survey the whole collection allows the later volumes, where essaylike letters predominate, to over-
shadow the 1645 volume, which presumably represents Howell's original intention. In 1645, Howell's preoccupation was with current events.
Approximately three out of five letters consist mainly or entirely of
news, and many begin, "The greatest news I have to tell you is . . ."
or some such phrase. Second, one really needs to read the 1645 volume in isolation to get the full impact of those preliminary features —
title page, dedication — that controlled its original reception. The 1645
Epistolae were described on the title page as "Familiar Letters Domestic and Forren; Divided into Six Sections, Partly Historicall, Politicall, Philosophicall, Upon Emergent Occasions; By J. H. Esq;: One
of the Clerks of His Majesties most Honourable Privy Councill."
Genre and structure were thus identified for the reader; but also certain intimations, reminiscent of the hermeneutics of censorship, were
given about the author and his motives. At a time when Howell was
already in prison, possibly as a royalist spy, and by the indefinite order
of the revolutionary House of Commons, the *Epistolae Ho-Elianae*
presented themselves as topical, royalist statement. Political bravado
was, however, mixed with discretion; the author's self-identification
was incomplete.

In later editions, Howell referred his readers equally to the Senecan and Ciceronian traditions of letter writing. This is especially true
of the 1650 title page with its symmetrical columns (see Fig. 5). But
in the 1645 edition, Howell had dedicated his letters to Charles I, and
clearly placed them in the highest Ciceronian tradition:

> Nor would these Letters be so Familiar, as to presume upon so
> high a Patronage, were not many of them Records of your own
> Royal Actions: And 'tis well known, that Letters can treasure
> up, and transmit Matters of State to Posterity, with as much
> Faith, and be as authentick Registers, and safe Repositories of
> Truth, as any Story [history] whatsoever.[23]

Anthony à Wood's remark, that despite their fraudulence, Howell's
letters "yet give a tolerable History of those times," was, therefore a
piece of malicious insight. My proposal differs only in giving Howell's intentions the benefit of the doubt, morally and intellectually.

Figure 5. Frontispiece, James Howell, Epistolae Ho-Elianae *(1645, 1650). By permission of the British Library.*

Read with his authorial directions as the key, the 1645 *Epistolae* deliver a version of royalist history that would not have been possible without formal manipulation. Howell's editing, his reinventing of history, were not the result of carelessness or poor memory, but rather of a need to give form and meaning to his experience, to give it (and hence his audience) the value of hindsight. When the dates were added in the 1650 edition, the incongruities were far too obvious to be mistakes.[24] What they should have alerted his readers to was the need to look closer, to examine the possible meaning of incongruity itself.

The six sections of the 1645 edition to which Howell's title page draws our attention are not arbitrary divisions, but signs of structuring activity that denote purpose. The first three cover Jacobean history, the second three Caroline. Each of the first four sections opens with a letter "To my Father" marking both a stage in Howell's travels and a new phase in the political history of his day. It gradually becomes clear that the emphasis on travel (the formal excuse for correspondence) is really a further excuse, for the introduction of Europe as the scene and cause, ultimately, of the English civil war. Section I is a youthful and conventional tour of Europe, which yet provides the basis for understanding what happens later. In Section II, the central issue is the loss of the Palatinate; in III, the Spanish marriage negotiations, of which Howell was an eyewitness, as part of Digby's entourage in Madrid, and which, quoting the Spanish ambassador, Gondomar, Howell presented as the only way "to regain the Palatinate, and to settle an eternal Peace in Christendom" (1:144). The failure of the match is the formal center of the book, and also a low point, the end of an era. With the death of James, closely followed by that of Sir Francis Bacon and Elizabeth of Bohemia's eldest son, Charles is proclaimed king "in a sad shower of Rain":

> And the Weather was suitable to the condition wherein he finds the Kingdom, which is cloudy: for he is left engag'd in a War with a potent Prince, the People by long desuetude unapt for Arms, the Fleet-Royal in quarter repair, himself without a Queen, his sister without a Country, the Crown pitifully laden with Debts . . . But God Almighty, I hope, will make him emerge, and pull this Island out of all the plunges, and preserve us from worser times. (1:217)

In this remarkable letter to his father, Howell inaugurates the reign of the king to whom he dedicates his history; and thereby indicates, one must suppose, its far from simple purpose.

In fact, the Caroline phase of Howell's history evinces a deep pessimism. Section IV, after that gloomy coronation, rises to a moment of exuberance with Charles's marriage to Henrietta Maria, and Howell's own hopes for preferment under Buckingham. But its major events are the loss of Breda, the "miscarriages" of the naval war against Spain, Parliament's attack on Buckingham, its resulting dissolution, the institution of forced loans ("they are imprison'd that deny to conform themselves," p. 243), and the sudden dismissal in disgrace of the queen's French household. A letter to his father signals the overall design, by finding Howell, in Section IV, "now the fourth time at a dead stand" (p. 239) in his career, having discovered Buckingham's antipathy to him. Section V opens buoyantly with Howell elected to the new parliament of 1628 (though not without fear of some penalty for not having paid the forced loan, p. 249). Optimism extends into the public sphere with the passage of the Petition of Right, "whereby the Liberty of the freeborn Subject is so strongly and clearly vindicated" (p. 252). Howell reports to the earl of Sunderland Buckingham's speech "in joy hereof"; yet *in the very next* letter he reports to the countess of Sunderland the "sad Tragedy" of Buckingham's assassination. The clash of tones, the classic tragic irony, which cannot be unintentional, is reinforced by the congruence between the addressees and, in the 1650 text, the incongruous dating. The letter to the earl is dated 25 September 1628; that to the countess 5 August 1628; the assassination actually took place on August 23.

We must, I think, assume that Howell knows exactly what he is doing. His subtlety is both ubiquitous and entirely justified. A typical letter reports that "there is fearful News come from Germany" about the fate of the Palatinate, and proceeds to interpret James's attitude to his son-in-law's predicament on the basis of a local incident:

> For whereas Dr. Hall gave the Prince Palsgrave the title of K. of Bohemia in his Pulpit-Prayer, he had a check for his pains; for I heard his Majesty should say, That there is an implicit Tie among Kings, which obligeth them . . . to stick to and right one another upon an insurrection of Subjects.

In other words, James was bound to support the emperor. Yet Howell concludes:

> But the fearful News I told you of at the beginning of this Letter is, that . . . the new King of Bohemia, having not worn the Crown a whole twelvemonth, was forc'd to fly with his Queen and Children, . . . This News affects both Court and City here with much heaviness. (1:101–3)

As compared with the open and militant propaganda of Thomas Scott, Howell's strategy is extremely demure. He combines political analysis with on-the-spot reporting, but pointedly informs his correspondent that public discussion of the crisis is restricted, judging by the "check" given Bishop Hall. He indicates a breach between public opinion and the king's response to the issue; and he implies his own sympathies for the Elector Palatine by proceeding to use the offending title, king of Bohemia, himself!

The allusion to restricted discourse is not casual. Section V concludes with an extraordinary letter describing the Spanish Inquisition, a proleptic and prophetic version of Howell's own arrest, the climactic event of Section VI. Here the procedures of censorship are given a peculiarly generic relationship to the medium in which they are described; for Howell explains how the Inquisition sends out an officer, called a "Familiar," to search out evidence of heterodoxy:

> When the said Familiar goes to any House, tho' it be in the dead of night (and that's the time commonly they use to come, or in the dawn of the day), all doors, and trunks, and chests fly open to him; and the first thing he doth, he seizeth the Party's breeches, searcheth his pockets, and taketh his keys, and so rummageth all his closets and trunks: And a Public Notary, whom he carrieth with him, taketh an Inventory of everything, which is sequestered . . . . The Party being hurry'd away in a close Coach, and clapt in prison . . . if he refuseth to swear, he convicteth himself, and tho' he swear, yet he is remanded to prison. (1:291)

Howell needs no explicit comment on the reverberation of the term "Familiar." In its stress on the invasion of privacy, this letter connects to the other, quoted above, complaining to Sir James Croft about the "Barbarismes" of censorship, the "interception and opening of Letters," that "plundering of the very brain." There, Howell wrote that "we have nothing left which may entitle us free Rationall creatures";

here there is also a breakdown of rational, even of sanctified, forms (the oath) of communication.

The same condition governed Howell's arrest in 1643. As he wrote to the earl of Bristol:

> One morning betimes there rush'd into my chamber five armed Men with Swords, Pistols, and Bills, and told me they had a Warrant from the Parliament for me: I desir'd to see their Warrant, they deny'd it: I desir'd to see the date of it, they deny'd it: I desir'd to see my name in the Warrant, they deny'd all . . . So they rush'd presently into my Closet and seiz'd on all my Papers and Letters, and anything that was Manuscript; and many printed Books they took also, and hurl'd all into a great hair Trunk, which they carry'd away with them. (1:355)

Despite an inspection of Howell's papers, with nothing found "that might have given offence," he was imprisoned on unspecified charges, and for an indefinite period. The letter to Bristol concludes, "God's will be done, and amend the times, and make up these ruptures which threaten so much calamity." If "ruptures" subsumes the breaches in both private space and public coherence, the desired amendment should reverse this cultural deprivation, reinstate the traditional distinctions between private and public forms of expression. Letters to friends would then have no need to go public, either in self-defense or in the service of the king. They could return to their venerable role of placing the self in its historical context, of reading history in the mirror of self.

The stress on amendment in Section VI helps to explain the somber tone of Howell's history, the growing implication that present trouble (the civil war) originated in past failures. In Letter 29 Howell closed down the tragic tale of the Palatinate with one last disaster, in the conviction that "there is some angry Star that hath hung over this business . . . from the beginning of these German Wars to this very day" (p. 330). Here superstition and formalism meet; the patterns visible in history are articulate as curses, activated by the mistakes and betrayals of the previous generation. This is history rewritten as prophecy. Yet the more this pessimism emerges as a theme, the more clearly Howell identifies himself as Jeremiah, the less we can understand his dedicating this volume to the king; unless, perhaps, warned by his self-identification as clerk of the *Privy Council,* we consider the possibility that counsel is being given. If so, what would it be, and what form does it take?

One example cannot, of course, provide an answer; but it is nevertheless startling to look again, with this question in mind, at a much-
quoted letter, which when it appeared in the 1650 edition was dated
3 June 1634, and which epitomizes Caroline culture. Howell begins
by thanking his correspondent for "the variety of News . . . sent me
so handsomely couch'd and knit together"; and then, to reciprocate,
gives three items of recent interest. First,

> the greatest News we have here is, that we have a gallant Fleet-
> Royal ready to set to Sea, for the Security of our Coast and
> Commerce, and for the Sovereighty of our Seas. . . . These are
> brave Fruits of the Ship-money.

Second, he reports that the Swedish army has been decimated at the
battle of Nordlingen by the Archduke Ferdinand, cardinal infante of
Spain. And third,

> the Court affords little News at present, but that there is a Love
> call'd Platonick Love, which much sways there of late; it is a
> Love abstracted from all corporeal gross Impressions and sen-
> sual Appetite, but consists in Contemplations and Ideas of the
> Mind . . . This Love sets the Wits of the Town on work; and
> they say there will be a Mask shortly of it, whereof Her Maj-
> esty and her Maids of Honour will be part. (1:317–18)

Modern readers have seen nothing in this letter other than useful docu-
mentation of a phase in the Caroline drama. Yet Howell invites more
circumspection. He too has "handsomely couch'd and knit together"
different kinds of news: "greatest" and "little" and events that will not
combine chronologically. The battle of Nordlingen took place on 6
September 1634; and the courtly masque referred to is almost certainly Aurelian Townsend's *Tempe Restored,* in which the queen performed on 14 February 1632. Linked by a false chronology, the show
of naval strength, the shattered Protestant campaign, the courtly ab-
stractions, are related to each other in unstated and provocative ways.
The letter asks us to consider how timing affects interpretation, what
it means when events are *out of order;* and, with the hindsight of 1645,
what has been the effect of these disordered priorities. With his queen
now fled for her own safety to France, how would the other chief author of the royal romance feel, reading of "a Love abstracted . . .
consist[ing] in Contemplations and Ideas"? What ironies would arise
from reconsidering the "brave Fruits of the Ship-money"? What did
Howell mean by this celebration of the "Fleet-Royal" as he sat incar-

cerated in the "Fleet" prison, a metaphor he later unpacks: "As far as I can see, I must lie at a dead anchor in this Fleet a long time, unless some gentle gale blow thence to make me launch out" (1:356). The gentle gale of deliverance that Howell awaited was surely part of his message, the other side of his jeremiad. Letter 50 hopes that "there will be sweet and gentle means us'd to preserve [the country] from Precipitation" (1:359). Letter 54 praises Bishop Juxon for unusual moderation, and attributes his survival of the national tempest to "being a Willow, and not an Oak" (1:366). Letter 51 is a confession of his own responsibility for the civil war: "When I make this scrutiny within myself, and enter into the closest Cabinet of my Soul, I find (God help me) that I have contributed as much to the drawing down of these Judgments on England as any other" (1:360). His message to the king, the royal oak, the only man who *had* to take responsibility for the revolution, seems unavoidable. The solution to past errors was moderation, conciliation, and self-scrutiny, the letter's province.

The 1645 *Epistolae* were dated at the end: "Imprimatur . . . June 9, 1645." On 14 June of the same year, Charles was conclusively defeated by the New Model Army at the battle of Naseby. At that time his own correspondence was seized and the king's cabinet opened to scrutiny, though not in the way that Howell had recommended. After Naseby, Charles would protest that the Long Parliament had published his letters in order "to make all reconciliation desperate"; and Milton would reply: "What he feares not by Warr and slaughter, should we feare to make desperate by op'ning his Letters?"[25] By the time these exchanges were published, in 1649, the king was dead, and the desperate situation that Howell had hoped to avert was fully manifest. He had failed in his attempt to alter the shape of future history by delineating that of the past, at least as he himself had experienced it; thereafter his letters would retreat to safer territory. He may not have been unreasonably or unseasonably self-protective. He certainly was not the fraud that Wood suggested he was; but his later volumes of *Epistolae* show little interest in presenting, as Fielding put it, "authentic Memorials of Facts" — doctored or otherwise — and a great deal of concern with "the Person himself."

Restoration letter writers: the case for natural genre

It is something of a relief, therefore, to turn to a group of "real" letter writers, even though the problems that they raise for genre theory may be greater still. In the correspondence of Andrew Marvell; of Henry Savile in one of his roles; of Halifax, his elder brother, writing to Henry, there appears to be a natural Ciceronianism of the letter, an analogy rather than a copy. These men were all writing in the 1670s, one of the most troubled and disillusioned decades of the Restoration. They were all active politicians, parliamentarians, each, to a different degree, opposed to Charles II's policies; by the accidents of historical circumstance and temperament they recreated in their own familiar letters, which they themselves never published, that powerful mixture of self-absorption and political generosity, candor and discretion, that Cicero and his Renaissance agents had stamped with generic form. This group becomes more interesting if one extends it to include Algernon Sidney and Rochester, both of them also writing to Henry Savile. In Sidney's the Ciceronian forms are muted, shadowy; they are muted by age, self-effacement, and perhaps by political absolutism. From Rochester's all Ciceronian preoccupations are deliberately excluded; they are incompatible with absolute cynicism and self-contempt.

Marvell's letters are already well recognized as historical documents of first importance. From a generic standpoint they are interesting because they too, like Cicero's, fall into two major categories. One collection, by far the largest, consists of his day-by-day reports as a member of Parliament to his constituents in Hull. In these he is resolutely impersonal, neutral in his reporting of debates, remarkably silent about his own role in the House, and usually in a tearing hurry. His position in these letters is well defined on one occasion when the contents of one letter have been circulated more widely than he intended:

> Although I object nothing to Mr. Cressets fidelity and discretion neither do I write deliberately any thing which I feare to have divulged yet seeing it is possible that in writing to assured friends a man may give his pen some liberty and the times are something criticall beside that I am naturally and now more by my Age inclined to keep my thoughts private, I desire that what I write down to you may not easily or unnecessarily returne to a third hand at London.[26]

As the representative of Hull he will assume trust and coincidence of views; but in the "criticall" environment of the 1670s he will write nothing that could not be published in the parliamentary journals;

and even what he does write he would prefer his constituents to keep to themselves. There could scarcely be a more telling expression of the effect of what we have been calling censorship, since what might have been a candid correspondence has been stripped to the bare bones, leaving nothing but "facts."

In his really familiar letters, Marvell's position is different in every way. We should ignore his famous but obsequious letter to Milton of 1654, and look rather at his correspondence with Philip, Lord Wharton, and Sir Edward Harley, both peers of the Country party and defenders of the Nonconformists; with Sir Henry Thompson and his younger brother Edward, both political figures in York; and above all with his beloved nephew William Popple in Hull.[27] All but one of these letters were written during the 1670s. In them, Marvell wrote as a member of the Opposition party in the House of Commons, and as an outspoken critic of Charles and his chief ministers. Although the relationship with Popple was intimate as the others were not, in all of these letters Marvell wrote to someone he felt he could trust, to whom he could (though there are degrees of trust) speak his mind.

We can take the long letter to Rolt, the friend in Persia, as characteristic of the form, the style, and the purpose of Marvell's familiar letters. There are a few personal preliminaries (his friends's sore hand) and then a warning, with respect to some business deal, that his friend should be cautious, "for in this world a good Cause signifys little, unless it be well defended." It appears, too, that a previous letter has "miscarried," and Marvell is concerned: "Tho there was nothing material in it, the Thoughts of Friends are too valuable to fall into the Hands of a Stranger." Then the subgenre is defined: it is to be a letter of political news, from one in the center, to one outside the periphery of action. "Now," writes Marvell, "after my usual Method, leaving to others what relates to Busyness, I address myself, which is all I am good for, to be your Gazettier" (2:323–24).

But the gazette which follows is far from neutral reporting. The subject is the corruption both of the Restoration court and the Cavalier Parliament which has abandoned its constitutional functions. "The King [has]," writes Marvell, "upon Pretence of the great Preparations of his Neighbours, demanded three hundred thousand Pounds for his Navy." Everyone suspects, however, that the money is really intended for various Court pockets. Members of Parliament are being bought off with such large bribes of money or land "that it is a Mercy they gave not away the whole Land, and Liberty, of England."

Buckingham is out of control in his affair with Lady Shrewsbury, "by whom he believes he had a Son, to whom the King stood Godfather," and "We truckle to France in all Things, to the Prejudice of our Alliance and Honour" (2:324–25). The news, in other words, is partly public scandal and partly candid reporting of events which have been quite differently presented in official propaganda. The tone, after the preliminary note of caution, is partly the sardonic drawl of the satirist, and partly the more dignified, tragic accent of the public orator presiding over the fall of the republic. There is no discernible structure, logical, rhetorical, or even chronological; as another letter puts it, Marvell stops when "the paper is full" (2:318).

But there is one characteristic of Marvell's letters totally alien to the *Letters to Atticus,* which are dominated by Cicero's self-concern, his ambitions, his fears, his irresolutions, his self-justifications and self-recriminations. From Marvell's familiar letters the ego is missing. In a letter to Harley recording the reception of his *Mr. Smirke,* Marvell's caution combines with his irony in an extraordinary gesture. Not only is the letter unsigned, but he refers to himself throughout in the *third* person: "The book said to be Marvel's makes what shift it can in the world but the Author walks negligently up & down as unconcerned" (2:346). The *I,* prerequisite of all epistolary discourse, one would think, has disappeared. In another letter to Harley of November 1677, not long before his death, Marvell actually apologized for his "indiscretion in talking so much and so extravagantly concerning my selfe in my last Letter" (2:356). Of course, if we had this last letter, we might have a different picture of this man, whose desire to travel incognito may well now seem exaggerated by the accidental survival of some letters and not others of quite a different kind. But there is some basis for believing that his view of the familiar letter did not include self-revelation. In that letter to Mayor Shires at Hull which marks the boundary between official and personal correspondence, Marvell spoke of his being "naturally and now . . . by . . . Age inclined" to keep his thoughts private. Even to Popple, he eschews self-exposure.

The closest approximation to a personal statement appears in a letter to Popple of July 1676, and a strange letter it is. The strangeness results from its division into two parts: the second half, in English, contains political news and criticism; the first half, in Latin, contains an enquiry as to his nephew's finances and a description of his own emotional state. The letter comes with a covering note to

Robert Thompson, a clerk in the Popple firm, requesting him to deliver the "backside of this letter . . . to my nephew yr M^r *you not reading it*" (italics added). In the context of this note the use of Latin appears to have been a protective device—protective, in more than one sense, of Marvell's personal self. It sets up an obstacle to other people's inquisitiveness, and it provides a degree of formalism which allows for, which sanctions, extravagance of sentiment:

> Ignoscas Gulielme curiositati meae sed non opus est ut satisfacias[.] tametsi si faceres secretum apud me inviolabile maneret[.] Cuperem scire quantum effeceris pecuniae et in solido collocaveris ut spes aliqua mihi etiam senescenti effulgeret te coram aliquando videndi fruendi antequam in pulverem nativum dissiper, imminuar, revertar, at saltem vano hoc prospe[ctu] liceat summo erga [te] affectui adulari. (2:348)[28]

> [William, you will forgive my curiosity, but you don't have to satisfy it anyway. If you confide in me, the secret will remain with me, inviolable. I would like to know how much money you have made and deposited in a secure form, so that some hope may shine on me even as I grow older of sometimes seeing you face to face, of enjoying you, before I am dissipated, diminished, returned to my native dust; but at least let me go on dreaming of this vain prospect in my extreme affection toward you.][29]

"I miss you; I wish you were here." That primary message of the familiar letter (so frequently expressed in Cicero's letters to Atticus) is all the more striking in this one letter of Marvell's because it is missing from the others.

One of Marvell's letters to Sir Henry Thompson, written in January 1674/75, ends with the following piece of scandal: "Rochester has lost his Bridge. The D[uke] forgives not Henry Savill but [he] is still forbid the Court" (2:338). The incident referred to, a phase in the extended quarrel between Rochester and Lord Mulgrave, was a duel provoked by Savile in a drunken fit and seconded by Rochester; it is typical of the group which Marvell, in another letter, referred to as "the merry gang." In yet another letter Marvell reported how Rochester "in a debauch at Epsome," having started a fight with a constable, panicked and hid when the situation got out of control. In the resulting fracas one of his friends was killed. This not-so-merry affair, and

Marvell's disapprobation, provide a convenient sign of the difference between his familiar correspondence and that which passed between Savile and Rochester. To use the terms of Cicero's letter to Curio, the Savile-Rochester letters are entirely jocose. Marvell would have called them irresponsible.

If one had only this part of Savile's correspondence to consider, it would be hard to imagine him capable of seriousness. Fat Harry Savile, known for his successful accommodations to the younger-brother syndrome, living by his wits successfully enough (despite temporary disgraces) to survive as courtier, diplomatist, and member of Parliament, presents himself, in his relationship to Rochester, as a Falstaff figure, an obsolescent Cavalier living in much too serious times. Yet there are signs that this role is, to some extent, a literary construct; and also that it is Rochester who determines and controls the tone of the relationship and its written expression. Rochester's stance is that of a professional cynic and underminer, with a drive toward self-annihilation rather than self-preservation. It is his sardonic view of experience, acting upon Savile's flexibility, which restricts them to the interchange of wit.

Writing to Savile in April 1676, in reply to a letter which has not survived, Rochester complains:

> You cannot shake off the Statesman intirely, for I perceive you have no Opinion of a Letter, that is not almost a Gazette: Now, to me, who think the World as giddy as my self, I care not which way it turns, and am fond of no News, but the Prosperity of my Friends, and the continuance of their Kindness to me.[30]

It seems that Savile partially accepted the correction. A letter from him of 17 December 1677 begins by describing the "sorte of mad-nesse" which the anti-French sentiment has spread through the court as war against France begins to seem inevitable. The tone is, however, of drawing room comedy: "Though the Parliament will occasion your comeing up within a month it were well enough worthy a journey sooner to see how the stile of the court is altered in this point, and to see his Majesty soe merry with the confederates in the Queen's withdrawing room whilst poor Barillon stands by neglected." Then, as it were, the cardinal irresponsibility of both life and letters is defined: "*The greatest newes I can send you* from hence is what the King told mee last night, that your Lordship has a daughter borne by the body of Mrs. Barry of which I give your honour joy" (p. 52; italics added). In the same parodic vein Savile sends bulletins to Rochester about the current state of his syphilis, a bond between them in more senses than one, and a symbol of familiarity carried to its logical conclusion.

Both Savile and Rochester deploy the topos of political censorship. So did Marvell. Writing to Popple in June 1672 he remarked that "there was the other Day . . . a severe Proclamation issued out against all who shall vent false News, or discourse it concerning Affairs of State. So that in writing to you I run the Risque of making a Breach in the Commandment" (2:328). But where Marvell alluded, although with some irony, to a risk he was actually taking, for Savile and Rochester the dangerousness of correspondence seems to be *merely* a ploy. Writing on 4 June 1678 when Charles had just been out-flanked by Louis XIV in Europe[31] and was facing a newly assembled recalcitrant parliament and an army that had to be paid before it could be disbanded, Savile makes light work of an inflammable political situation, which would, in September, be set ablaze by the Popish Plot:

> For Parliament affaires to-morrow is appointed in your house for the utmost decision whether my Lord Purbeck bee a viscount or noe. . . . Wee the poor Commons goe gently on towards disbanding the army and discharging the fleet . . . As for court newes you know all prudent persons have ever been wary of writing, especially since Mr. Lane was once turned out about it, but since I am out allready I will venture att one small piece of intelligence, because one who is allways your friend and sometimes (especially now) mine, has a part in it that makes her now laughed att and may one day turne to her infinite disadvantage. (pp. 55–56)

This piece of "intelligence" turns out to be Lady Hervey's "civill plott" to introduce a new mistress to Charles at the expense of Nell Gwyn.

On 1 November 1679, it is now Savile who is out of earshot as envoy extraordinary to France, while Rochester writes from Whitehall, at the center of events. This was the year of the first Exclusion Bill, of Charles's dangerous illness, of the duke of York's return from exile and Monmouth's enforced departure; but Rochester's response to these events is that of "The Careless Good Fellow" portrayed in Oldham's satirical ballad, who "minds[s] not grave asses who idly debate / About right and succession, the trifles of state."[32] He begins by professing stylistic doubts,

> I Am in a great straight what to write to you; the stile of Business I am not vers'd in, and you may have forgot the familiar one we us'd heretofore;

moves quickly into satirical detachment,

> My own ill-nature . . . inclines me very little to pity the Misfortunes of malicious mistaken Fools, and the Policies of the Times;

and escapes with a gesture of mock discretion,

> The News I have to send, and the sort alone which could be so to you, are things *Gyaris & carcere digna,* which I dare not trust to this pretty Fool the Bearer. (p. 72)

The letter then resolves its genre with some suggestive remarks about the "pretty Fool" and how serviceable he could be to Savile if both should choose so. It is entirely appropriate to Rochester's self-characterization that his reference to the risks of news letters ("things worthy of exile and imprisonment") should be a quotation from Juvenal.[33]

Although Rochester seems to control the tone of the correspondence, its status in any theory of the familiar letter is perhaps best defined by Savile. Precisely because he is uncertain of his own status, because his relationship with Rochester is only one of his roles, Savile is able to articulate the problem of genre and style which for him remains unsettled. Writing on 18 June 1678 Savile apologizes to Rochester, in effect, for not being Rochester, for not being totally irresponsible:

> As to your opinion in that state matter I mentioned to you I do very much approve it, and have myselfe been of late see [soe] battered in politicks that if there bee a man alive who ought to retire from businesse and have noe more civill plotts it is myselfe. Butt what would you have? The lease of my house lasts above two years longer and the steame of Guy's wisdome dos soe fly into my head, that I cannot but attempt notable undertakings, and wanting ballast to sayle steadily upon the least foule weather, I am apt to oversett. *This is matter of fact and as well the truth as the stile politicall.* (p. 58; italics added)

The "state matter" to which Savile refers is probably the "civill plott" of Lady Hervey, but the battering in politics involved a much more serious matter—Savile's speech in the House of Commons on 8 May against Lauderdale, the king's tyrannical high commissioner in Scotland (and the villain also of several of Marvell's familiar letters). Charles's rage on this occasion was so extreme that it not only resulted in Savile's personal disgrace (yet again) but constituted a psychological setback to the Lauderdale opposition in the Commons, and caused an immediate prorogation of Parliament.[34]

In these circumstances (none of which Savile had reported to Rochester) his admission to being engaged, to finding retirement alluring but less so than "civill plotts" and "notable undertakings," is recognizably an admission of the Ciceronian ethos, however wryly qualified. That is what Savile means by the "stile politicall"; it is focused by one of Cicero's most characteristic tropes, the politician as sailor, or as himself a miniature ship of state. When Henri Estienne wished to illustrate the philosophical gravity of Cicero's letters, he gathered together all the ship-of-state passages from both collections.[35] Savile proceeds to parody his own political style by parodying that venerable symbol:

> Such a collier as Manchester will ride safe upon the Dogger Banke when, it may bee, such a pretty pinke as your Lordship shall bee in danger, and where such a dungboate as Lauderdale rides admirall, what vessell of valew or worth can thinke it calme weather; God send him in Charon's ferry boate to end this melancholy sea voyage quickly.

Not all of the seriousness inherent in the metaphor, however, can be thus disposed of. It seeps into the playful language ("this melancholy sea voyage"); and its center is Savile's extraordinary statement: "This is matter of fact and as well the truth as the stile politicall." His own experience can be identified in traditional terms, expressed as a choice between styles of discourse; but its very actuality revalidates the old language, prefixes *style* with *life-* and *expression* with *self-*. Where could this happen, if not in a familiar letter?

The best proof of Savile's split personality comes, of course, from his correspondence with other men. The friend whose personality was most dissimilar to Rochester's was Algernon Sidney, who was to be tried and executed in 1683, on ostensible suspicion of connection with the Rye House Plot, but in fact as an example of the likely fate of republican thinkers, however discreet. Sidney's unbending republican principles had expressed themselves chiefly in prolonged self-imposed

exile and in the private manuscript answer to Filmer's *Patriarcha* which
was found in his rooms and cited in evidence against him. When in
1679 he entered into an agreement with Savile (in France) to send him
a weekly letter from London, it was clearly because Savile needed
someone he could absolutely trust to send him the news. For Sidney,
"news" excluded court scandal, was to be distinguished from rumor,
and certainly prohibited satirical comment and epistolary gamesmanship. On 31 October 1679, the month in which Charles began another
of his long prorogations of Parliament to stave off the Exclusionists,
Sidney wrote to Savile defining the correspondence:

> We are in a busy time, and how empty soever any man's head
> hath formerly been, the variety of reports concerning things in
> agitation do so fill it, at the least with an imagination of con-
> tributing something to other men's inventions, that they have
> little leisure to do anything else. This obligeth me to write in
> haste, and without any other consideration than of the agree-
> ment made between you and me, *to set down nothing but truth.*
> (italics added)[36]

In the long run, however, Sidney's definition of the letter as containing nothing but news, and of news as "nothing but truth," made
for restrictiveness, while at the same time his discretion, his absolute
restraint of self, led toward formality, rather than familiarity. He was,
moreover, by his age and political disposition, an outsider in the 1670s.
In the summer of 1679 he had sent Savile an apology for what is,
in effect, a failure in his chosen genre:

> If I had a mind to play the Politick, like a house of Commons
> man newly preferred to be a privy Counsellor, I should very
> gravely excuse myself for not writing to you by the last post,
> and lay the fault upon my want of leisure, . . . but having at
> their costs learnt, that those who make such discourses, cheat
> none but themselves, I ingenuously confess, I had nothing to
> say; and that now the Parliament is prorogued and the Court
> at Windsor, I hear little more than I shall do when I am dead.
> (p. 126)

This is an old man's voice. The Ciceronian accent is very faded. At
his trial, even Sidney's enemies adopted, in their satire against him,
the same elegiac tone:

> Welcome, kind Death: my long tired spirit bear
> From hated monarchy's detested air;
> . . . .
> View my hacked limbs, each honorable wound,
> The pride and glory of my numerous scars
> In Hell's best cause, the old republic wars.[37]

Synchronically with Sidney's correspondence, Savile was receiving letters of still another kind from his older brother, George, marquis of Halifax, who in April 1679, as a leading member of the reconstituted Privy Council, had suddenly become a major political figure. On 1 May 1679, he wrote to Savile in Paris:

> We are here every day upon high points: God send us once at an end of them! Impeachments of ministers [Danby], tryalls of peers for their life, discourses and votes too concerning the heir presumptive, are the only things our thoughts are employ'd about. And I that have dream't this half year of the silence and retirement of old Rufford [his country estate], find myself engaged in an active and an angry world, and must rather take my part in it with grief then avoid it with scandal. Whatever passes is sent to you of course, so that I shall never write any news to you except you bid me.[38]

The tone of this inter-Savile correspondence, in other words, is to be contemplative, a cut above the letter of mere news; its terms, whether self-consciously or not, are to be those of Ciceronian dialectic, political responsibility versus philosophical retirement. What will rescue it from the charge of imitation is the remarkable relevance of this topos to Halifax's actual situation in the next few months. When Charles prorogued Parliament until November 1680, Halifax, who had been attempting to mediate the Exclusionist crisis, was forced to take a stand. The stand he took was retirement to Rufford, symbolic of the Country party's disapproval of Court policy. Men like Burnet, Thynne, and Coventry wished him to stay there, because "they believed that by remaining in the country until the meeting of Parliament he should most clearly express the reality of his discontent."[39]

In October 1680, Halifax returned to London for the new session and the renewed Exclusionist battle; but by 25 January 1681 he was back in Rufford, in retreat from the fury of the House of Commons over what was perceived as his cooption by Charles. The letter he wrote to Henry on this occasion deserves quotation almost in full, because in it we hear the great tropes of Ciceronian self-justification occurring quite naturally:

> Though I cannot absolutely agree to your prescriptions of a looser morality in things that relate to the publick, yet I am enough convinced, and was so even before my late experience, that there is a good deal of hazard in opposing the torrent of a House of Commons; but on the other side, it being the only definition of an honest man to be a lover of justice with all its inconveniences, I do not very well know how things of this kind are to be avoided . . . I have had the good luck to have every unpopular thing imputed to me in the first place, and by going a strait way without any bypass, or engaging in any faction, one part of the world hath been much more violent against me than the other hath been in my defence. All these disadvantages did not move me so as to quit my ground whilst the Parlt. sat. I thought myself restrain'd by a necessary point of honour not to do that by compulsion which perhaps in itself was the thing in the world I most desir'd; but now that the Parliament is dissolved, I am going down to Rufford to breathe a little, and enjoy some quiet, which will be a very welcome thing to me; and when we meet again at Oxford I must venture to go into the storm, and receive the shot once more of an angry House of Commons. (1:277)

So had Cicero, against Atticus's prudential advice, and after much indecision, thrown in his lot with Pompey in 49 B.C., citing his duty throughout. But it is worth remembering that Cicero was also the first great articulate trimmer. "We should move with the times," he had written to Lentulus in 54 B.C.:

> For never have the distinguished men who steer the ship of state been praised for an undeviating persistence in one opinion. But just as in sailing it takes one kind of skill to run before the storm, even if you fail to make the port, when you could certainly get there by trimming your sails, and as it is downright stupid to keep your original course with all its dangers rather than change it and still arrive at your destination, so in state administration, while we should all aim at . . . peace with honour [cum

dignitate otium] that vision need not always be expressed in the same way.[40]

When Halifax circulated his *Character of a Trimmer* in 1684 he was still possessed by the same vision of an honorable peace; but the extent to which his expression of it had changed can be measured by what has become of the ship of state, in the pamphlet's governing metaphor:

> This innocent word Trimmer signifieth no more than this, that if men are together in a boat, and one part of the company would weigh it down of one side, another would make it lean as much to the contrary; it happeneth there is a third opinion of those who conceive it would do as well if the boat went even, without endangering the passengers.[41]

The range of what I have been calling natural "Ciceronianism" is, it should now be apparent, fairly wide. It extends from Marvell's passionate and satirical "gazettes" to Algernon Sidney's sober news letters; it accommodates Henry Savile's embarrassed allusions to "notable undertakings" as well as his brother's rotund protests about the burdens of state. What connects these ethicopolitical stances and the styles which carry them is the sense of a real relationship between sender and receiver, one in which trust is a prerequisite, and of a real need for the letter, which goes beyond "keeping in touch," and far beyond the formal or utilitarian contacts outlined in epistolary manuals. These are all letters written in times of crisis, and though they are not devoid of posturing, the pressure of events makes even their postures look natural. Although there are marked differences between them, they are alike enough in their assumptions, motifs, and metaphors to constitute a distinct category of familiar letter — in other words, a genre.

In a rather different sense, the "political letter to a friend" was actually recognized as a genre in the seventeenth century. In the 1640s political pamphlets began to be published as "Letters," exploiting any or all of these features: the difference in perspective between city and country, the sending of news, the giving of advice, the confidential sharing of political views. The genre established itself so quickly that its motifs could be used ironically or parodically. *A Letter sent From A Private Gentleman To A Friend in London, In Justification of his own adhering to His Majestie in these times of Distraction* (1642) is clearly a royalist tract, and the "friend" to whom it is addressed is clearly on the other side:

> Sir, I have receiv'd your Letter, and the Newes you sent me; though I have either seene or heard it all before, yet I give you many thanks for it. I would that either there were lesse newes, or better stirring. In your last letter I received nothing but chiding invectives. I wish you to examine your selfe how farre the profession of so much faith (as those of your opinion are full of) can stand with so little charity. (p. 2)

During the second Dutch war there appeared an anonymous *Lettre d'un Marchand de Londres A son amy a Amsterdam* (1666) attributed to Sir William Temple. Written in French, the letter plays ironically on the trust motif ("Aux amis il faut ouvrir le coeur . . . Parlons en confiance") to develop the theme that France was a false friend to England, that the French were promoting the Dutch war in order to weaken both sides in the interests of their own imperialism. The letter's object is to have its audience recognize "que les ennemis ouverts sont moins dangereux que les amis dissimulez." (p. 11)

But it was during the embattled 1670s and 1680s that this genre really became recognized and its examples ubiquitous. One of the most famous was the *Letter From a Person of Quality, To His Friend in the Country,* published in 1675 to make public the debates in the House of Lords over the infamous Non-Resisting Bill, or Test Act. Usually attributed to Shaftsbury, but sometimes to Marvell, it offers its recipient a firsthand account of the debate, in lively, colloquial, and personal terms, so that "your curiosity may be satisfied" (p. 31), and maintains the epistolary fiction with some care.[44] Other tracts, however, assert membership in the class by their title alone, and make no other gesture toward familiarization. This is very obviously the case with the 1681 *Letter from a Person of Quality to his Friend concerning His Majesties late Declaration touching the Reasons which moved him to dissolve the Two last Parliaments at Westminster and Oxford*! And when Halifax wrote his own reply to this pamphlet, he included in his attack a comment of its misuse of the genre:

> Out cometh a Letter to a Friend, which of late signifieth little less than a Proclamation set out by the Authority of the high and mighty Conservators of England, there is only this difference which is for their advantage, that if these Letters take in

the world, they are imputed to the wisdom of these great Governors; if not, they are easily laid upon some foolish fellow that would be scribling.[42]

Halifax's own exercise in this genre, the *Letter to a Dissenter* published in 1687, was both scrupulously epistolary in form and thematically decorous, since his appeal was for solidarity between Protestants as opposed to the seductive "new friendships" with Roman Catholics offered to the Dissenters under James's Declaration of Indulgence. Nothing could better illustrate the difference between the two conceptions of genre, formal and natural, than a comparison between this *Letter* and one to Henry Savile, written in March 1681. "Ask leave to come over for ten days," wrote Halifax, "and it must be done immediately, because of the uncertainty of the continuance of the (Parlt.). The end of this is, that you may see and consider the scene now that it is changed, examine how many of your old friends deserve to be kept, and what new ones are necessary to be made . . . It is not possible to write the particular reasons, but I think if you can prevail with yourself to do it, it may be very advantagious to you."[43] It must have been the experience of writing or receiving letters like this — full of advice, immediacy, affection, caution — which gave the pamphlet "Letters" some initial advantage in the competition for readers, some claims on people's attention; while the very proliferation of these imitative forms suggests the importance, in seventeenth-century political life, of the "real" thing.

Afterwords

*Three Sidneys, John Dryden,
and Jean-Jacques Rousseau*

The questions raised in the preceding chapter concerning the genre of familiar letters may not, as questions, be fully answerable. Are there natural genres in "the written universe"? Can a text be a member of a class without its author's claim, expressed or otherwise, to such membership? How can we determine the cultural assumptions that were actively a component of authorial intention? The value of posing such questions about the letter, however, despite their ultimate recalcitrance, is the exposure thereby gained on the methods of literary analysis in general. What we *must* see when we look at the familiar letter is a tangle of forces or causes that determine its production, its general form and function, its special and peculiar instances: education, which gives access to classical texts or intellectual traditions, and which makes possible the stance of "being a writer" or "being an intellectual"; political and social circumstances, which both demand and inhibit private, written communication; and last but certainly not least, the differentiating force of character and temperament. It is no coincidence that these three forces correspond, respectively, to methods of investigation often practiced separately: the study of literary tradition (including genre) as an intertextual system; "historical" or sociopolitical criticism; and biographical or psychoanalytical study of individual authors. What the familiar letter reminds us, in fact, is that the three kinds of story we have been told — of books and their influence; of public events, power, and money; and of individual careers, beliefs, allegiances, anxieties — are all aspects of a single inquiry.

I wish, therefore, to tie up this study of reading and writing in the

241

light of censorship with one last knot, which connects the letter back again to some of the issues raised in my introduction. This knot has three strands, each of which involves, at least slightly, a Sidney, and between them they span the period, returning us for a moment to the *Arcadia,* leaping to the end of the seventeenth century for a brief colloquy with John Dryden, and then expanding both geographically and chronologically to conclude with Rousseau. In the course of this final piece of selectivity, my own ideological commitments, at least with respect to the stance of "being a writer," should themselves cross over from the safe territory of the oblique, in which we have spent so much time, and make a bold face of it, whatever the consequences.

The first Sir Philip Sidney could well have taken a place in my discussion of the familiar letter, for several reasons. He was certainly well aware of the cultural significance of the letter. His Huguenot friend and mentor, Hubert Languet, had (in a letter) advised him to study both volumes of Cicero's correspondence, "not only for the beauty of the Latin, but also for the very important matter they contain. There is nowhere a better statement of the causes that overthrew the Roman republic."[1] Sidney had also met Henri Estienne, editor of the *Ad familiares,* in 1573, and was given or sent several of his publications.[2] He had himself written one notorious letter, advising Elizabeth against her projected marriage to Alençon; and in revising the *Arcadia* he had converted the advice of Philanax to Basilius (advice which if taken would have canceled the entire action of the romance) from a speech into a letter.

This did not, however, increase its authority. It had no more effect on Basilius than the speech; and Sidney ensured that its status as a document was presented to the reader as highly problematic. What we read is a text read to Musidorus by Kalander, who has acquired, so he says, an unauthorized copy of the original, through his son Clitophon:

> This sonne of mine (while the Prince kept his court) was of his bed-chamber; now since the breaking up thereof, returned home, and shewed me . . . the coppy which he had taken of a letter: which when the prince had read, he had laid in a window, presuming no body durst looke in his writings: but my sonne not only took a time to read it, but to copie it. In trueth I blamed Clitophon for the curiositie, which made him break his duetie in such a kind, whereby kings secrets are subject to be revealed:

but since it was done, I was content to take so much profite, as to know it.[3]

The representation of the purloined letter as a breach of privacy, the king's secrets revealed, might have been a subtle extension of the Ciceronian tradition that letters are the real stuff of which history is made; but the undermining of this letter's reliability (we read its text at three removes from the original, if there ever was one) places it squarely on the epistemological boundary between history and fiction, precisely that territory inhabited by the *Arcadia* as a whole. If Sidney also intended to allude to his own unsuccessful letter of advice to Elizabeth, that specific historical connection was only one aspect of his grasp of the central problem. In literary theory, as in historiography, the categories of "real," "forged," and "doctored" are extremely hard to distinguish.

A century and a decade later, John Dryden published a play, *Don Sebastian,* that he also advertised as written on the interface between history and fiction. Its historical subject was the story of Sebastian, king of Portugal, his defeat at the battle of Alcazar in 1578, and his possible survival as a stateless exile in Europe; but as Dryden said of his play, "'Tis purely fiction; for I take it up where the History has laid it down."[4] The story had considerable romantic potential, which had been fully explored by interpreters prior to Dryden, and which Dryden himself exploited; but it had also had a prehistory in the hermeneutics of censorship. Philip Massinger's *Believe As You List* had originally been written as a version of the Sebastian story; initially prohibited by Sir Henry Herbert, it was licensed for production only after Massinger had recast it in a Carthaginian setting.[5]

In 1690, two years after the revolution that expelled James II and brought in the Protestant William III, Dryden was writing in a far more dangerous environment than Massinger, especially because of his own recent and public conversion to Roman Catholicism. He was, therefore, particularly careful that his play not be capable of any obvious political allegorization, such as an identification of Sebastian with the recently deposed James.[6] In his plot, the crucial question of legitimacy is left indeterminate, complicated by the purely fictional incest that is the skeleton in Sebastian's family closet. Yet Dryden went out of his way to protect himself against misinterpretation, pointing out in his preface that the earl of Dorset, now Lord Chamberlain, "was pleas'd to read the Tragedy twice over before it was Acted; and did me the favour to send me the word, that . . . he was displeas'd any thing shou'd be cut away" (15:70–71). In other words, it had passed an inspection by one of the pillars, moderate but influential, of the new regime.

Still more to my point, however, was Dryden's dedication of the play in its printed version to Philip Sidney, third earl of Leicester, and grandnephew of *our* Sir Philip. The form or genre of the dedication was a familiar letter, chosen, as we shall see, for ideological reasons. For what Dryden creates in his epistle is a complicated typology that depends on his knowledge of the letter as a genre, and conveniently obscures his own political circumstances. First, he identifies Leicester as a second Atticus, implicitly proposing himself as a second Cicero, republican ethos and all. Second, he recalls the first Philip Sidney, and his patronage of Edmund Spenser. Notwithstanding the disclaimer that "there can never be another Spencer to deserve the Favor" of the second Sidney (15:63), the effect is to ally himself with writers known as Protestant activists.[7] The reader is therefore utterly confused as to where Dryden has stood, and now stands, ideologically.

More cleverly still, Dryden confuses the issue of where Leicester himself might be expected to stand in 1690. Once a member of the Long Parliament and advisor to Cromwell, now a retired aristocrat and literary patron, Leicester might well be seen as someone whose turn had now come round again on the slippery wheel of political fortune. Dryden specifically forbids such a prognosis. Both the first and the second Atticus, he argues, were mediatorial figures:

> Both of them born of Noble Families in unhappy Ages, of change and tumult; both of them retiring from Affairs of State: Yet, not leaving the Common-wealth, till it had left it self; but never returning to publick business, when they had once quitted it; tho courted by the Heads of either party . . . Their Philosophy on both sides, was not wholly speculative, for that is barren, and produces nothing but vain Ideas of things which cannot possibly be known; . . . but it was a noble, vigorous, and practical Philosophy, which exerted it self in all the offices of pity, to those who were unfortunate, and deserv'd not so to be. The Friend was always more consider'd by them than the cause: And an Octavius, or an Anthony in distress, were reliev'd by them, as well as a Brutus or a Cassius; For the lower-

most party, to a noble mind, is ever the fittest object of good
will. (15:61–62)

So Dryden, now himself suddenly a member of the lowermost party,
acknowledges the instability that Jonson had recorded in the *Under-
wood* poems, recalls, as Cowley had done in his *Brutus* ode, the slip-
periness of a Roman typology. The philosophy to which Dryden appeals is pragmatism, moderated by decency. "In every turn of State,
without meddling on either side," Leicester has "always been favor-
able and assisting to opprest Merit" (15:62). Without such generous
flexibility, it is the intellectuals who express themselves on every turn
of State who will become the victims of history.

There is considerable pathos, too, in the conclusion of Dryden's
epistle, where, as Miner has shown, he "brilliantly fuses" the endings
of two of Cicero's letters to Atticus, written in 58 B.C. when his best
prospect was immediate exile:

> Me, O Pomponi, valdè poenitet vivere: tantùm te oro, ut quo-
> niam me ipse semper amâsti, ut eodem amore sis; ego nimirum,
> idem sum. Inimici mei mea mihi non meipsum ademerunt.

> [I indeed, Pomponius, can scarcely bear to live on. One thing
> only I beg of you, since you have always loved me for myself,
> keep your love as it stands. I am still the same. My enemies have
> not robbed me of myself.][8]

As the ultimate protection against "turns of State," Dryden evoked
the idea of self, discovered as a point of stability *because* of "change
and tumult," the conditions he had lived with all his life. The voice
happens to be Cicero's; but it could just as easily be Jonson's, or
Donne's, or Marvell's, or Milton's.

Or the voice of Jean-Jacques Rousseau. For if there were ever a
paradigmatic figure in which the story of censorship connects with
the story of self-definition, that figure is Rousseau. It is not without
interest, however, that the study of Rousseau has been to a remarkable degree central to the development of postmodernist criticism.
In Jacques Derrida's *Of Grammatology* an argument is made for
following the trace of a particular term, the dangerous "supplement,"
the "blind spot" in certain of Rousseau's writings that revealed his
lack of faith in the existence of a "real" world, in anything except

writing itself.[9] And in Paul de Man's *Allegories of Reading,* such evidences of self-conscious textuality, of self-concealment, as the second preface to *Julie* (another epistolary novel) are defined as a new, postmodernist type of allegory, or irony, "no longer a trope but the undoing of the deconstructive allegory of all tropological cognitions, the systematic undoing, in other words, of understanding."[10] Again, as with *Don Quixote,* I do not wish to challenge these readings as a whole, a task which would take me into purely philosophical territory; but the historical logic of this study allows me, indeed requires me, to introduce the last strand of the knot of the letter's intersection with censorship.

Letters are a crucial part of the Rousseau canon; and none were more crucial than his extraordinary correspondence with Malesherbes, Director of the Book Trade, whose appointment to that position in 1750 had seemed to signal a great cultural liberation.[11] Rousseau introduces him (and the correspondence) in Book X of the *Confessions* as a man who governs "autant de lumières que de douceur, et à la grande satisfaction des gens de lettres."[12] In this same section, he explains how Malesherbes assisted him in the importation of his Amsterdam edition of *Julie* into France, and how he actually arranged for a specially printed "exemplaire" intended for Mme. de Pompadour to be expurgated, so that a particular phrase he thought would be objectionable to her would disappear. Rousseau describes this constructive act of censorship as a "tour de passe-passe."

A little later in Book X, however, the question arises as to how and where *Emile* is to be published; and Rousseau recounts an argument between himself and Mme. de Luxembourg:

> une longue dispute, moi prétendant que la permission tacite était impossible à obtenir, imprudente même à demander, et ne voulant point permettre autrement l'impression dans le royaume; elle soutenant que cela ne ferait pas même une difficulté à la censure, dans le système que le gouvernement avait adopté. (1:327)[13]

To Rousseau's surprise, Malesherbes, we are told, involved himself in the dispute, and wrote him "une longue lettre tout à sa main," in which he persuaded him that a French edition of the work was by no means out of the question, it being "précisément une pièce faite pour avoir partout l'approbation du genre humain, et celle de la Cour dans la circonstance." It was, of course, the eventual publication of

Emile in two editions, one in Holland and one in France, that resulted in Rousseau's public condemnation and banishment from his country.

But letters lead also to letters. In anxious anticipation of the consequences of this decision, which had to some extent been taken out of his own hands, he wrote the *Quatres lettres à M. le Président de Malesherbes contenant le vrai tableau de mon caractère et les vrais motifs de toute ma conduite,* letters designed to "suppléer aux mémoires" and which were indeed the embryo of the *Confessions.*[14] And in 1764 he published his *Lettres écrites de la montagne,* in answer to the burning of *Emile* and of the *Contrat social* in Geneva, and specifically to the hostile *Lettres écrites de la campagne* of Jean-Robert Tronchin, procurator general of Geneva. In that parodic version of the genre that had developed in the seventeenth century as a vehicle of political controversy, he tackled one after another the principles of freedom of expression, beginning with the question of authorial intention, and the right, therefore, of the author to be heard in his own cause:

> Des principes établis, la chaîne d'un raisonnement suivi, des conséquences déduites manifestent l'intention de l'auteur, et cette intention dépendant de sa volonté rentre sous la juridiction des lois. (3:403)

And in the sixth letter he compared himself not only to Locke and to Montesquieu, who had expressed with impunity theories similar to his own in the *Contrat Social,* but also to Sir Algernon Sidney, executed for suspected involvement in the Rye House Plot, and cited for possession of a manuscript refuting Filmer's *Patriarcha.* The difference between Sidney and himself, according to Rousseau (who had read with care Montesquieu's analysis of censorship in the *Esprit des lois*), was that Sidney was condemned for actions, himself for words alone: "L'infortuné Sydney pensait comme moi, mais il agissait; c'est pour son fait et non pour son livre qu'il eut l'honneur de verser son sang" (3:454).

Rousseau's definition of self, from the beginning of the 1760s, was thus a circular process, circumscribed by letters (in both senses) which led to his convictions (in both senses) and therefore to "lettres sur lettres," as he put it in the *Confessions* (1:339). His books became, because of the extraordinary developments in the censorship system, events, which in turn provoked more writing, more self-definition and self-justification. The "permission tacite," which, as I have argued, was the normal *implicit* relationship between writers and the authorities in early modern Europe, had actually been formalized as a bureaucratic procedure in France and, under Malesherbes's liberal regime, was regularly put to use;[15] but in this instance, the result of the "permission tacite," in conjunction with Rousseau's own eccentricities and the impending confrontation between the French government and the Jesuits, was a situation of impenetrable intricacy and injustice. Rousseau found himself responsible for publishing in Paris a clandestine edition of *Emile,* under a Dutch imprint, an arrangement at which Malesherbes had himself connived; and because he thought that he was thereby protected, because he had originally intended the book to be printed only in Holland, and therefore refused to have it subjected to expurgation by the French censors, Rousseau found that he had provoked the very confrontation he had hoped to avoid. The final, classic irony was that, in distaste for the web of subterfuge into which he had been drawn, he refused to publish *Emile* anonymously; and it was precisely that gesture, apparently, that provoked the Paris *parlement* to take action for his arrest. The warrant stated "that it was important, in view of the fact that he had not concealed his identity, that justice should take the opportunity of making an example."[16] Small wonder that, in the face of such dangerous paradoxes, Rousseau should have imagined himself the victim of a conspiracy; nor that he should have been propelled by this experience into a lifelong meditation on the meaning of authorship and the rights of the self to expression.

In the *Lettres écrites de la montagne* he would later deliver a scathing attack on the principle of the *permission tacite,* on anonymous publication, and the social bad faith thereby promoted; and in the course of this attack he made some crucial observations about authorship which bear repeating, particularly in the light of our own critical climate in the 1980s:

> La distinction . . . entre le livre et l'auteur est inepte, puisqu'un livre n'est pas punissable. Un livre n'est en lui-même ni impie ni téméraire; . . . Quand on brûle un livre, que fait là le bourreau? Déshonore-t-il les feuillets du livre? qui jamais ouït dire qu'un livre eût de l'honneur?
>
> Voilà l'erreur: en voici la source: un usage mal entendu.
>
> On écrit beaucoup de livres; on en écrit peu avec un désir sincère d'aller au bien. De cent ouvrages qui paraissent, soixante

au moins ont pour objet des motifs d'intérêt ou d'ambition. . . .
Dix, peut-être, et c'est beaucoup, sont écrits dans de bonnes vues:
on y dit la vérité qu'on sait, on y cherche le bien qu'on aime.
Oui: mais où est l'homme à qui l'on pardonne la vérité? Il faut
donc se cacher pour le dire. Pour être utile impunément, on lâche
son livre dans le public, et l'on fait le plongeon.

De ces divers livres, quelques-uns des mauvais et à peu près
tous les bons sont dénoncés et proscrits dans les tribunaux: la
raison de cela se voit sans que je la dise. Ce n'est, au surplus,
qu'une formalité, pour ne pas paraître approuver tacitement ces
livres. Du reste, pourvu que les noms des auteurs n'y soient pas,
ces auteurs, quoique tout le monde les connaisse et les nomme,
ne sont pas connus du magistrat. . . . De cette façon la sûreté
ne coûte rien à la vanité. (3:455)

[The distinction between the book and the author is unusable,
because a book is not punishable. A book is in itself neither
impious nor rash. When a book is burned, what does the exe-
cutioner accomplish? Does it dishonor the pages of the book?
Who ever heard tell that a book has honor?

Here is the error; and here is its source—a misunderstood
practice.

Many books are written, but few with a sincere desire to do
good. Out of every hundred published works, sixty at least have
for their objective motives of interest or ambition . . . Ten, perhaps, and that is generous, are written with good aims: one
speaks the truth that one knows, one seeks the good that one
loves. Yes: but where is the man who may be forgiven for his
truthfulness? In order to speak truth, it is necessary to hide.
To be useful with impunity, one casts one's book at the public,
and ducks one's head.

Of these various books, some of the bad ones and almost
all of the good ones are denounced and proscribed by the tribu-
nals. The reason for this is clear without my having to explain
it. It is only, at the most, a formality, not to appear to give tacit
approval. For the rest, provided that the names of the authors
are not given, these authors, although everybody knows who
they are and identifies them, are not "known" to the magistrate.
. . . In this manner, one can have safety at no cost to one's
vanity.]

It is in the light of these statements, and the experience that gave rise to them, that we need to reassess Rousseau's extraordinary unreliability as a historian of the self, which is so at variance with his obsession with the truth, as expressed in his personal motto: "Vitam impendere vero." In this late development of the hermeneutics of censorship, the always-difficult art of sincerity was made virtually impossible by the accepted norms and procedures of publication, norms and procedures which the Director of the Book Trade had himself, with the best of intentions, rendered totally arcane.

We might, therefore, compare with a deconstructive reading of Rousseau's work in general a passage which opens the twelfth book of the *Confessions,* where he pauses to reflect on the consequences of his publication of *Emile.* Here, in the language of darkness, veiling, cloud, and obscurity which is typical of his representation of this passage in his life,[17] Rousseau handed over to the reader the responsibility for interpreting the material that has just been passed before him:

> Ici commence l'oeuvre de ténèbres dans lequel depuis huit ans je me trouve enseveli, sans que de quelque façon que je m'y sois pu prendre il m'ait été possible d'en percer l'effrayante obscurité. Dans l'abîme de maux où je suis submergé, je sens les attentes des coups qui me sont portés, j'en aperçois l'instrument immédiat, mais je ne puis voir ni la main qui dirige, ni les moyens qu'elle met en oeuvre. . . . Ces causes primitives sont toutes marquées dans les trois précédents livres; tous les intérêts relatifs à moi, tous les motifs secrets y sont exposés. Mais dire en quoi ces diverses causes se combinent pour opérer les étranges événements de ma vie: voilà ce qu'il m'est impossible d'expliquer, même par conjecture. Si parmi mes lecteurs il s'en trouve d'assez généreux pour vouloir approfondir ces mystères et découvrir la verité, qu'ils relisent avec soin les trois précédents livres, qu'ensuite à chacque fait qu'ils liront dans les suivants ils prennent les informations qui seront à leur portée, qui'ils remontent d'intrigue en intrigue et d'agent en agent jusqu'aux prémiers moteurs de tout, je sais certainement à quel terme aboutiront leurs recherches, mais je me perds dans la route obscure et tortueuse des souterrains qui les y conduiront. (1:348)

Because it would ruin this passage to translate it, let me simply suggest that this disclaimer, this formal transfer of the interpretive responsibility, while a move entirely characteristic of Rousseau, is also characteristic of many of the texts examined elsewhere in this book; that the stress on the difficulty of understanding is a sign of the hermeneutics of censorship, and appears *additionally* powerful if we recognize it as coming at the end of a long tradition, a tradition of self-restraint and evasive tactics. It is also interesting to note Rousseau's ambiguous use (twice) of the word "oeuvre," the work of darkness in which for the last eight years he has found himself enshrouded, and in which books and events are inextricably involved. And finally, it is surely not without relevance to the subsequent history of Rousseau criticism that he himself, in this passage, speaks of the "abîme" of evils, bad things, in which he is submerged, and which, whatever else may be said of him, he did not excavate for himself unilaterally. Facing such a passage, it is hard to conceive how a theory of his work could have been constructed on the premise that "there is nothing outside the text," that it is the concept of the supplement and textuality itself, in an indefinitely multiplied structure, that constitutes the state of being "en abyme," and that "this abyss is not a happy or unhappy accident."[18]

This book of mine, then, is written in defense of the cluster of principles to which Rousseau declared himself committed, and to which his career, however imperfectly and ambiguously, bears witness. Especially as enlarged by the careers and principles of the other writers discussed in earlier chapters, we recognize this cluster conceptually under the title of liberal humanism, and we recognize it also as a tradition with very long roots, going back to classical antiquity. It is, however, a concept and a tradition that has been recently much under attack, even within our own profession. Whatever other motives inevitably enter into any publication of this kind, I hope they will be forgiven in the light of my stated intentions; for if we in the academy do not defend the tradition of liberal humanism, it is not clear from what direction such a defense might come, or whether it will be in time.

Notes
Index

Notes

Introduction

1. The best introduction to English censorship is F.S. Siebert, *Freedom of the Press in England, 1476–1776* (Urbana, 1952). See also, on England, Virginia Gildersleeve, *Government Regulation of the Elizabethan Drama* (1908; rpt. Westport, Conn., 1975); Charles Gillett, *Burned Books: Neglected Chapters in British History and Literature*, 2 vols. (New York, 1932); Lawrence Hanson, *Government and the Press, 1695–1763* (London, 1936); Donald Thomas, *A Long Time Burning: The History of Literary Censorship in England* (London, 1969); Leona Rostenberg, *The Minority Press and the English Crown: A Study in Repression, 1558–1625* (Niewkoop, 1979); G. R. Elton, *Policy and Police* (Cambridge, 1972); Denis B. Woodfield, *Surreptitious Printing in England, 1550–1640* (New York, 1973); D. M. Loades, "The Theory and Practice of Censorship in Sixteenth-Century England," *Transactions of the Royal Historical Society*, 5th ser., 24 (1974): 141–57. For France in the early modern period, see H.-J. Martin, *Livre, pouvoirs et société à Paris au XVIIe siècle (1598–1701)*, 2 vols. (Geneva, 1969); Alfred Soman, "Press, Pulpit, and Censorship in France before Richelieu," *Proceedings of the American Philosophical Society* 120, no. 6 (1976): 439–63; and for at least one major area of Italian censorship, Paul Grendler, *The Roman Inquisition and the Venetian Press, 1540–1605* (Princeton, 1977), which provides valuable insight into the compromises made between the Holy Office, the political interests of the Venetian republic, and the practical needs of the bookmen for survival.
2. For this early crisis in French censorship, see David T. Pottinger, *The French Book Trade in the Ancient Regime, 1500–1791* (Cambridge, Mass., 1958), pp. 56–57. For Marot's involvement, see P. M. Smith, *Clément Marot:*

255

Poet of the French Renaissance (London, 1970), pp. 17–31; and C. A. Mayer, *Clément Marot* (Paris, 1972), pp. 258–375.

3. Clément Marot, *Les Epîtres,* ed. C. A. Mayer (1958; rpt. London, 1964), pp. 202–03.

4. See Smith, *Clément Marot,* pp. 71–77; and Mayer, *Clément Marot,* pp. 83–131, especially p. 130, where the gesture is interpreted as symbolic defiance of the Roman Catholic church.

5. Marot, *Oeuvres Satiriques,* ed. C. A. Mayer (London, 1962), pp. 68–69.

6. Marot, *Oeuvres Lyriques,* ed. C. A. Mayer (London, 1964), pp. 343–53.

7. Václav Havel, "History of a Public Enemy," *New York Review of Books* 37, no. 9 (May 31, 1990):38.

8. In 1976 Havel, having involved himself in a campaign for the release of a group of hippy singers, The Plastic People, repudiated "the world of 'rear' exits," as he called the artificial protection of writers with a reputation outside Czechoslovakia; but it was not until the following year, when he helped to organize the famous Charter 77, a human rights document, that the authorities instituted the series of arrests and releases that finally culminated in his four-year prison term, beginning in May 1979.

9. Václav Havel, *Letters to Olga,* trans. Paul Wilson (New York, 1989). See also "The Trial of Alyosha," a review of the *Letters* by Janet Malcolm, *New York Review of Books* 37, no. 10 (June 14, 1990):35–38.

10. Havel, *Letters to Olga,* p. 262.

11. Malcolm, "Trial of Alyosha," p. 35.

12. *Epistolae Ho-Elianae: The Familiar Letters of James Howell,* ed. Joseph Jacobs, 2 vols. (London, 1892), p. 469.

13. Soman, "Press, Pulpit, and Censorship," p. 455.

14. Philip J. Finkelpearl, " 'The Comedians' Liberty': Censorship of the Jacobean Stage Reconsidered," *English Literary Renaissance* 16 (1986):123–38. This article adopts mainly the inefficiency and venality thesis, and only in its last paragraph takes cognizance of "arcane codes mastered by the cognoscenti" (p. 138).

15. See my *Shakespeare and the Popular Voice* (Oxford, 1989), pp. 80–88.

16. Elizabeth's comment was "I am Richard II. Know ye not that?" See *Richard II,* ed. Peter Ure (Cambridge, Mass., 1956), pp. lvii–lxii. For the stage history of *A Game at Chess,* see R. C. Bald's edition (Cambridge, 1929), pp. 19–25; for the revision required in Massinger's *Believe As You List,* see Philip Edwards and Colin Gibson, eds., *The Plays and Poems of Philip Massinger,* 5 vols. (Oxford, 1976), 3:293.

17. Lord Chesterfield, in *Versions of Censorship,* ed. John McCormick and Mairi MacInnes (Chicago, 1962), p. 323.

18. See L. W. Conolly, *The Censorship of English Drama, 1737–1824* (San Marino, 1976), pp. 109–10.

19. Alexsandr Nikitenko, *Diary of a Russian Censor,* trans. Helen Sallis Jacobsen (Amherst, 1975), pp. 64–65.

20. John Tasker, "Censorship in the Theatre," in *Australia's Censorship Crisis*, ed. Geoffrey Dutton and Max Harris (Melbourne, 1970), p. 38.

21. Frederick M. Ahl, *Lucan: An Introduction* (Ithaca, 1976), especially pp. 25–35: "The Man of Letters in a Totalitarian Society." The quotation from Quintilian is from *Institutio Oratoria*, IX.ii.67.

22. *A Myrrour for Magistrates* (1559), ed. L. B. Campbell (Cambridge, 1938; rpt. New York, 1960), p. 66. See also L. B. Campbell, "The Suppressed Edition of *A Mirror for Magistrates*," *Huntington Library Bulletin* 6 (1934):1–16.

23. Sir Francis Bacon, *Essays*, ed. Michael Kiernan (Cambridge, Mass., 1985), p. 44.

24. Francis Bacon, *A Wise and Moderate Discourse, concerning Church-affairs* (1641), p. 11. Though first printed posthumously as a comment on the Smectymnuan controversy, Bacon's pamphlet was written in 1589. The quotation from Tacitus is from the *Annals* IV, 35.

25. Daniel Balmuth, *Censorship in Russia, 1865–1905* (Washington, D.C., 1979), pp. 141–43.

26. "I, the censor," from *Censorship and Political Communications in Eastern Europe*, ed. George Schöpflin (London, 1983), p. 107.

27. Nikitenko, *Diary of a Russian Censor*, pp. 82–83.

28. Ibid., p. 167: "There is *lighting* progress and *gradual* progress. If I had to label myself according to one of these categories, I would call myself a moderate progressive. I have little faith in those doctrines which promise society infinite happiness and perfection, but I do believe in mankind's need to develop."

29. Ibid., p. 208: "I come from the ranks of the people. I am a plebeian from head to toe, but I do not accept the idea that it is wise to give the people power. Not everybody in this world can be content, educated, or virtuous."

30. Christopher Hill, review in *Literature and History*, 12, no. 2 (Autumn, 1986):252–53.

31. Mario Vargas Llosa, "The Writer in Latin America," in *They Shoot Writers, Don't They?*, ed. George Theiner (London and Boston, 1984), p. 168. The purpose of Llosa's essay, however, is to argue that this *expectation* of social purpose from the Latin American writer constitutes another kind of censorship for those who (like Borges) only wish to write about metaphysics and fantasy.

32. Leo Strauss, *Persecution and the Art of Writing* (Westport, Conn., 1952).

33. Toland seems to have been at best a scamp with libertarian instincts and at worst an arduous plagiarizer and time-server. See A. B. Worden, ed., *Edmund Ludlow: A Voice from the Watch Tower* (Camden Society, 4th Series, Vol. 21 London, 1978), pp. 22–80.

34. For a devastating account of Straussianism, see Shadia Drury, *The Political Ideas of Leo Strauss* (New York, 1988). See also Stephen Holmes, "Truths for Philosophers Alone?" *Times Literary Supplement* 1–7, (December,

1989):1319–24, which builds on Drury's critique, but substitutes for her clarity and forthrightness a brilliant and blistering humor.

35. Leo Strauss, *What Is Political Philosophy? and Other Studies* (Glencoe, 1959), pp. 221–22.

36. For a brief biography of Leo Strauss, see Allan Bloom, "Leo Strauss: September 20, 1889–October 18, 1973," *Political Theory* 2, no. 4 (November 1974):372–92. Strauss left Germany in 1932, first for France and England, and then, in 1938, for the United States, where he taught at the New School for Social Research in New York, and then, from 1949 to 1968, at the University of Chicago, where his influence was profound.

37. Strauss, *Persecution and the Art of Writing,* p. 33.

38. Hans-Georg Gadamer, *Truth and Method* (New York, 1975), p. 488. Originally published as *Wahrheit und Methode* (Tübingen, 1960).

39. Louis Althusser, "Ideology and Ideological State Apparatuses," in *Lenin and Philosophy and Other Essays* (New York, 1972), pp. 127–92.

40. Michel Foucault, *The Archeology of Knowledge,* trans. A.M. Sheridan Smith (New York, 1976), pp. 34–38, 224. See also the elucidation of this concept by Frank Lentricchia, *After the New Criticism* (Chicago, 1980), pp. 190–99.

41. Jacques Lacan, *Écrits* (Paris, 1966), p. 158. Lacan identifies the factor of displacement or *Verschiebung* (the veering off of signification) which takes place in metonymy as one of the major devices employed by the unconscious to *elude* censorship, and compares it, with a reference to Strauss, to the function of metonymy in circumventing the obstacles of social censure.

42. I am uncomfortable, therefore, with the use that has been made of my theory by Kevin Sharpe, in *Criticism and Compliment: The Politics of Literature in the England of Charles I* (Cambridge, 1987), where unquestionable evidence of "allowances" in the theater leads Sharpe to the assertion that "there is little substance to the spectre of censorship that stalks Butler's (and others') pages" (p. 39), and even to the self-canceling statement "We know of no voice that was silenced" (p. 37).

43. Soman, "Press, Pulpit, and Censorship," p. 456.

44. Christopher Hill was, I believe, the only reviewer to complain that I *underemphasized* the negative effect of censorship, mentioning my omissions of the Martin Marprelate pamphleteers, many of whom were executed; George Wither, who spent years in prison; John Lilburne, who was imprisoned and flogged. Indeed, the list could be almost indefinitely extended, especially if one includes the trials of Jesuits or the treatment of political figures, like Sir John Hoskyns, who made allusions in the House of Commons that James I did not care for. My point, however, was to list not the victims of censorship but rather its literary consequences. Hill, whose "Censorship and English literature," in *Collected Essays* (Brighton, Sussex, 1986), 1:32–71, should be consulted by anyone interested in the subject, writes primarily from the perspective of a historian, whereas I was attempting to mediate between the two disciplines.

45. It really needs to be doubled in length. A full treatment of the topic, with
respect to early modern England alone, would certainly now include a chapter
on Milton, especially *Paradise Lost,* which invokes the *Myrroure's* concept of the "ancient liberty" of literature in its opening comments on blank
verse, a "key" to the politics of the poem. Some omissions I have dealt
with elsewhere. The extremely important case of the 1587 "Holinshed"
was drawn to my attention by Elizabeth Story Donno's article "Some Aspects
of Shakespeare's Holinshed," *Huntington Library Quarterly* 50 (1987):
229–47, provoking a paper delivered at the English Institute. My interest
in the genre of the beast fable—the origins of Aesopian writing—led first
to an essay, "Fables of Power," in *Politics of Discourse,* ed. Kevin Sharpe
and Steven Zwicker (Berkeley and Los Angeles, 1987), pp. 271–96, and
then to a monograph, forthcoming from Duke University Press. The "secret
meaning" of Spenser's *Shepheardes Calender* is discussed in my *Pastoral
and Ideology* (Berkeley and Los Angeles, 1987), pp. 118–31; but the
"calling-in" of Spenser's *Complaints,* his hostile relationship with Burghley,
and its effects on *The Faerie Queene,* need to be thoroughly reinvestigated.
   In the interim, the problems of theatrical control or allowance have been
further explored by Martin Butler, in *Theatre and Crisis, 1632–1642* (Cambridge, 1984); by William Empson, *Faustus and the Censor,* ed. J. H. Jones
(Oxford, 1987); and by Janet Clare, " 'Greater Themes for Insurrections
Arguing': Politic Censorship of the Elizabethan and Jacobean Stage," *Review
of English Studies* 38 (1987):169–83. In *Secret Rites and Secret Writings:
Royalist Literature, 1641–1660* (Cambridge, 1989), Lois Potter has much
advanced the discussion of writing produced by royalists during the Commonwealth and Protectorate. Apart from essays on the meaning (and censorship) of Marvell's *Miscellaneous Poems* in 1681 (in *The Political Identity of Andrew Marvell,* ed. Conal Condren and A. D. Cousins [Berkeley,
1990]), and on the censorship of Sir Robert Howard's *The Country Gentleman*
(*Studies in English Literature* 25 [1985]:491–509), which should really be
included here, I have still not fully grappled with 1660–1770; but the gap
has already been partly and tantalizingly filled by Steven Zwicker's *Politics
and Language in Dryden's Poetry: The Arts of Disguise* (Princeton, 1984),
and by Richard Ashcraft's *Revolutionary Politics and Locke's* Two Treatises
of Government (Princeton, 1986), which contains an important chapter on
"The Language of Conspiracy."
46. See Patterson, "Intention," in *Critical Terms for Literary Study,* ed. Frank
Lentricchia and Thomas McLaughlin (Chicago and London, 1990),
pp. 135–46.
47. *The Rehearsal Transpros'd,* ed. D. I. B. Smith (Oxford, 1971), p. xxii.
48. Ibid., p. xx.

1. "Under . . . pretty tales": Intention in Sidney's Arcadia

1 C. S. Lewis, *English Literature in the Sixteenth Century* (Oxford, 1954),
p. 339.

2 Fulke Greville, *The Life of the Renowned Sir Phillip Sidney* (London, 1652), p. 18.

3 *A Discourse of Syr Ph. S. To The Queenes Majesty Touching Hir Marriage With Monsieur* survives in a number of manuscripts, but was first published only in 1663. See *The Complete Works of Sir Philip Sidney,* ed. A. Feuillerat, 4 vols. (Cambridge, 1912; rpt. 1969), 3:51–60, 385–86.

4 J. E. Neale, *Elizabeth I and Her Parliaments, 1559–1581* (New York, 1953), 1:393–98.

5 Evidence for dating is discussed by William Ringler, ed., *The Poems of Sir Philip Sidney* (Oxford, 1962), p. 365; and by Jean Robertson, ed., *The Countess of Pembroke's Arcadia* (The Old Arcadia) (Oxford, 1973), pp. xv–xvii. On their painstaking analysis of the text and manuscript tradition all serious analysis of the *Arcadia* depends. Where they differ, as on the date of completion of the *Old Arcadia* and of the beginning of work on the *New,* I lean toward Robertson, whose edition I cite throughout this chapter.

6 Greville reported in a letter to Walsingham that Sidney had left with him the only manuscript of the *New Arcadia,* along with directions for its editing, but did not specify further. Ringler, on the basis of manuscript evidence and the prefatory note to the 1590 edition, concluded that it was left entirely up to the editors to insert or delete the eclogues "they considered appropriate" (p. 372). This conclusion can be accepted only with qualifications.

7 *Complete Works of Sir Philip Sidney,* 3:132, 1:3–4. All quotations from the *New Arcadia* are from *Complete Works,* Vol. 1.

8 *The Countesse of Pembrokes Arcadia* (London, 1593), ¶4.

9 Sir Philip Sidney, *An Apology for Poetry,* ed. Geoffrey Shepherd (London, 1965), p. 116.

10 George Puttenham, *Arte of English Poesie* (1589), eds. G. D. Willcock and A. Walker (Cambridge, 1936), p. 38.

11 Edwin Greenlaw, "Sidney's Arcadia as an Example of Elizabethan Allegory," *Kittredge Anniversary Papers* (New York, 1913), pp. 327–37.

12 "Then will the Princes of Christendom be forced to wake up from their deep sleep"; "Our princes are enjoying too deep a slumber; nevertheless, while they indulge in this repose, I would have them beware that they fall not into that malady, in which death itself goes in hand with its counterpart." Letters of 15 April and 7 May 1574, *The Correspondence of Sir Philip Sidney and Hubert Languet,* ed. Steuart Pears (London, 1854), pp. 48, 59. The Sidney-Languet correspondence was first published in Latin in Frankfurt in 1633. Translations were provided by Pears and by James Osborn, *Young Philip Sidney, 1572–1577* (New Haven, 1972).

13 The *Life*'s subtitle was "The True Interest of England as it then stood in relation to all Forrain Princes: And particularly for suppressing the power of Spain."

14 Neil Rudenstine, *Sidney's Poetic Development* (Cambridge, Mass., 1967). Rudenstine's opening chapters do, however, relate the *Arcadia*'s contents to the Sidney-Languet correspondence, implying an expressive theory of literature. The *Arcadia* "reveals itself . . . as a fictional extension of Sid-

ney's letters in defense of relaxation, reflection, and a life of dignified ease" (p. 46), in other words, as a fictional defense of pastoral *otium,* rather than a critique of it.

15 Walter Davis and Richard Lanham, *Sidney's Arcadia* (New Haven and London, 1965), p. 197.

16 Dorothy Connell, *Sir Philip Sidney: The Maker's Mind* (Oxford, 1977), pp. 102–13.

17 Richard McCoy, *Sir Philip Sidney: Rebellion in Arcadia* (New Brunswick, N.J., 1979), p. x.

18 Compare Dennis Moore, *The Politics of Spenser's Complaints and Sidney's Philisides* (Salzburg Elizabethan and Renaissance Studies No. 101).

19 W. D. Briggs, "Political Ideas in Sidney's *Arcadia." Studies in Philology* 28 (1931): 137–61; and "Sidney's Political Ideas," *Studies in Philology* 29 (1932): 534–42.

20 Irving Ribner, "Sir Philip Sidney on Civil Insurrection," *Journal of the History of Ideas* 13 (1952): 257–65.

21 Ringler, *Poems,* p. 413; endorsed by Robertson, *Countess of Pembrokes Arcadia,* p. 464.

22 Andrew Weiner, *Sir Philip Sidney and the Poetics of Protestantism* (Minneapolis, 1978), pp. 135–38.

23 Ringler, *Poems,* p. 414, points out that the tale combines Aesop's fable with the late-classical myth of how Prometheus created man, as told by Horace, *Carmina* I, 16. Readers would also, no doubt, have assumed an allusion to 1 Samuel 8:5 ff.

24 John Ogilby, *The Fables of Aesop Paraphras'd in Verse* (1668), ed. Earl Miner (Los Angeles, 1965), p. 31.

25 *Jacopo Sannazaro: Arcadia and Piscatorial Eclogues,* trans. Ralph Nash (Detroit, 1966), pp. 116, 118–19.

2. Prynne's Ears; or,
The Hermeneutics of Censorship

1 For accounts of Hayward's *Life* and its consequences, see F. J. Levy, *Tudor Historical Thought* (San Marino, 1967), pp. 261–62; S. L. Goldberg, "Sir John Hayward, 'Political Historian,'" *Review of English Studies* 6 (1955): 233–44; and Margaret Dowling, "Sir John Hayward's Trouble over His Life of Henry IV," *The Library,* 4th ser., 11 (1931): 212–24.

2 *Letters of John Chamberlain,* ed. Norman McLure, 2 vols., (Philadelphia, 1939), 1:70.

3 Thomas Scott, *Vox Regis* (London, 1622), pp. 34–35.

4 Examples that bear directly on the materials of this chapter or its methodology are: David Bevington, *Tudor Drama and Politics* (Harvard, 1968), especially the chapter entitled "Some Approaches to Topical Meaning," pp. 8–25; Barbara de Luna, *Jonson's Romish Plot: A Study of "Catiline" and Its Historical Contexts* (Oxford, 1967), which explains Jonson's Roman plays as a means "of covertly commenting on, and criticizing, the events" of an era of censorship (p. 1); Stephen Orgel, *The Illusion of Power* (Berkeley and Los Angeles, 1975), a highly influential introduction to the political implications of Caroline court drama and masque; Dale Ran-

dall, *Jonson's Gypsies Unmasked* (Durham, N.C., 1975), which contains a brief rationale for topical readings (pp. 12–16); Margot Heinemann, *Puritanism and Theatre: Thomas Middleton and Opposition Drama under the Early Stuarts* (Cambridge, 1980); and Jonathan Goldberg, *James I and the Politics of Literature* (Baltimore, 1983), a Foucauldian account of the discursive rules established by James I, by rhetorical example rather than by institutional pressures in the usual sense.

5 John Southerden Burn, *The Star Chamber: Notices of the Court and Its Proceedings* (London, 1870), p. 129. The ritual element of such punishment has been brilliantly described by Alfred Soman, "Press, Pulpit, and Censorship in France before Richelieu," *Proceedings of the American Philosophical Society* 120, no. 6 (1976): 439–63, especially p. 452. The ritual function of such acts of mutilation, book burning, or press smashing was equally understood in England. Soman draws attention to a diplomatic letter from Sir Dudley Carleton, ambassador to the Hague, in February 1618, in which he complained about the inadequate response of the States General to his protest against Venator's *Theologia vera & mera:* "The book, of which I have so much complained as scandalous to his majesty, and seditious in respect of this state, is translated into French, with the addition of a satirical preface and a scornful prefixion of the motto of the garter; which hath forced me to speak to the states general in this subject. . . . Upon my complaint hereof to mons. Barnevelt, he acquainted the states of Holland therewith and they caused certain copies to be sent for from the stationers (where they were publicly sold for the space of three days without controlment) and burnt them in the chamber of their assembly; which, if it had been done in the market-place, had been some satisfaction: but of an execution *a huis clos* the world cannot take knowledge," *Letters from and to Sir Dudley Carleton* (London, 1757), p. 243.

6 John Hayward, *The first part of the life and raigne of King Henrie the IIII . . . by J. H.* (London, 1599), Aiir: "(illustrissime comes) cuius nomen si Henrici fronti radiaret, ipse & laetior & tutior in vulgus prodiret . . . Hunc igitur si laeta fronte excipere digneris, sub nominis tui umbra (tanquam sub Aiacis clipio Teucer ille Homericus) tutissime latebit."

7 C. H. Herford, P. Simpson, and E. Simpson, eds., *Works,* 11 vols. (Oxford, 1925–52), 11:253.

8 See Jonas Barish, ed., *Sejanus His Fall* (New Haven, 1965), pp. 16–17; and Herford and Simpson, *Works,* 1:36–37.

9 Goldberg, *James I and the Politics of Literature,* argues that "Roman" drama in this period was primarily the result of James's own preference for seeing himself in imperial terms. This causes certain problems of chronology, since the English interest in Roman history as a source of plot, theme, metaphor, and even ideology neither began nor ended with the reign of James; witness Shakespeare's *Elizabethan* Roman plays, the liminal status of the 1603 *Sejanus,* the tendentious use of Lucan during the civil war, or Marvell's use of Suetonius as a metaphor for the cultural climate of the 1670s. The point could be more safely made in more general terms: as English intellectuals tried to come to terms with different styles of monarchical absolutism, they constantly returned, for a

frame of reference, to the most relevant sections of the history of imperial Rome.

10 Jonson, *Works*, 11:314, 316–17. On these poems, see also Norbert Platz, "'By Oblique Glance of His Licentious Pen,'" in *Recent Research on Ben Jonson* (Salzburg, 1978), pp. 72–76.

11 This is the argument used by Bevington, *Tudor Drama and Politics*, pp. 8–25, to *limit* the scope of topical reading.

12 Tacitus, *Annals*, IV, 34.

13 Francis Bacon, *A Wise and Moderate Discourse, concerning Church-affairs* (1641), p. 11. Though first printed posthumously as a comment on the Smectymnuan controversy, Bacon's pamphlet was written in 1589 with reference to the Admonition controversy.

14 Orest Ranum, *Artisans of Glory: Writers and Historical Thought in Seventeenth-Century France* (Chapel Hill, N.C., 1980), pp. 282–91.

15 Richard Baker, trans., Vergilio Malvezzi, *Discourses upon Cornelius Tacitus*, Preface; cited by Alfred Alvarez, *The School of Donne* (London, 1961), p. 40.

16 Henry Savile, *The Ende of Nero and Beginning of Galba. Fower Bookes of the Histories of Cornelius Tacitus* (Oxford, 1591).

17 F. J. Levy, *Tudor Historical Thought* (San Marino, 1967), pp. 251, 261–62. For the ambiguous reputation of Tacitus in England, see also M. F. Tenney, "Tacitus in the Politics of Early Stuart England," *Classical Journal* 37 (1941): 151–63; and Edwin B. Benjamin, "Milton and Tacitus," *Milton Studies* 4 (1972):117–40.

18 *Lords Journal*, 3:617–24. See also Harold Hulme, *The Life of Sir John Eliot* (London, 1957), pp. 135–44.

19 See *Epigrammes*, No. 65: *The Under-wood*, Nos. 14, 23, 47.

20 Glynne Wickham, "From Tragedy to Tragi-comedy: 'King Lear' as Prologue," *Shakespeare Survey* 26 (1973): 33–48.

21 See Rosalie Colie, "Reason and Need: *King Lear* and the Crisis of the Aristocracy," in R. L. Colie and F. T. Flahiff, eds., *Some Facets of King Lear* (Toronto, 1974); Sidney Shanker, *Shakespeare and the Uses of Ideology* (The Hague, 1975), pp. 137–77; Paul Delaney, "*King Lear* and the Decline of Feudalism," *Publications of the Modern Language Society of America* 92 (1977): 429–40; David Aers and Gunther Kress, "The Language of Social Order: Individual, Society and Historical Process in *King Lear*," Aers and Kress, eds., *Literature, Language and Society in England 1580–1680* (Totowa, N.J., 1981), pp. 75–99; Franco Moretti, "'A Huge Eclipse': Tragic Form and the Deconsecration of Sovereignty," in Stephen Greenblatt, ed., *The Power of Forms in the English Renaissance* (Norman, Okla., 1982), pp. 7–40; Jonathan Dollimore, *Radical Tragedy: Religion, Ideology and Power in the Drama of Shakespeare and his Contemporaries* (Chicago, 1984), pp. 195–203.

22 Frank Kermode, ed., *Shakespeare*: King Lear: *A Casebook* (London: Macmillan and Co., 1969), p. 13.

23 Wickham, "From Tragedy to Tragi-comedy," pp. 36–43.

24 In June 1607 the Venetian ambassador reported that James "leaves all government to his Council and will think of nothing but the chase . . . so

one may say that he is sovereign in name and in appearance rather than in substance and effect," *Venetian State Papers,* 1603–1607, pp. 513, 510.

25 *King Lear* (1608), Shakespeare Quarto Facimiles (London, 1939), Dlr. All subsequent citations refer to the quarto text.

26 Gary Taylor and Michael Warren, eds., *The Division of the Kingdoms* (Oxford, 1984).

27 Taylor, "Monopolies, Show Trials, Disaster, and Invasion: *King Lear* and Censorship," pp. 75–117.

28 W. W. Greg, "Time, Place, and Politics in *King Lear,*" in *Collected Papers,* ed. J. C. Maxwell (Oxford, 1966), p. 333; Madeleine Doran, *The Text of "King Lear"* (Stanford, 1931), pp. 73–76.

29 Taylor, "A New Source and an Old Date for *King Lear,*" *Review of English Studies* 33 (1982): 396–413.

30 G. P. V. Akrigg, *Shakespeare and the Earl of Southampton* (Cambridge, Mass., 1968), pp. 254–55.

31 *The King's Maiesties Speech, as it was delivered by him in the upper house of the Parliament, . . . On Munday the 19 day of March 1603: Being the first day of this present Parliament, and the first Parliament of his Maiesties Raigne* (London, 1604). Cited from C. H. McIlwain, *The Political Works of James I* (Cambridge, Mass., 1918), p. 272. It is one of the zanier coincidences of scholarship that the Folger Shakespeare Library owns a copy of the speech, with "Shakespeare's" signature on the title-page, and on the final page the following annotation: "Thys speche as those of our kyngs owne generalle follye dothe speake onne everie mattere litle thatte he shoulde. W. S." (See Fig. 2) The manuscript additions are assumed to be in the hand of William Henry Ireland, the remarkable eighteenth-century forger, who though a knave was certainly no fool, at least with respect to his knowledge of Shakespeare.

32 *Rapta Tatio: The Mirrour of his Maiesties present Government, tending to the Union* (London, 1604), B1.

33 Wallace Notestein, *The House of Commons 1604–1610* (New Haven and London, 1971), p. 63.

34 J. R. Tanner, ed., *Constitutional Documents of the Reign of James I 1603–1625* (Cambridge, 1930), p. 230; and see also Notestein, *House of Commons,* pp. 125–40.

35 Compare, for example, the possibility that George Wilkins' play, *The Miseries of Enforced Marriage* (S. R. 12 June, 1605) was the source for the Fool's famous phrase (found only in the folio), "I'll go to bed at noon." See Taylor, "A New Source," p. 412. The problem in such instances is, obviously, of determining who borrowed from whom. But whereas play-wrights frequently borrowed from each other, bishops were unlikely to borrow their metaphors from the theater.

36 The lexical similarity is much more convincing than in the passage from Samuel Harsnett's *Declaration of Egregious Popishe Impostures* (London, 1603), "fire him out of his hold, as men smoke out a Foxe out of his burrow," suggested by Kenneth Muir, ed., *King Lear* (Cambridge, Mass., Arden edition), pp. 200, 255; and in addition Thornborough's and Shakespeare's metaphors share the same context of separation and re-union.

37 *Journals of the House of Commons,* 1:315.
38 It would be difficult for an audience in 1606 not to see here, an addition, some problematic allusion to Prince Henry, Duke of Cornwall, and Prince Charles, Duke of Albany until November 1605. See Wickham, "From Tragedy to Tragi-comedy," p. 36.
39 Muir, *King Lear,* p. 47.
40 One cannot ignore the extraordinary coincidence between Shakespeare's version of the Lear story and the real-life story of Sir Brian Annesley and his three daughters. Yet since Cordell Annesley did not marry into the family of the Earl of Southampton until early 1608, the episode can scarcely be reckoned as a *motive* for Shakespeare's choice of subject.
41 Taylor, *"King Lear:* The Date and Authorship of the Folio Version," pp. 351–468.
42 McIlwain, *Political Works,* p. 308.
43 Chamberlain, *Letters,* ed. McLure, 1:301.
44 Heinemann, *Puritanism and Theatre,* p. 203.
45 For Scott, minister at Norwich in 1620 and in Utrecht from 1622, see Heinemann, *Puritanism and Theatre,* pp. 156–59, 167; and L. B. Wright, "Propaganda against James I's Appeasement of Spain," *Huntington Library Quarterly* 6 (1942–43): 149–72.
46 Chamberlain, *Letters,* 2:396: Proclamations "Against Excesse of lavish and licentious Speeche of Matters of State" were issued on 24 December 1620 and 21 July 1624: "against the disorderly Printing, uttering and dispersing of Books, Pamphlets, etc." on 25 September 1623; against "Seditious, Popish and Puritanical Bookes and Pamphlets" on 16 August 1624.
47 Chamberlain, *Letters,* 2:411.
48 *Proceedings and Debates of the House of Commons in 1620 and 1621* (Oxford, 1766), 2:277.
49 *Vox Coeli,* described as "Printed in Elizium," was an imaginary debate between the spirits of Henry VIII, Edward VI, Prince Henry, Elizabeth I, Mary Tudor (!), and Queen Anne on the (un)desirability of the Spanish match. *Tom Tell Troath or A free discourse touching the manners of the tyme* appears to have been first written under James, revised to include a letter from the pope, dated 4 September 1626, published once c. 1630, and again in 1642, when the "manners" of the title were replaced by "murmurs." The attribution of both *Vox Coeli* and *Tom Tell Troath* to Scott is, however debatable.
50 See G. E. Bentley, *The Jacobean and Caroline Stage,* 7 vols. (Oxford, 1941–68), 5:1412: "Probably one can assume that [it] was a play with political reflections." See also 7:56, on a letter of submission by the King's Company to Sir Henry Herbert, the licenser.
51 Bentley, *Jacobean and Caroline Stage,* 5:1455–56. J. T. Murray, *English Dramatic Companies, 1558–1642* (London, 1910), 2:348, states that the play was forbidden and one of the actors arrested.
52 For the stage history and interpretation of the play, see Heinemann, *Puritanism and Theatre,* pp. 151–71; and R. C. Bald, ed., *A Game at Chess* (Cambridge, 1929), pp. 1–25.
53 *The Noble [Spanish] Soldier* (1634), ed. J. S. Farmer (New York: Tudor Facsimiles, 1970), D4.
54 Bentley, *Jacobean and Caroline Stage,* 1:182–86.

55 Richard Brathwaite, *An Age for Apes*, p. 228. This satire formed the second part of a volume entitled *The Honest Ghost, or a Voice from the Vault* (London, 1658).

56 Philip Edwards and Colin Gibson, eds., *The Plays and Poems of Philip Massinger*, 5 vols. (Oxford, 1976), 1:liii–lxi.

57 S. R. Gardiner, "The Political Element in Massinger," *New Shakespeare Society Transactions* 2 (1875–76): 314–31.

58 *His Majesties Speach in the Upper House of Parliament, on Munday, the 26 of March, 1621* (London, 1621) B3v. For the currency of the topos in connection with James, see William Loe, *Vox Clamantis* (1621), p. 23; Samuel Buggs, *Miles Mediterraneus. The Mid-Land Souldier* (1622), pp. 2–3; and Richard Brathwaite's retrospective account, "Solomon's Reign," in *The History of Moderation* (1669), p. 112.

59 Massinger, *Plays and Poems*, 1:105–6.

60 Ibid., 1:303.

61 Bentley, *Jacobean and Caroline Stage*, 1:182–86.

62 Massinger, *Plays and Poems*, 3:293. Perhaps even more telling is Herbert's report on Massinger's *The King and the Subject*, to the effect that Charles I himself read the play text and wrote against one passage that referred to forced taxation, "This is too insolent, and to be changed."

63 Massinger, *Plays and Poems*, 3:297.

64 *The Roman Actor; or, The Drama's Vindication. A Prelude. Compressed from Massinger's Celebrated Play* (London, 1822), pp. 11–12. The playlet was presented as a curtain raiser on Kean's benefit night, and the proceeds went to the "distressed" Irish.

65 William Lee Sandidge, ed., *The Roman Actor* (Princeton, 1929), p. 23.

66 Goldberg, *James I and the Politics of Literature*, pp. 203–9.

67 This ambiguity is increased by the statement that the play occurs at "the end of the Jacobean period" and can be seen as a response to "the high Roman style of Jacobean absolutism" (ibid., p. 203).

68 Massinger, *Plays and Poems*, 3:16.

69 John Donne, *Poems*, ed. H. J. C. Grierson, 2 vols. (Oxford, 1912) 1:154.

70 Donne, *Pseudo-Martyr* (London, 1610), ¶2r.

71 Donne, *Letters to Severall Persons of Honour* (1651), ed. M. Thomas Hester (Delmar, N.Y.: Scholar's Facsimiles, 1977), pp. 160–61.

72 See ibid., p. 76.

73 Izaak Walton, *The Lives of John Donne, etc.*, ed. G. Saintsbury (London, 1927), p. 53.

74 *The Sermons of John Donne*, eds. George R. Potter and Evelyn M. Simpson, 10 vols. (Berkeley and Los Angeles, 1953–62), 4:202.

75 Noted by Potter and Simpson, *Sermons*, 4:34.

76 Richard Montague, canon of Windsor and later bishop of Chichester, published *Appello Caesarem* (1625) as an expression of his own high Church principles. Parliament had protested the book's licensing, and tried to engage Abbot on their side.

77 William Prynne, *Histriomastix* (London, 1633; facsimile edition, ed. Arthur Freeman, New York, 1974), p. 848.

78 S. R. Gardiner, ed., *Documents Relating to the Proceedings against Wil-*

liam Prynne (London, 1877; rpt. London and New York: Camden Society Publications, n.s., Vol. 18, 1965), pp. 10–16.

79 *The Works of Sir John Suckling,* ed. L. A. Beaurline, 2 vols. (Oxford, 1971), 2:23. Beaurline notes (p. 250) that Hazlitt saw a reference to Prynne here, but himself doubted "if Suckling would be coming to the defence of Prynne." Yet the allusion is compatible both with Beaurline's dating, between 1632 and 1637, and with the play's recognized critique of Jacobean and Caroline misgovernment.

80 As noted by Stephen Orgel, *Inigo Jones: The Theatre of the Stuart Court,* 2 vols. (London and Berkeley, 1973), 1:164–65.

81 See Rhodes Dunlap, ed., *The Poems of Thomas Carew* (Oxford, 1949), pp. 274–75.

82 On Carew's skepticism, as expressed by Momus, see also M. P. Parker, "Comely Gestures: Thomas Carew and the Creation of a Caroline Poetic," Ph.D. diss., Yale University, 1979, pp. 82–86.

83 Fredric Jameson, *The Political Unconscious* (Ithaca, 1981), pp. 84, 85.

84 This was Milton's conclusion to the sonnet *On the New Forcers of Conscience Under the Long Parliament.*

85 John Milton, *Complete Prose Works,* ed. D. M. Wolfe et al., 8 vols. (New Haven, 1953–80), 3:561.

86 Cf. *Paradise Lost,* III, 183–84: "Some I have chosen of peculiar grace / Elect above the rest," where Milton's intellectual elitism qualified his general rejection of Calvinist predestination.

87 Milton was quoting Bacon's *Wise and Moderate Discourse;* see n. 13, above.

88 Tacitus, *Histories and Annals,* ed. and trans. C. H. Moore and J. Jackson, 5 vols. (London and Cambridge, Mass.: Loeb Classical Library, 1937–69), 3:63. E. B. Benjamin did not find this, or any other, reference to Tacitus "unmistakably" in Milton's republican tracts; but he pointed out an interesting note, "perhaps by Milton," in the margin of Sir Richard Baker's translation of Vergilio Malvezzi's commentary on Tacitus (London, 1642); Milton (?) wrote that Elizabeth, like Tiberius, censored discussion of the succession ("lege cavit, ne quis sub poenâ capitis, mentionem faceret haeredis regni") and cited Tacitus, *Historia,* I. This recall of the "statute of silence" was surely one of the seeds of *Areopagitica.*

89 *The Tragedies of Euripides,* trans. Arthur S. Way (London, 1894), 1:382.

90 See R. C. Jebb, *The Attic Orators,* 2 vols. (London, 1893), 2:206–14; J. A. Wittreich, Jr., "Milton's *Areopagitica:* Its Isocratic and Ironic Contexts," *Milton Studies* 4 (1972): 101–13.

91 *The Laws of Plato,* trans. Thomas L. Pangle (New York, 1980), p. 45.

92 F. S. Siebert, *Freedom of the Press in England, 1476–1776* (Urbana, 1952), p. 196.

93 Donald Thomas, *A Long Time Burning: The History of Literary Censorship in England* (London, 1969), p. 14.

94 Siebert, *Freedom of the Press in England,* gives the most complete coverage, while noting (p. 196) the insignificance of Milton's tract in its own time. Jeremy Taylor's scriptural focus placed him outside Siebert's frame of reference; but his arguments for free theological debate share some

of the same roots as Milton's, including Tacitus. Against the banning and burning of books he cites the opening of Tacitus's *Agricola* and concludes: "It is but an illiterate Policy to think such indirect and uningenuous proceedings can amongst wise and free men disgrace the Authors, and disrepute their Discourses" (*The Liberty of Prophesying* [London, 1647], pp. 35–36).

95 Thomas, *A Long Time Burning*, p. 57.
96 Lawrence Hanson, *Government and the Press, 1695–1763* (London, 1936), pp. 25–26.
97 Ibid., p. 24.
98 *A Faithful Report of a Genuine Debate Concerning the Liberty of the Press* (London, 1740), p. 37.

3. Lyric and Society

1 The chief victims were John Marston and Thomas Dekker. See C. H. Herford, P. Simpson, and E. Simpson, eds., *Works*, 11 vols. (Oxford, 1925–52) 1:432–37, 9:533–35; R. A. Small, *The Stage-Quarrel between Ben Jonson and the So-Called Poetasters* (Breslau, 1899), pp. 25–28, 62–132.
2 According to the 1616 folio; Jonson, *Works*, 4:193.
3 T. S. Eliot, *The Three Voices of Poetry* (London, 1953), p. 17.
4 W. R. Johnson, *The Idea of Lyric: Lyric Modes in Ancient and Modern Poetry* (Berkeley, Los Angeles, and London, 1982), p. 1.
5 Theodor Adorno, "Rede über Lyrik und Gesellschaft," *Akzente* 4 (1957): 8–26; reprinted in *Noten zur Literatur*, 3 vols. (Frankfurt, 1958–65), 1:79–80: "Die grossen Dichter der früheren Vergangenheit, die nach literargeschichtlichen Begriffen der Lyrik zurechnen, Pindar etwa und Alkaios, . . . sind unserer primären Vorstellung von Lyrik ungemein fern." Translation by Margaret E. Kennington.
6 Ibid., pp. 77–78: "Ihr Affekt hält daran fest, dass es so bleiben soll, dass der lyrische Ausdruck, gegenständlicher Schwere entronnen, das Bild eines Lebens beschwöre, das frei sei vom Zwang der herrschenden Praxis, der Nützlichkeit, vom Druck der sturen Selbsterhaltung. . . . Sie impliziert den Protest gegen einen gesellschaftlichen Zustand, den jeder Einzelne als sich feindlich, fremd, kalt, bedrückend erfährt."
7 Ibid., pp. 90, 76.
8 Ibid., pp. 82–83: Das geschichtliche Verhältnis des Subjekts zur Objektivität, des Einzelnen zur Gesellschaft im Medium des subjecktiven, auf sich zurückgeworfenen Geistes seinen Niederschlag muss gefunden haben. Er wird um so volkommener sein, je weniger das Gebilde das Verhältnis von Ich und Gesellschaft thematisch macht, je unwillkürlicher es vielmehr im Gebilde von sich aus sich kristallisiert."
9 Ibid., p. 83.
10 Paul Fry, *The Poet's Calling in the English Ode* (New Haven and London, 1980), pp. 1, 61. For the implications of deconstruction as a strategy of textual criticism, see Jonathan Culler, *On Deconstruction* (Ithaca, 1982).
11 But see my *Marvell and the Civic Crown* (Princeton, 1978), pp. 59–68.
12 In *Timber; or, Discoveries* Jonson makes poetry and lyric coextensive un-

der the etymological sign *carmina,* yet lists as separate kinds "an Epick, Dramatic, Lyrike, Elegiake, or Epigrammatike Poeme" (*Works,* 8:635). Within *Under-wood* there is more apparent inconsistency. Poems are designated as songs, elegies, odes, epigrams, epistles, sonnets, even an "execration" and a "fit"; *A Speach according to Horace* imitates *Odes* III, 24 conceptually but not formally. If challenged, Jonson would probably have reverted to the broadest possible definition of lyric.

13 For a discussion of the original text in relationship to the frontispiece, see Margaret Corbett and Ronald Lightbown, *The Comely Frontispiece: The Emblematic Title-Page in England, 1550–1660* (London, 1979), p. 135.

14 See Leonard Tennenhouse, "Sir Walter Ralegh and the Literature of Clientage," in Guy Fitch Lytle and Stephen Orgel, eds., *Patronage in the Renaissance* (Princeton, 1981), pp. 248–58.

15 See J. W. Williamson, *The Myth of the Conqueror: Prince Henry Stuart: A Study of 17th Century Personation* (New York, 1978), especially pp. 75–129.

16 Compare Tennenhouse's theory that "the *History* ends with the events of 168–167 B.C. because Ralegh's copy-text adopted Livy's chronology; this is precisely the point where the last extant book of Livy ends," "Sir Walter Ralegh and the Literature of Clientage," p. 256.

17 Walter Ralegh, *The History of the World,* ed. C. A. Patrides (Philadelphia, 1971), p. 80. It was almost certainly Ralegh's preface that gave the greatest affront, for it did in fact provide an account of previous English history, replete with criticism of the behavior of earlier monarchs. In a letter to Sir Robert Carr, Earl of Somerset, James mentioned "Sir Walter Ralegh's description of the kings that he hates, of whom he speaketh but evil"; and John Chamberlain reported in a letter that the *History* was "called in by the Kinges commaundment, for divers exceptions, but specially for beeing too sawcie in censuring princes," *Letters of John Chamberlain,* ed. Norman McLure, 2 vols. (Philadelphia, 1939), 1:568. See John Racin, *Sir Walter Ralegh as Historian* (Salzburg, 1974), pp. 5–11.

18 Racin, *Sir Walter Ralegh as Historian,* p. 7. These transactions are documented in *Records of the Court of the Stationers Company, 1602–1640,* ed. William A. Jackson (London, 1957), p. 357.

19 In his conversations with Drummond of Hawthornden, Jonson later remarked that Ralegh had not given credit to those who had helped him with the *History:* "The best wits in England were Employed . . . Ben himself had written a peice for him of ye punick warre which he altered and set in his booke" (*Works,* 1:138).

20 Fry, *Poet's Calling in the English Ode,* p. 29.

21 Philip Sidney, *The Countess of Pembroke's Arcadia,* ed. Jean Robertson (Oxford, 1973), p. 86.

22 B. Dew Robert, *Mitre and Musket: John Williams, Lord Keeper, Archbishop of York* (London, 1938), pp. 94–117.

23 In *Timber* (*Works,* 8:603), Jonson wrote under the heading *De Gratiosis* (Of Favors): "When a vertuous man is rais'd, it brings gladnesse to his friends: griefe to his enemies, and glory to his Posterity. Nay, his honours are a great part of the honour of the times: when by this meanes he is

grown to active men, an example; to the sloathfull, a spurre; to the envious, a Punishment."

24 Richard S. Peterson, *Imitation and Praise in the Poems of Ben Jonson* (New Haven and London, 1981), p. 103.

25 Compare Peterson's view that the conversion into "apt compliment" was complete (ibid., p. 104). That Jonson revised the quotation suggests an anxiety about its connotations. The Newcastle MS reads, "his body then, not boughs, projects his shade," an earlier version where, as Herford and Simpson suggest, the idea of decay was too close to the surface (*Works*, 11:98).

26 The best example of this premise is found in Thomas M. Greene, "Ben Jonson and the Centered Self," *Studies in English Literature* 10 (1970): 325–48; but see also Earl Miner, *The Cavalier Mode from Jonson to Cotton* (Princeton, 1971), pp. 70–74; Johnson, *Idea of Lyric,* p. 180, who remarks on the hegemonic implications of the idealizing mode; and Richard Helgerson, *Self-Crowned Laureates: Spenser, Jonson, Milton and the Literary System* (Berkeley, Los Angeles, London, 1983), who accepts the idealist account of Jonson's interest in circles while providing a more problematic account of his career (pp. 169–84). Helgerson does not, however, deal directly with the ode.

27 Fry, *Poet's Calling in the English Ode,* pp. 16–30.

28 Richard Fanshawe, trans., *Il Pastor Fido* (London, 1648), p. 310. On Horace's poetry of accommodation, see Steele Commager, *The Odes of Horace* (New Haven and London, 1962), especially pp. 170–71, 203, 255–56.

29 C. M. Bowra, *Pindar* (Oxford, 1964), pp. 110–17.

30 Abraham Cowley, *Pindarique Odes, Written in Imitation of the Stile & Manner of the Odes of Pindar* (London, 1656), p. 1.

31 The Latin for the first passage reads: "Quot in terrâ interfecturus esset quot in mari belluas perniciosas, & cuinam hominum cum obliquâ insolentiâ incedenti, inimicissimo mortem daret," (ibid., p. 17). The emphasis on tyranny is Cowley's own. The second passage has no basis in the original at all.

32 *Translatio* was, of course, the Latin term for metaphor. George Puttenham, in the *Arte of English Poesie* (1589), defined metaphor as "the figure of transport."

33 See Paul Hardacre, "Cromwell and the Royalists," in Ivan Roots, ed., *Cromwell: A Profile* (New York, 1973), pp. 32, 44–45.

34 *Constitutional Documents of the Puritan Revolution, 1625–1660,* ed. S. R. Gardiner (Oxford, 1906), p. 391. The oath was established 2 January 1650.

35 Announced in *Mercurius Politicus* for 19 January 1654: "An Ordinance for repealing several Acts, and Resolvs of Parliament, made for, or touching the subscribing or taking the Engagement." In *The English Revolution,* III, *Newsbooks* 5, Vol. 8, *Mercurius Politicus 1653–1654,* p. 24.

36 David Underdown, *Royalist Conspiracy in England, 1649–1660* (New Haven, 1960), pp. 30–51, 73–96.

37 *Calendar of the Clarendon State Papers,* ed. O. Ogle et al., 5 vols. (Oxford, 1869–1932), 2:149. Quoted in ibid., p. 56.

38 *Life of Edward Earl of Clarendon* (Oxford, 1857), quoted in ibid., p. 87.
39 A. H. Nethercot, *Abraham Cowley: The Muses' Hannibal* (Oxford and London, 1931), pp. 112-17. The other major biography is Jean Loiseau, *Abraham Cowley: Sa vie, son Oeuvre* (Paris, 1931).
40 Nethercot, *Abraham Cowley,* pp. 188-91, details the negotiations by which Cowley and his supporters tried, on the eve of the Restoration, to explain it away.
41 Cowley, *Poems* (London, 1656), a4.
42 A manuscript of the complete poem was discovered by Allan Pritchard in 1967 among the Cowper family papers. See Pritchard, ed., *The Civil War* (Toronto, 1973).
43 Thomas Sprat, *The Works of Mr. Abraham Cowley* (London, 1668), a3v.
44 Nethercot, *Abraham Cowley,* p. 156.
45 Ibid., pp. 189-90.
46 Humphrey Prideaux, *The Judgment of Dr. Prideaux in Condemning the Murder of Julius Caesar* (London, 1721).
47 Richard Lovelace, *Poems,* ed. C. H. Wilkinson (Oxford, 1925), 2:143.
48 Thomas May, *The History of the Parliament of England,* (Oxford, 1854), pp. 271-72.
49 *A Defence of Liberty Against Tyrants,* ed. Harold J. Laski (London, 1924), p. 60. According to the author of the *Vindiciae,* who wrote under the pseudonym of the other famous Brutus (Lucius Junius), "no man can justly reprehend Brutus, Cassius, and the rest who killed Caesar before his tyrannical authority had taken any firm rooting," p. 194.
50 John Milton, *Complete Prose Works,* ed. D. M. Wolfe et al., 8 vols. (New Haven, 1953-80), 3:212-13.
51 [William Sanford], *Modern Policies* (London, 1652), C6.
52 Loiseau, *Abraham Cowley,* p. 189.
53 See T. R. Langley, "Abraham Cowley's 'Brutus': Royalist or Republican?" *Yale English Studies* 6 (1976):41-52; James J. Keough, "Cowley's Brutus Ode: Historical Precepts and the Politics of Defeat," *Texas Studies in Language and Literature* 19 (1977): 382-91. Langley's argument, that Brutus is the portrait of a royalist intellectual, is based on Cowley's allusion to himself as Brutus in the 1656 preface, as well as his apparent identification, in the 1661 *Discourse . . . concerning the Government of Oliver Cromwell,* of Octavius and Antony with the revolutionary leaders. Such arguments presuppose that topical allusions, once made, are rigid, and that writers are always consistent.
54 This polysemy must include the divergence between my own interpretation and that of Paul Korshin, in *From Concord to Dissent* (Menston, N.Y., 1973), p. 28: "The analogies of Rome-England and Brutus-Cromwell are immediately clear beneath the allegorical presentation. The generality of the Pindaric has been replaced by the precision of the Roman ode. By this modification of his style, Cowley rejects ambiguity of political reference, which had been the usual method in Elizabethan and Metaphysical poetry, introducing this plainness of allusion to historical events which his audience could easily interpret. . . . Its very forthrightness emphasizes his sense of doctrinal certainty."

272   Notes to Pages 165–172

55 Abraham Cowley, *Works* (London, 1668), p. 19. Compare Commager, *Odes of Horace,* p. 234: "The tough and massive structure of the semi-allegorical Odes of the early twenties was necessary to sustain the complexities of Horace's attitude towards an already complex situation. In like fashion, the easy similes and lifeless catalogues of the last book are symptomatic of the relaxed and almost perfunctory response that was by then all that was called for."

4. The Royal Romance

1 Sir Francis Bacon, *In Felicem Memoriam Elizabethae Angliae Reginae,* trans. James Spedding, *Works,* Vol. 6 (London, 1861), p. 317.
2 Cited from a medieval life of Gregory the Great, in W. J. S. Sayers, "The Beginnings and Early Development of Old French Historiography," Ph.D. diss., University of California—Berkeley, 1966, p. 477. This is an invaluable source of information on medieval romance and historiography.
3 See Willem de Briane, *Historia Turpini,* ed. André de Mandach, as *Chronique de Turpin* (Geneva, 1963), p. 53: "Ici commence la veraye estoyre si cum li fort roys Charlemain . . . e sachunt certeynement tous ceus ke le orrunt kel l'estoyre est verai . . . e cruee de clers et de lais. Ly bons archesweke Turpyn de Reyns, ke fut compagnoun de Charles en Espayne . . . escrist a Vienne." ("Here begins the true history of the great king Charlemagne . . . and certainly everyone who hears it knows that the history is true . . . and believed by clerics and laymen. The good archbishop Turpin of Rheims, who accompanied Charles in Spain . . . wrote it in Vienne.")
4 See Bernard Weinberg, *A History of Literary Criticism in the Italian Renaissance,* 2 vols. (Chicago, 1961), 2:954–1073.
5 Giovanni Battista Pigna, *I Romanzi* (Venice, 1554); Giovannbattista Giraldi Cinthio, *Discorso intorno al comporre dei romanzi* (1554), trans. H. L. Snuggs (Lexington, Ky., 1968).
6 Loosely based on the history of the first crusade, the *Gerusalemme* has a fabulous soft center, complete with earthly paradise, seductive enchantress, magic forest with talking trees, and sexually fallen but eventually regenerate heroes.
7 Torquato Tasso, *Discourses on the Heroic Poem,* trans. Mariella Cavalchini and Irene Samuel (Oxford, 1973), pp. 27, 40, 58.
8 Or so I argue in "*Paradise Regained* as Romance," in Joseph Wittreich, Jr., and Richard Ide., eds., *Composite Orders: Essays on "Paradise Lost," "Paradise Regained," and "Samson Agonistes," Milton Studies* 17 (1983): 187–208.
9 The textual history of the *Arcadia,* and its original ten-book structure, suggest its genesis in separate, neo-Vergilian eclogues; but debts to Greek romance via Boccaccio's *Ameto* and *Filocolo* have also been documented. See Michele Scherillo, ed., *Arcadia* (Turin, 1888), pp. cxiii–cxxxv.
10 Jacques Amyot, trans., *L'Histoire aethiopique de Heliodorus* (Paris, 1547), Aiiv.
11 Michel Foucault, *The Order of Things,* (New York, 1970): his translation of *Les mots et les choses.*

12 M. de Cervantes Saavedra, *The Adventures of Don Quixote,* trans. J. M. Cohen (Penguin, 1950), p. 59.

13 Ben Jonson, *An Execration upon Vulcan, Works,* eds. C. H. Herford, P. Simpson, and E. Simpson, 11 vols. (Oxford, 1925–52), 8:203–6.

14 Letter from James to Charles and Buckingham of February 1623; British Library, Harl. MS 6987, fol. 13.

15 James Howell, *Epistolae Ho-Elianae: The Familiar Letters,* ed. Joseph Jacobs, 2 vols. (London, 1892), 1:164, 166.

16 Ibid., 1:182.

17 *Expans'd Hieroglyphicks: A Critical Edition of Sir John Denham's "Coopers Hill,"* ed. Brendan O Hehir (Berkeley and Los Angeles, 1969), p. 118.

18 Richard Lovelace, *Poems,* ed. C. H. Wilkinson (Oxford, 1925), p. 155.

19 John Donne, *Letters to Severall Persons of Honour* (1651), ed. M. Thomas Hester (Delmar, N.Y.: Scholar's Facsimiles, 1977), pp. 235–36.

20 Editions of *Argalus and Parthenia* appeared in 1629, 1630, 1632, 1647, 1651, 1654, 1656, 1659, etc.

21 William Prynne, *Histriomastix* (London, 1633; facsimile edition, ed. Arthur Freeman, New York, 1974), p. 913. See also pp. 915, 923.

22 Richard Fanshawe, *Il Pastor Fido* (1647), ed. Walter F. Staton, Jr., and William E. Simeone (Oxford, 1964), p. 109.

23 *The Dramatic Works in the Beaumont and Fletcher Canon,* ed. Fredson Bowers, 5 vols. (Cambridge, 1976), 3:493.

24 W. W. Greg, *Pastoral Poetry and Pastoral Drama* (New York, 1959), pp. 273–74.

25 Fanshawe, *Il Pastor Fido,* p. 4.

26 See Barbara Breasted, "Comus and the Castlehaven Scandal," *Milton Studies* 3 (1971): 201–24; Rosemary Mundhenk, "Dark Scandal and the Sun-Clad Power of Chastity," *Studies in English Literature* 15 (1975): 141–52.

27 John Milton, *Complete Prose Works,* ed. D. M. Wolfe et al., 8 vols. (New Haven, 1953–1980), 1:597.

28 See Barbara K. Lewalski, "Milton: Revaluations of Romance," in Herschel Baker, ed., *Four Essays on Romance* (Cambridge, Mass., 1971), p. 64.

29 Lord Ernle, *The Light Reading of Our Ancestors* (London, 1927), p. 154. Sir Walter Raleigh, *The English Novel* (New York, 1899), pp. 106–7, declared these romances "an innocent and fanciful pastime for the very prolonged and unrelieved leisure of highborn ladies." This verdict was repeated by Ernest Baker, *The History of the English Novel* (London, 1929), 3:11–37, and by Thomas Haviland, *The Roman de Longue Haleine on English Soil* (Philadelphia, 1931), p. 21.

30 *John Barclay His Argenis, Translated Out of Latine Into English: The Prose Upon His Majesties Command . . .* (London, 1629), p. 485.

31 A. C. Baugh, ed., *A Literary History of England* (New York, 1948), p. 477.

32 *Commons Debates 1628,* ed. Robert Johnson et al., 3 vols. (New Haven and London, 1977). See especially 3:470–72, for the text of the Remonstrance against tonnage and poundage.

33 John Davies, trans., *The Extravagant Shepherd. The Anti-Romance* (London, 1653), pp. 75–76.

34 Henry Cogan, trans., *Ibrahim, Or the Illustrious Bassa* (London, 1652), A3v.

35 Dorothy McDougall, *Madeleine de Scudéry* (London, 1939), p. 74. See also the accounts of de Scudéry's motives and political involvements in Georges Mongrédien, *Madeleine de Scudéry et son salon* (Paris, 1946), and Erica Harth, *Ideology and Culture in Seventeenth-Century France* (Ithaca, 1983), pp. 96–102.

36 John Davies, trans., *Clelia. An Excellent New Romance* (London, 1656), Part II, Book 2, p. 59.

37 See Philip Knachel, *England and the Fronde* (Ithaca and New York, 1967), p. 112.

38 *Artamenes* (London, 1653), a4v. See also the anonymous *Theophania: Or Severall Modern Histories Represented by way of Romance: and Politickly Discours'd upon; By an English Person of Quality* (London, 1655), an early attempt to write an English version of a Scuderian allegory. The message of "The Stationer to the Reader" suggested that "if under some seeming Grotesques, you can find such a glass as will represent you real and excellent figures, you will add to the pleasure I intend you, and I believe be a gainer by it" (A4v). The romance represents English history from the reign of Elizabeth to the moment of publication, told from the point of view of the third earl of Essex, outraged ex-husband of Lady Frances Howard, and justifies the revolution in terms of a long series of royal failings, beginning with Elizabeth's destruction of the second earl of Essex ("my unfortunate father," p. 105); "the too peaceful inclinations of Seleucus (James); The unlimited power of favourites, the unseasonable mildness of Antiochus (Charles), . . . his too great indulgence to Eudoxia (Henrietta Maria)"; and his "seeking with rewards to appease the turbulencie of factious discontented spirits" (p. 192). Yet it seems to be addressed to Charles II, and to argue for the restoration of a reformed monarchy.

39 *Cassandra: the fam'd romance . . . by an honorable person* (London, 1652), was incomplete. Cotterell produced a complete translation in 1661, and dedicated it to Charles II. Cotterell collaborated with William Aylesbury in translating Enrico Davila's *Historia delle guerre civili di Francia* (Venice, 1630). *The Historie of the civill warres of France* was published in London in 1647–48, showing clear signs of having been commissioned by Charles for its value as historical analogy to the situation in England.

40 All citations are from the 1661 edition.

41 Compare Sidney's attack on the historian as "authorising himself (for the most part) upon other histories, whose greatest authorities are built upon the notable foundation of hearsay; having much ado to accord differing writers and to pick truth out of partiality." *An Apology for Poetry*, ed. Geoffrey Shepherd (London, 1965), p. 105.

42 See Benjamin Boyce, "History and Fiction in *Panthalia: or the Royal Romance,*" *Journal of English and Germanic Philology* 57 (1958): 478, n. 3.

43 The British Library catalogue lists the following as Brathwaite's pseudonyms: M. Silesio, Philogenes Panedonius, Corymbacus, Hesychius Pamphilus, Parthenius Osiander, Musophilus, Musaeus Palatinus, Clitus Alexandrinus, and Eucapnus Nepenthiacus Neapolitanus!

44 Boyce, "History and Fiction in *Panthalia,*" p. 489.

45 Sir Walter Scott, *Waverley* (London: Everyman, 1969), p. 11.

5. Letters to Friends: The Self in Familiar Form

1 John Barth, *Letters* (New York, 1979), p. 654.

2 See, for example, Jacques Lacan's "Seminar on 'The Purloined Letter,'" trans. Jeffrey Mehlman, *French Freud, Yale French Studies* 48 (1972): 38–72; Homer O. Brown, "The Errant Letter and the Whispering Gallery," *Genre* 10 (Winter 1977): 573–99; and Jacques Derrida's attack on Lacan's "Seminar," in *La carte postale* (Paris, 1980), "Le facteur de la vérité," pp. 441–524.

3 Cited by Brown, "Errant Letter," p. 581, from *The Criticism of Henry Fielding,* ed. Ioan Williams (New York, 1970), p. 131.

4 See L. D. Reynolds and N. G. Wilson, *Scribes and Scholars* (Oxford, 1974), p. 120.

5 Henri Estienne, ed., *M. T. Ciceronis Epistolarum Volumen, quae Familiares olim dictae, nunc rectius Ad Familiares apellantur* (Paris, 1577), p. 216. For Henri Estienne, scholar-publisher, see A. Firmin Didot, *Les Estienne* (Paris, 1858), pp. 517–53.

6 *M. Tullii Ciceronis Epistolarum Libri XVI Ad Familiares,* ed. J. Graevius, with annotations by Victorinus, Paulus Manutius, etc. (Amsterdam, 1677), 1:1.

7 Cicero, *Epistulae ad familiares,* trans. W. Glynn Williams, 3 vols. (London and New York: Loeb Classical Library, 1927), 1:101.

8 Cicero, *Letters to Atticus,* trans. E. O. Winstedt, 3 vols. (Cambridge, Mass.: Loeb Classical Library, 1967), 1:131.

9 Ibid., 1:165–71.

10 Roger Ascham, *The Scholemaster* (1570), p. lv.

11 John Brinsley, *Ludus Literarius; or, The Grammar Schoole* (1627), ed. E. T. Campagnac (London and Liverpool, 1917), p. 166.

12 The British Library owns Harvey's copy of the 1563 Aldine edition (*M. Tullii Ciceronis Epistolae ad Atticum, ad M. Brutum, ad Quinctum fratrem*) interleaved and annotated, but with the letters to Atticus missing. In the Spenser-Harvey *Letters,* Harvey satirizes the decay of classical education: "What Newes al this while at Cambridge? . . . betwene the learned, and unlearned, Tully, and Tom Tooly, [no difference] at all,"*Spenser's Prose Works,* ed. Rudolph Gottfried (Baltimore, 1949), p. 460.

13 Letter to Beatus Rhenanus, May 1520, *The Epistles of Erasmus from His Earliest Letters to His Fifty-first Year Arranged in the Order of Time,* trans. F. M. Nichols, 3 vols. (1901), 1:lxxx. Quoted in W. H. Irving, *The Providence of Wit in the English Letter Writers* (Durham, N.C., 1955), p. 39.

14 John Donne, *Letters to Severall Persons of Honour,* ed. M. Thomas Hester (Delmar, N.Y.: Scholar's Facsimiles, 1977), pp. 105–6.

15 *Epistolae Ho-Elianae: The Familiar Letters of James Howell,* ed. Joseph Jacobs, 2 vols. (London, 1892), 1:14.

16 Francis Bacon, *Works,* ed. James Spedding, Vol. 14 (London, 1874), pp. 546–47.

17 *Letters of Sir Henry Wotton to Sir Edmund Bacon* (London, 1661), pp. 126–27.

18 Howell, *Epistolae*, 2:658. The letter is presented as introducing Howell's *Apologs or Fables*, first published anonymously in 1643 with a fake Paris imprint, as *Parables reflecting upon the Times.*

19 *Rump: or an exact collection of the choycest poems and songs relating to the late times* (London, 1662), 1:170. It is interesting to see the cause of intellectual privacy connected metaphorically to that of private land-ownership and enclosure policy, versus the public "Commons." The ideological basis of literary and genre theory often emerges (unintentionally?) in such small lexical choices.

20 Anthony à Wood, *Athenae Oxonienses*, 3 vols. (London, 1691), 3:744.

21 Jacobs, *Epistolae*, 1:lxxx–lxxxi. See also Verona M. Hirst, "The Authenticity of James Howell's Familiar Letters," *Modern Language Review* 54 (1959): 558–61.

22 See, for example, Douglas Bush, *English Literature in the Earlier Seventeenth Century* (Oxford, 1962), pp. 206–7.

23 Jacobs, *Epistolae*, 1:4.

24 Compare Leo Strauss, *Persecution and the Art of Writing* (Glencoe, Ill., 1952), p. 30. "If a master of the art of writing commits such blunders as would shame an intelligent high school boy, it is reasonable to assume that they are intentional." In this one instance, Strauss's methodology seems to merge with mine.

25 John Milton, *Complete Prose Works*, ed. D. M. Wolfe et al., 8 vols. (New Haven, 1953–80), 3:542–43; Milton also puns on the generic point, "that it is with none more *familiar* then with Kings, to transgress the bounds of all honour and civility" (3:539; italics added).

26 Andrew Marvell, *The Poems and Letters*, ed. H. M. Margoliouth, rev. P. Legouis, 2 vols. (Oxford, 1971), 2:156.

27 It is symptomatic of the apolitical nature of modern criticism that Irving, in *The Providence of Wit*, mentions none of these, referring only to Marvell's letter to Sir John Trott, a textbook consolation that could have been written by and to anybody.

28 Marvell, *Poems and Letters*, 2:348. I cannot understand Margoliouth's declaration (2:394) that this is not a separate letter but part of a previous letter to Popple. He printed from a seventeenth-century copy (Lambeth Palace Library, Codices Gibsoniani, v. 88). It seems clear the the copyist combined one long letter (beginning "Deare Will," signed "Andrew Marvell," and dated "London, July 15") with a short one (beginning "Ignoscas Gulielme," unsigned, and dated "July 17, 76"). It is surely the second, short letter which carried the superscription to Robert Thompson, the longer one being *too* long for the "backside" there mentioned.

29 I owe the translation to my familiar friend Barry Weller.

30 *The Rochester-Savile Letters, 1671–1680*, ed. J. H. Wilson (Columbus, Ohio, 1941). p. 41.

31 In December 1677 Charles had signed a defensive treaty with William of Orange; in May 1678 he signed a treaty of neutrality with France. This double-dealing backfired when, also in May, the States General accepted

Louis's peace terms, resulting in the Treaty of Nimeguen in July, from which Charles was excluded.

32 See George de F. Lord, ed., *Anthology of Poems on Affairs of State* (New Haven and London, 1975), pp. 246–48.

33 Juvenal, *Satires,* I, 73. Gyaros or Gyara was a small island in the Aegean, one of the Cyclades, where the Romans under the Empire used to send political prisoners.

34 See *Common Debates* for 9 May 1678; *The Lauderdale Papers,* ed. O. Airy, 3 vols. (London, 1885), 3:139–40; and the account by J. H. Wilson, *Rochester-Savile Letters,* p. 20.

35 Estienne, *M. T. Ciceronis Epistolarum Volumen,* pp. 133–35.

36 *Letters of The Honourable Algernon Sydney . . . 1679* (London, 1742), p. 158.

37 "Algernon Sidney's Farewell," from Lord, *Anthology of Poems on Affairs of State,* pp. 361–62.

38 H. C. Foxcroft, *Life and Letters of Sir George Savile,* 2 vols. (London, 1898), 1:156.

39 Ibid., 1:208.

40 Cicero, *Epistulae ad familiares,* I.ix.21 (my translation).

41 Foxcroft, *Life and Letters of Sir George Savile,* 2:281.

42 George Savile, marquis of Halifax, *Observations Upon a late Libel,* ed. Hugh Macdonald (Cambridge, 1940), p. 15.

43 Foxcroft, *Life and Letters of Sir George Savile,* 1:283–84.

Afterwords: Three Sidneys, John Dryden, and Jean-Jacques Rousseau

1 Cited in W. H. Irving, *The Providence of Wit in the English Letter Writers* (Durham, N.C., 1955), p. 43.

2 See John Buxton, *Sir Philip Sidney and the English Renaissance* (London, 1954), pp. 56–59.

3 *The Countesse of Pembrokes Arcadia* (1590), ed. Albert Feuillerat, *Complete Works of Sir Philip Sidney,* 4 vols. (Cambridge, 1912; rpt. 1969), 1:23.

4 *The Works of John Dryden,* Vol. 15, ed. Earl Miner and George Guffey (Berkeley, Los Angeles, and London, 1976), p. 67.

5 See Chapter 2, p. 86, above.

6 I am much indebted here to Earl Miner's judicious account of the play's context of reception, and the manner in which Dryden controlled its interpretation. See *Works of John Dryden,* 15:404–8.

7 The connection with Spenser was, however, made earlier, in Dryden's *The Hind and the Panther* (1687), which cites as one of its models for the "mysterious writ" or political beast fable Spenser's *Mother Hubberds Tale.* See *Works,* 3:161.

8 Dryden, *Works,* 15:64, 411; translation mine.

9 Jacques Derrida, *Of Grammatology,* trans. Gayatri Spivak (Baltimore and London, 1974, 1976), pp. 141–74.

10 Paul de Man, *Allegories of Reading: Figural Language in Rousseau, Nietzsche, Rilke, and Proust* (New Haven and London, 1979), especially pp. 193–209.

11 On the appointment of C.-G. de Lamoignon de Malesherbes to the position of Director, see David T. Pottinger, *The French Book Trade in the Ancient Regime, 1500–1791* (Cambridge, Mass., 1958), pp. 66–70.

12 Jean-Jacques Rousseau, *Oeuvres Complètes,* eds. Jean Fabre et Michel Launay, 3 vols. (Paris, 1967–71), 1:318.

13 For an explanation of the "permission tacite" as a procedure, see Pottinger, *French Book Trade,* p. 67: "This device had been more or less in use ever since the end of the reign of Louis XIV to cover books for which the Director did not want to take full responsibility. It was issued on the advice of a censor and registered in the Chancellor's office, in the headquarters of the guild, and with the lieutenant of police. But it was not sealed with the Great Seal; and since it was not printed in the edition itself, the public did not see the name of the censor."

14 See Rousseau, *Oeuvres,* 1:117.

15 Pottinger, *French Book Trade,* p. 67.

16 See Jean Guéhenno, *Jean-Jacques Rousseau,* trans. John and Doreen Wightman, 2 vols. (New York and London, 1966), 2:85.

17 Compare Rousseau, *Oeuvres,* 1:105, 112, 339.

18 Derrida, *Of Grammatology,* p. 163.

Index

279